THE MORGAN KAUFMANN SERIES IN DATA MANAGEMENT SYSTEMS

Series Editor, Jim Gray

Database Modeling and Design: The Entity-Relationship Approach
Toby J. Teorey (University of Michigan)

Readings in Object-Oriented Database Systems
Edited by Stanley B. Zdonik (Brown University) and
David Maier (Oregon Graduate Center)

Readings in Database Systems
Edited by Michael Stonebraker (University of California, Berkeley)

Deductive Databases and Logic Programming
By Jack Minker (University of Maryland)

DATABASE MODELING AND DESIGN:
The Entity-Relationship Approach

Toby J. Teorey
University of Michigan

Morgan Kaufmann Publishers, Inc.
San Mateo, California

Editor   Bruce Spatz
Production Editor   Sharon E. Montooth
Typesetter   Merry Finley, Desktop Productions
Cover Designer   Gary Head
Text Designer   Gary Head
Art Director   Gary Head
Copy Editor   Toni Murray

Library of Congress Cataloging-in-Publication Data

Teorey, Toby J.
   Database modeling and design : the entity-relationship approach /
Toby J. Teorey.
     p.   cm. -- (Morgan Kaufmann series in data management systems,
ISSN 1046-1698)
  ISBN 1-55860-134-1
  1. Relational data bases. 2. Data base design. 3. Data base
management. I. Title. II. Series.
QA76.9.D3T424 1990
005.75'6--dc20

Morgan Kaufmann Publishers, Inc.
Editorial Office:
   2929 Campus Drive
   San Mateo, CA 94403
Order from:
   P.O. Box 50490
   Palo Alto, CA 94303-9953

94   93   92   91   90   5   4   3   2   1

Dedication

To Matt, Carol, and Marilyn

Contents

6   Physical Design Fundamentals   129

7   An Example of Relational Database Design   165

Preface

Entity-relationship (ER) modeling is a popular method for representing data requirements and for conceptual database design. Currently there is no standard ER model, and many papers and textbooks have introduced various semantics to include in this approach. This book presents a comprehensive set of semantic definitions for ER models and a corresponding notation that combines the most readable original constructs from Peter Chen with a computer screen representation for large complex databases developed by David Reiner.

The database life cycle is described in Chapter 1, along with a real-life case study that is used throughout most of the text. ER modeling constructs are presented at two levels: the simple level that is currently used in most computer-aided software engineering (CASE) tools and which satisfies requirements for end-user readability, and a complex level that is useful to database designers who want to clearly define complex relationships. The ER approach is presented in a straightforward way in Chapter 2. Fundamental constructs are described in Section 2.1 and advanced constructs in Section 2.2.

Chapters 3 and 4 show how to use ER concepts in the database design process. Chapter 3 is devoted to direct application of ER modeling in logical database design. Chapter 4 explains the transformation of the ER model to the relational model and to SQL syntax specifically. Chapter 5 is devoted to the fundamentals of database normalization, showing the functional equivalence between the ER model and the relational model. Chapter 6 introduces the concepts of physical design and illustrates with an example how to modify a relational schema to be more efficient when usage for specific applications is well known. The case study in Chapter 7 illustrates and summarizes the techniques presented in Chapters 2 through 6 with a new problem environment.

Chapters 8 and 9 present two approaches to distributed database allocation strategies. Chapter 8 presents the fundamentals of fragmentation and data allocation in a distributed database system, and the case study in Chapter 9 illustrates the connection between logical design and distribution of data in a relational database system.

Chapter 10 introduces the concept of ER clustering, a technique for bottom-up abstraction of a large ER model so it can eventually be represented on a single page. For a large complex model, this technique is vital to end-user communication and for the documentation required by the database designer and programmer.

This book can be used by the database practitioner as a useful guide to ER modeling and its application to database designs from the business and office environments to scientific and engineering databases. Whether you are a novice database user or an experienced professional, this book offers new insights into database modeling and the ease of transition from the ER model to the relational model, including the building of standard SQL data definitions. Thus, whether you are using DB2, SQL/DS, Oracle, Ingres, Sybase, NonStop SQL or any other SQL-based system, the design rules set forth here will be applicable. The case study used for the examples throughout most of the book is a real-life database that was designed using the principles formulated in this book. The other case studies, used in Chapters 7 and 9, are quite different in scope, but have been extensively tested in the classroom.

This book can also be used by the advanced undergraduate or beginning graduate student to supplement a course textbook in introductory database management or data models or for an advanced course in database design.

Acknowledgments

I wish to acknowledge the cooperation of Mathematical Reviews and Bill Woolf for providing the case study and especially John Koenig and Deb Bolton who designed and implemented the database and provided important feedback on the ER modeling techniques and clustering methodology. Pando Yosifovski assisted by preparing many of the clustering figures. I also wish to acknowledge my coauthors in several relevant papers that contributed to the continuity of this book: Yang Dongqing, Jim Fry, Wei Guangping, Amjad Umar, Jarir Chaar, Kunle Olukotun, and Marilyn Mantei. Jim Gray provided valuable technical criticism. Dick Spencer provided some very precise basic definitions, which may lead to ER standards in the future. The Star Trek problem was designed by Paul Helman and Marilyn Mantei; and the ER model solution was provided by Carol Fan, Nayantara Kalro, and Dan O'Leary. I wish to thank the Department of Electrical Engineering and Computer Science (EECS) and the Center for Information Technology Integration (CITI) and the University of Michigan for providing computer resources for writing and revising. The entire manuscript was written using MacWrite and FullPaint. Pat Corey and Ann Gordon provided excellent detailed critiques of the entire manuscript, and Rosemary Metz was always there for anything that needed fixing. Finally, thanks to Julie for offering Ludington, and not giving up.

1

Introduction

Database technology began to replace file systems in the mid 1960s. Since that time database design has slowly evolved from an art to a science that has been partially implementable as a set of software design aids. Many of these design aids have appeared as the database component of computer-aided software engineering (CASE) tools, and many of them offer interactive modeling capability using a simplified entity-relationship (ER) approach.

Schema diagrams were formalized in the 1960s by Bachman [Bach69, Bach72]. He used rectangles to denote record types and directed arrows from one record type to another to denote a one-to-many relationship among instances of records of the two types. The ER approach for conceptual database modeling was first described in 1976 by Peter Chen [Chen76]. He used rectangles to specify entities, which are somewhat analogous to records. He also used diamond-shaped objects to represent the various types of relationships, which were differentiated by numbers or letters placed on the lines connecting the diamonds to the rectangles. Since the original definition of entities and relationships, the ER modeling technique has undergone a variety of changes and extensions, including the implementation of experimental database management systems (DBMSs) using the ER data model.

The overriding emphasis in ER modeling is on simplicity and readability. The goal of conceptual schema design, where the ER approach is most useful, is to capture real-world data requirements in a simple and meaningful way that is understandable by both the database designer and the end-user. The end-user is the person responsible for accessing the database and executing queries and updates through the use of DBMS software; therefore, the end-user has a vested interest in the database design process.

The ER model has two levels of definition, one which is quite simple and another which is considerably more complex. The simple level is the one used by most current CASE tools. It is quite helpful to the database designer in communicating with end-users about their data requirements. At this level, one simply describes, in diagram form, the entities, attributes, and relationships that occur in the system to be conceptualized and whose semantics are definable in a data dictionary. Specialized constructs, such as "weak" entities or mandatory/optional existence notation, are also usually included in the simple form. But very little else is, in order to avoid cluttering up the ER diagram while the designer's and end-user's understanding of the model are being reconciled.

From the database practitioner's standpoint, the simple form of the ER model is the preferred form for both database modeling and end-user verification. It is easy to learn, and it is applicable to a wide variety of design problems one might encounter in industry and small businesses. We will also see that the simple form is easily translatable into Structured Query Language (SQL) database definitions, and thus it has an immediate use as an aid for database implementation.

The complex level of ER model definition includes concepts that go far beyond the original model. It includes concepts from the semantic models of artificial intelligence (AI) and from competing conceptual data models such as the binary relationship model and NIAM methodology (see Chapters 2 and 10 for an overview of some NIAM concepts) [NvS79]. ER modeling at this level helps the database designer capture more semantics without having to resort to narrative explanations. It is also useful to the database application programmer because certain integrity constraints defined in the ER model relate directly to code—code that checks range limits on data values and null values, for example. However, such detail in very large ER diagrams actually detracts from end-user understanding. Therefore, the simple level is recommended as a communication tool for database design verification.

We will investigate ER modeling at each of these levels. Let us now see how ER modeling fits into the database life cycle at all the steps of logical database design. This includes the evolution of a database schema from the ER conceptual model to the relational schema.

1.1   The Database Life Cycle

The database life cycle incorporates the basic steps involved in designing a global schema of the logical database, allocating data across a computer network, and defining local DBMS-specific schemas. Once the design is completed, the life cycle continues with database implementation and maintenance. This chapter contains an overview of the database life cycle. In the succeeding chapters, we will focus on the database design process from ER modeling of requirements through distributed data allocation (steps I through IV). The ER approach will be used extensively in steps I and II.

I. *Requirements analysis*. The database requirements are determined by interviewing both the producers and users of data and producing a formal requirements specification. That specification includes the data required for processing; the natural data relationships; and constraints with respect to performance, integrity, and security. It also defines the hardware and software platform for the database implementation.

II. *Logical design*. The *global schema*, which shows all the data and their relationships, is developed using conceptual data modeling techniques such as ER. The data model constructs must ultimately be transformed into normalized (global) relations. The global schema development methodology is the same for either a distributed or centralized database.

   a. *ER modeling*. The data requirements are analyzed and modeled by using an ER diagram that includes, for example, semantics for optional relationships, ternary relationships, and subtypes (categories). Processing requirements are typically specified using natural language expressions or SQL commands along with the frequency of occurrence.

   b. *View integration*. Usually, when the design is large and more than one person is involved in requirements analysis, multiple views of data and relationships result. To eliminate redundancy and inconsistency from the model, these views must eventually be consolidated into a single global view. View integration requires the use of ER semantic tools such as identification of synonyms, aggregation, and generalization.

c. *Transformation of the ER model to SQL relations.* Based on a categorization of ER constructs and a set of mapping rules, each relationship and its associated entities are transformed into a set of candidate relations. We will show these transformations in standard SQL in Chapter 4. Redundant relations are eliminated as part of this process.

d. *Normalization of candidate relations.* Functional dependencies (FDs) are derived from the ER diagram. They represent the dependencies among data elements that are keys of entities. Additional FDs and multivalued dependencies (MVDs), which represent the dependencies among key and nonkey attributes within entities, can be derived from the requirements specification. Candidate relations associated with all derived FDs and MVDs are then normalized to the highest degree desired by using standard normalization techniques. Finally, redundancies that occur in normalized candidate relations are analyzed further for possible elimination, with the constraint that data integrity must be preserved.

III. *Usage refinement.* In this step the global schema is refined in limited ways to reflect processing requirements if there are obvious large gains in efficiency to be made. Usage refinement consists of selecting dominant processes on the basis of high frequency, high volume, or explicit priority; defining simple extensions to relations that will improve query performance; evaluating total cost for query, update, and storage; and considering the possible effects of denormalization. The justification for this approach is that, once local site physical design begins, the logical schema is considered to be fixed and is thus a constraint on efficiency. The database designer would like to remove this inflexibility if possible. Nevertheless, the usage refinement step makes assumptions about the physical design environment such that one may consider it to be actually an advanced stage of physical design.

IV. *Data distribution.* Data fragmentation and allocation are also forms of physical design because they must take into account the physical environment, that is, the network configuration. However, this step is separate from local schema and physical design, because design decisions for data distribution are still made independently of the local DBMS.

A *fragmentation schema* describes the one-to-many mapping used to partition each global relation into fragments. Fragments are logical portions of global relations, which are physically located at one or several sites of the network. A data *allocation schema* designates where each copy of each fragment is to be stored. A one-to-one mapping in the allocation schema results in nonredundancy; a one-to-many mapping defines a replicated distributed database.

Three important objectives of database design in distributed systems are

- the separation of data fragmentation and allocation
- control of redundancy, and
- independence from local database management systems

The distinction between designing the fragmentation and allocation schema is important: The first one is a logical mapping, but the second one is a physical mapping. In general, it is not possible to determine the optimal fragmentation and allocation by solving the two problems independently since they are interrelated. However, near-optimal solutions can be obtained with separable design steps, and this is the only practical solution available today.

V. *Local schema and physical design*. The last step in the design phase is to produce a DBMS-specific physical structure for each of the site databases and to define the *external user schema*. In a heterogeneous system, local schema and physical design are site dependent. The logical design methodology in step II simplifies the approach to designing large relational databases by reducing the number of data dependencies that need to be analyzed. This is accomplished by inserting ER modeling and integration steps (steps IIa and IIb) into the traditional relational design approach. The objective of these steps is an accurate representation of reality. Data integrity is preserved through normalization of the candidate relations created when the ER model is transformed into a relational model.

VI. *Database implementation, monitoring, and modification.* Once the design is completed, the database can be created through implementation of the formal schema by using the data definition language (DDL) of a DBMS. Then, as the database begins operation, monitoring will indicate whether performance requirements are being met. If they are not being satisfied, modifications should be made to improve performance. Other modifications may be necessary when requirements change or end-user expectations increase with good performance. Thus the life cycle continues, with monitoring, redesign, and modifications.

1.2 Case Study: Mathematical Reviews Publishing Application

A single case study is used throughout the text to show how ER concepts can be applied to the database design process. The case is especially instructive because it is large enough to illustrate most of the concepts but small enough to be quickly absorbed by the reader. It also has the advantage of being a real-life database design and implementation problem. The project is briefly introduced in this section. The text does not go into an excessive amount of detail about this particular application but merely uses it to illustrate the basic concepts of ER modeling and database design.

Mathematical Reviews produces a journal of bibliographic citations and reviews for mathematical papers. The database supports a series of steps through which submissions pass, including initial order and receipt, editorial screening of papers to be reviewed, selection of specific mathematicians to be reviewers, and final publishing. It is used to produce author and subject indexes in addition to the periodical.

Although the database is moderate in size (it contains information on approximately 180,000 papers, 70,000 authors, and 10,000 reviewers and grows physically by approximately 100 megabytes per year), it is a reasonable prototype for larger databases because it presents examples of most of the ER constructs presented in the following chapters.

To support the publication activities described, the database manages information about

- mathematical journals, books, and series
- publishers of journals, books, and series
- sources from whom the materials are obtained
- bibliographic and internal processing information about papers selected for review
- authors
- reviewers

The details of the requirements specification of this application are not of particular interest here. The text will, however, define the requirements necessary to explain the modeling constructs and present summaries of the database design at appropriate points. The description in the following chapters is based closely, but not exactly, on the actual Mathematical Reviews publication database. Certain liberties have been taken with the actual specifications to clarify the text or to illustrate important concepts not implemented in the original database.

1.3   Summary

ER modeling is an important technique for database practitioners, because of its simplicity and readability. The simple form is used in most CASE tools and is easy to learn and apply to a variety of industrial and business applications. It is also a very useful tool for communicating with the end-user about the conceptual model and verifying the assumptions made in the modeling process. The complex form is useful for the more experienced designer who wants to capture greater semantic detail in diagram form and avoid having to write long and tedious narrative to explain certain requirements and constraints over and over again.

The database life cycle shows what steps are needed in a methodical approach to database design from logical design, which is independent of the system environment, to data distribution in a computer network and to local physical design, which is based on the details of the database management system chosen to implement the database. The detailed steps in the database life cycle are illustrated using a case study taken from a real-life database. In the next chapter we look first at the basic ER modeling concepts, then—starting in Chapter 3—we apply these concepts to the database design process.

Literature Summary

Database design textbooks that adhere to a significant portion of the database life cycle described in this chapter are [TeFr82, Howe83, Hawr84, Wied83, Yao85]. For general textbooks on database systems, consult [Spro76, Ullm88, Date86, Ever86, KoSi88, ElNa89, Maci89]. Some of the early research in CASE tools for the ER model was done by [TeHe77, CFT84, Rein85].

[Bach69]   Bachman, C.W. "Data Structure Diagrams," *Database* 1,2(1969), pp. 4–10.

[Bach72]   Bachman, C.W. "The Evolution of Storage Structures," *Comm. ACM* 15,7(July 1972), pp. 628–634.

[Chen76]   Chen, P.P. "The Entity-Relationship Model—Toward a Unified View of Data," *ACM Trans. Database Systems* 1,1(March 1976), pp. 9–36.

[CFT84]   Cobb, R.E., Fry, J.P., and Teorey, T.J. "The Database Designer's Workbench," *Information Sciences* 32,1(Feb. 1984), pp. 33–45.

[Date86]   Date, C.J. *An Introduction to Database Systems*, Vol. 1 (4th Ed.), Addison-Wesley, Reading, MA, 1986.

[ElNa89]   Elmasri, R., and Navathe, S.B. *Fundamentals of Database Systems*, Addison-Wesley/Benjamin/Cummings, Redwood City, CA, 1989.

[Ever86]   Everest, G.C. *Database Management: Objectives, System Functions, and Administration*, McGraw-Hill, New York, 1986.

[Hawr84]   Hawryszkiewycz, I. *Database Analysis and Design*, SRA, Chicago, 1984.

[Howe83]   Howe, D. *Data Analysis and Data Base Design*, Arnold, London, 1983.

[KoSi88]   Korth, H.F. and Silberschatz, A. *Database System Concepts*, McGraw-Hill, New York, 1986.

[Maci89]   Maciaszek, L. *Database Design and Implementation*, Prentice-Hall International, 1989.

[NvS79]   Nijssen, G., van Asscher, F., and Snijders, J. "End User Tools for Information Systems Requirement Definition," *Formal Models and Practical Tools for Information System Design*, H. Schneider (editor), North-Holland, 1979.

[Rein85]   Reiner, D., Brodie, M., Brown, G., Friedell, M., Kramlich, D., Lehman, J., and Rosenthal, A. "The Database Design and Evaluation Workbench (DDEW) Project at CCA," *Database Engineering* 7,4(1985), 10–15.

[Spro76]   Sprowls, R.C. *Management Data Bases*, Wiley/Hamilton, Santa Barbara, CA, 1976.

[TeHe77]   Teichroew, D., and Hershey, E.A. "PSL/PSA: A Computer Aided Technique for Structured Documentation and Analysis of Information Processing Systems," *IEEE Trans. Software Engr.* SE-3,1(1977), pp. 41–48.

[TeFr82]   Teorey, T., and Fry, J. *Design of Database Structures*, Prentice-Hall, Englewood Cliffs, NJ, 1982.

[Ullm88]   Ullman, J. *Principles of Database and Knowledge-Base Systems*, Vols. 1 and 2, Computer Science Press, Rockville, MD, 1988.

[Wied83]   Wiederhold, G. *Database Design* (2nd Ed.), McGraw-Hill, New York, 1983.

[Yao85]   Yao, S.B. (editor). *Principles of Database Design*, Prentice-Hall, Englewood Cliffs, NJ, 1985.

2

The ER Model:
Basic Concepts

This chapter defines all the major entity relationship concepts that can be applied to the database life cycle. In Section 2.1, we will look at the simple level of ER modeling that was described in the original work by Chen and extended by others. This work is the basis for effective communication with the end-user about the conceptual model. Section 2.2 presents the more advanced concepts that are less generally accepted but useful to describe certain semantics that cannot be constructed with the simple model.

2.1   Fundamental ER Constructs

2.1.1   Basic Objects: Entities, Relationships, Attributes

The basic ER model consists of three classes of objects: entities, relationships, and attributes.

Entities are the principal data objects about which information is to be collected; they usually denote a person, place, thing, or event of informational interest. (This book drops the older term *entity set* and uses *entities* to represent entity types.) A particular occurrence of an entity is called an entity instance, or sometimes referred to as an entity occurrence. In our case study, authors, editors, publishers, journals, papers, books, institutions, and standing orders are all examples of entities. For easy reference, entity names will henceforth be capitalized throughout this text: Author, Editor, and so forth. The entity construct is a rectangle as depicted in Figure 2.1.

Relationships represent real-world associations among one or more entities, and as such, have no physical or conceptual existence other than that which is inherited from their entity associations. A particular occurrence of a relationship is called a relationship instance or, sometimes, relationship occurrence. Relationships are described in terms of degree, connectivity, cardinality, and existence. These terms are defined in the sections that follow. The most common meaning associated with the term *relationship* is indicated by the connectivity between entity occurrences: one-to-one, one-to-many, and many-to-many.

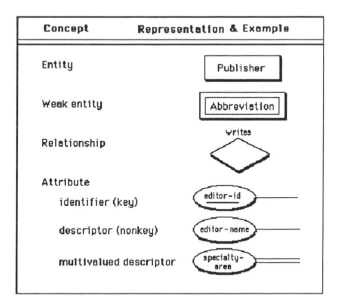

Figure 2.1
Fundamental ER constructs: basic objects.

A role is defined as the function an entity plays in a relationship. For example, the role "edits" defines the function of the entity Editor in the relationship between Editor and Paper in Figure 2.2. The role name and

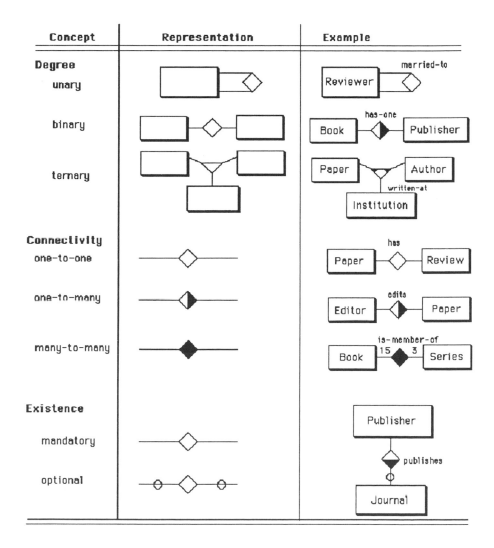

Figure 2.2
Fundamental ER constructs: relationship types.

relationship name are equivalent. Convention dictates that role names should act as verbs (if possible) between the nouns for entity names and, for readability, should be read from left to right or top to bottom in ER diagrams. In the example we read "Editor edits Paper" as a way of describing the relationship. Unfortunately, we cannot always set up our role names so easily, but we try!

Attributes are characteristics of entities or relationships that provide descriptive detail about them. These relationships are needed within the enterprise. A particular occurrence of an attribute within an entity or relationship is called an *attribute value*. Attributes of an entity such as Author may include name, address, id-number, phone, institution, and so on. An attribute of a relationship such as the is-member-of relationship between the entities Book and Series could be membership-id or date-of membership. In this case, a given membership-id or date-of-membership is common only to an instance of the membership of a particular Book in a particular Series, and it would be multivalued when assigned to either the Book or the Series entity alone. Performance and storage utilization would be optimized at database implementation time by assigning these attributes to the relation-ship rather than the entities, because each instance of a membership-id associated with a Book must carry information about the Series with it, creating unnecessary redundancy of data.

There are two types of attributes: identifiers and descriptors. An *identifier* (or key) is used to uniquely determine an instance of an entity; a *descriptor* (or nonkey attribute) is used to specify a nonunique characteristic of a particular entity instance. Both identifiers and descriptors may consist of either a single attribute or some composite of attributes. For example, an identifier or key of Editor is editor-id, and a descriptor of Editor is editor-name or specialty-area. Key attributes are underlined in the ER diagram, as shown in Fig. 2.1. Some attributes, such as specialty-area, may be multival-ued. The notation for multivalued attributes is shown with a double attach-ment line, as shown in Fig. 2.1.

Entities have internal identifiers that uniquely determine the existence of entity instances, but *weak entities* derive their identity from the identifying attributes of one or more "parent" entities. Weak entities are often depicted with a double-bordered rectangle (see Fig. 2.1), which denotes that all oc-currences of that entity are dependent for their existence in the database on the existence of an associated (strong) entity. For example, in Fig. 2.1 the weak entity Abbreviation could be related to an entity such as Publisher or Publication, and dependent upon the other entity for its own existence. Typically, a weak entity could be alternatively modeled as a multivalued attribute associated with an entity or a many-to-many relationship between two entites, so that the identity dependence is more obvious.

2.1.2   Degree of a Relationship

The *degree* of a relationship is the number of entities associated in the relationship. Unary, binary, and ternary relationships are special cases where the degree is 1, 2, and 3, respectively. An n-ary relationship is the general form for any degree n. The notation for degree is illustrated in Fig. 2.2.

The *binary relationship*, an association between two entities, is by far the most common type in the natural world. In fact, many modeling systems use only this type. In Fig. 2.2 we see many examples of the association of two entities in different ways: books and publishers, papers and reviews, editors and papers, and so on. The *unary relationship*—for example, married-to in Fig. 2.2—relates a particular reviewer to another reviewer by marriage. It is called unary because it involves only a single entity type. It is also called recursive in some data modeling systems, because the entity relates only to itself. A *ternary relationship* relates three entities to each other in such a way that it cannot be decomposed into equivalent binary relationships. Sometimes a relationship is mistakenly modeled as ternary, when it could be decomposed into two or three equivalent binary relationships. When this occurs, the ternary relationship should be eliminated to achieve both simplicity and semantic purity. Ternary relationships are discussed in greater detail in Sections 2.2 and 5.5.

2.1.3   Connectivity and Cardinality of a Relationship

The *connectivity* of a relationship describes the mapping of the associated entity occurrences in the relationship. Values for connectivity are either "one" or "many." For a relationship between entities Publisher and Book, a connectivity of one for Publisher and many for Book means that there is at most one entity occurrence of Publisher associated with many occurrences of Book.

The actual number associated with the term *many* is called the *cardinality* of the relationship connectivity. Cardinality describes the constraint on the number of entity instances that are related through a relationship. For example, in Fig. 2.2 the entity Book in the many-to-many relationship may be a member of a maximum of three Series; thus, the maximum cardinality is 3 on the Series side of the is-member-of relationship. Reading from right to left in the same relationship, we may be told that the entity Series may contain a maximum of 15 Books. Thus, 15 is the maximum cardinality of Book in the is-member-of relationship. The minimum cardinalities in all relationships of any type are either zero or one, depending on whether the relationship is optional or mandatory, respectively (see Section 2.1.4). In this case the minimum cardinalities are one for both Series and Book.

Figure 2.2 shows the basic constructs for connectivity for binary relationships: one-to-one, one-to-many, and many-to-many. The shaded area in the binary relationship diamond represents the "many" side; the unshaded area represents the "one" side. In the one-to-one case, the entity Paper has exactly one Review and each Review is for exactly one Paper. Therefore, the minimum and maximum cardinalities on the "has" relationship are exactly one for both Paper and Review.

In the one-to-many case, the entity Editor is associated with ("edits") many Papers. The maximum cardinality is not given on the Paper (many) side, but the minimum cardinality is defined as one. On the Editor side the minimum and maximum cardinalities are both one, that is, each Paper is edited by exactly one Editor.

In the many-to-many case, the entity Book may be a member of many Series and each Series may contain many Books. We saw that the maximum cardinality for Book and Series was 15 and 3, respectively, and the minimum cardinalities were each defined as 1. In the next section we will define the minimum cardinality more succinctly.

2.1.4   Existence of an Entity in a Relationship

Some enterprises have entities whose existence depends on the existence of another entity. This is called *existence dependency*, or just *existence*.

Existence of an entity in a relationship is defined as either mandatory or optional. If an occurrence of either the "one" or "many" side entity must always exist for the entity to be included in the relationship, then it is mandatory. When an occurrence of that entity need not exist, it is considered optional. For example, the entity Author may or may not have written a Book, thus making the entity Book in the "writes" relationship between Author and Book optional. Optional existence, defined by a 0 on the connectivity line between an entity and a relationship, defines a minimum cardinality of zero; mandatory existence defines a minimum cardinality of one. Maximum cardinalities are defined explicitly on the ER diagram as a constant (if a number is shown on the ER diagram next to an entity) or variable (by default if no number is shown on the ER diagram next to an entity). For example, in Fig. 2.2 the relationship "publishes" between the entity Publisher and Journal implies that a Publisher may publish from zero to some variable maximum (n) number of Journals, but a Journal must be published by exactly one Publisher.

Existence is often implicit in the real world. For example, an entity Employee associated with a dependent (weak) entity, Dependent, cannot be optional, but the weak entity is usually optional. Being a weak entity is a stronger form of existence dependency than optional existence. In optional existence, an entity occurrence may be able to exist in other relationships even though it is not participating in this particular relationship.

At this point we need digress briefly to look at other ER constructs that are commonly used today and compare them with the approach selected for this book. Connectivity in the ER model is commonly expressed by the classical notation originally described by Chen (see Fig. 2.3a), in which each entity in a relationship can be explicitly described as 1 or N, representing the "one" or "many" side, respectively. The circle on the connectivity line of the relationship denotes optional existence. The constructs for entities, weak entities, and attributes are basically the same for these two approaches; the differences between them for binary and unary relationships is minor.

A popular alternative form of one-to-many or many-to-many relationships uses "crow's foot" for the "many" side (see Fig. 2.3b). Fortunately, any of these forms is reasonably easy to learn and read, and the equivalence for the basic ER concepts is obvious from the diagrams. Unfortunately, however, there is currently no standard for the ER model, and many other constructs are being used today in addition to the three types shown here.

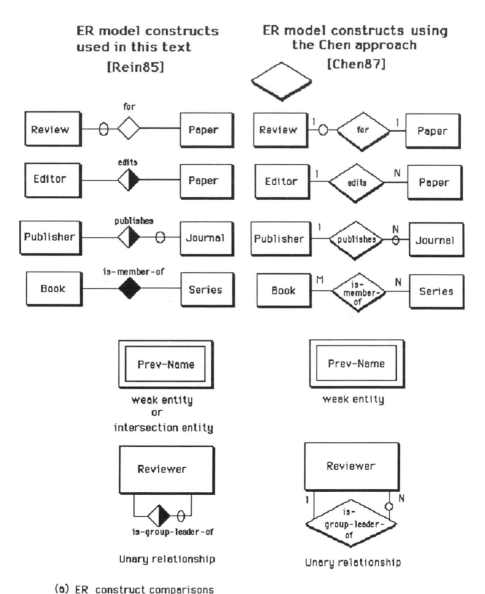

(a) ER construct comparisons

Figure 2.3
Comparison of ER construct conventions.

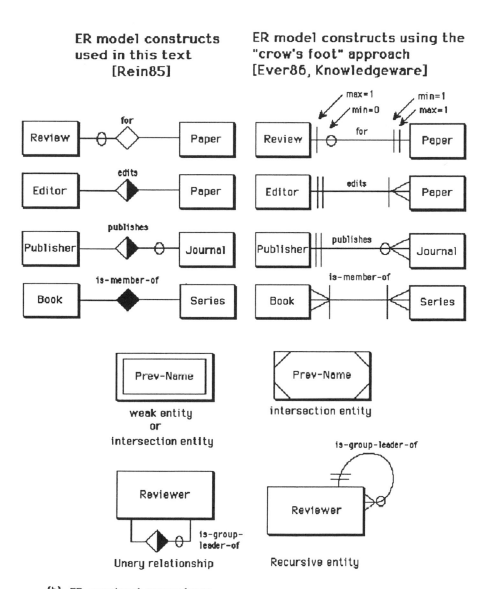

(b) ER construct comparisons

Figure 2.3, continued

Although standards efforts are currently underway, it will be several years before standardization will be achieved. Developers of CASE tools would certainly benefit from standardization, and in turn most database developers should welcome it.

2.1.5   Generalization: Supertypes and Subtypes

The original ER model has been effectively used for communicating fundamental data and relationship definitions with the end-user for a long time. However, using it to develop and integrate conceptual models with different end-user views was severely limited until it could be extended to include database abstraction concepts such as generalization. The *generalization relationship* specifies that several types of entities with certain common attributes can be generalized into a higher-level entity type:

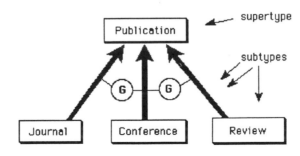

(a) Notation used throughout this book

(b) Alternate notation popularly used

Figure 2.4
Generalization constructs.

a generic entity, or superclass entity, which is more commonly known as a *supertype entity*. The lower levels of entities—*subtypes* in a generalization hierarchy—are generally assumed to be disjoint subsets of the supertype entity. For example, in Fig. 2.4a the entity Publication is a higher-level abstraction of Journal, Conference, and Review—all of which are disjoint types of publications. We denote the generalization relationship with the letter G, as shown in Fig. 2.4a. An alternate (equivalent) construct for generalization is shown in Fig. 2.4b.

A supertype entity in one relationship may be a subtype entity in another relationship. When a combination of supertype/subtype relationships comprise a structure, the structure is called a *supertype/subtype hierarchy*, or *generalization hierarchy*. Generalization can also be described in terms of *inheritance*, which specifies which attributes of a supertype are propagated down the hierarchy to entities of a lower type. An entity E is a generalization of the entities E1,E2,...,En, if each instance of E is also an instance of one and only one of the entities E1,E2,...,En. Generalization occurs when a generic entity, which we call the supertype entity, is partitioned by different values of a common attribute. For example, in Fig. 2.4a the entity Publication could be a generalization of Journal, Conference, and Review over the attribute publication_type in Publication. The inheritance property of generalization hierarchies states that all attributes defined for the supertype entity are inherited by all the subtype entities.

When the subtypes are really overlapping subsets, such as with Author and Reviewer as subtypes of Individual in Fig. 2.5, we call it *subset generalization* and denote it as a variation of generalization by the notation G_s. The

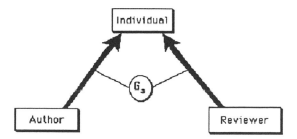

Figure 2.5
Generalization with overlapping subsets.

same inheritance properties apply to both generalization and subset generalization. Also, in both cases, each subtype entity may have additional special attributes that pertain only to it, and not to the supertype.

2.2 Advanced ER Constructs

2.2.1 Ternary and Higher n-ary Relationships

We will use an n-sided polygon between entities to represent n-ary relationships for n>2. Each corner of the n-sided polygon connects to an entity. A shaded corner denotes a "many" side and an unshaded corner denotes a "one" side. This device enables us to show graphically both the degree and connectivity of the relationship.

Ternary relationships

The ternary relationship is somewhat more complex. An entity in a ternary relationship is considered to be "one" if only one instance of it can be associated with one instance of each of the other two associated entities. It is "many" if more than one instance of it can be associated with one instance of each of the other two associated entities. In either case, one instance of each of the other entities is assumed to be given.

As an example, the relationship "written-at" in Fig. 2.6c associates the entities Author, Paper, and Institution. The entities Author and Paper are considered "many"; the entity Institution is considered "one." This is represented by the following assertions:

Assertion 1: *One author*, writing at *one institution*, could write *many papers*.

Assertion 2: *One paper*, written at *one institution*, could have *many authors*.

Assertion 3: *One author*, writing *one paper*, must credit only a *single institution*.

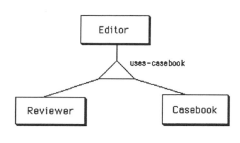

(a) one-to-one-to-one ternary relationship

An editor will use one casebook for a given reviewer. Different editors use different casebooks for the same reviewer. No editor will use the same casebook for different reviewers, but different editors can use the same casebook for different reviewers.

Functional dependencies

editor_id, rvr_id -> book_no
editor_id, book_no -> rvr_id
rvr_id, book_no -> editor_id

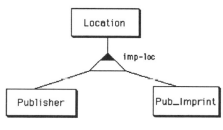

(b) one-to-one-to-many ternary relationship

Each publisher/location pair must have one imprint. Each publisher imprint/location pair may refer to only one publisher. Each publisher and publisher imprint may occur at multiple locations.

Functional dependencies

loc_addr, pub_id -> pub_imp_id
loc_addr, pub_imp_id -> pub_id

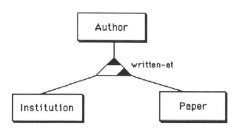

(c) one-to-many-to-many ternary relationship

Authors can work at one or more institutions, but can credit at most one institution to a given paper.

Functional dependencies

auth_id, paper_id -> inst_name

Figure 2.6
Types and properties of ternary relationships.

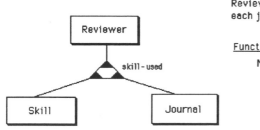

Reviewers use a wide range of skills on each journal they review for.

Functional dependencies

None

(d) many-to-many-to-many ternary relationship

Figure 2.6, continued

Assertion 3 could also be written in another form, using an arrow (–>) in a kind of shorthand form called a functional dependency. For example:

author_id, paper_id –> inst_name

where author_id is the primary key associated with the entity Author, paper_id is the primary key associated with the entity Paper, and inst_name is the primary key of the entity Institution. In general, for an n-ary relationship, each entity considered to be a "one" has its key appearing on the right side of exactly one functional dependency (FD). No entity considered "many" ever has its key appear on the right side of an FD.

All four forms of ternary relationships are illustrated in Fig. 2.6. In each case the number of "one" entities implies the number of FDs used to define the relationship semantics, and the key of each "one" entity appears on the right side of exactly one FD for that relationship.

General n-ary relationships

Generalizing this form to higher-degree relationships, an n-ary relationship that describes some association among n entities is represented by anywhere from zero to n FDs, depending on the number of "one" entities. The FDs that describe an n-ary relationship must have n components: n–1 on the left side (determinant) and 1 on the right side. A ternary relationship (n=3), for example, has two components on the left and one on the right, as we saw in the example in Figure 2.6. In a more complex database, other types of FDs may also exist within an n-ary relationship. When this occurs, the ER model does not provide enough semantics by itself, and it must be supplemented with a narrative description of these dependencies (see Chapter 5).

2.2.2   ER Constraints:
Extensions from the NIAM Model

Conceptual modeling of databases is by no means confined to the ER approach. A number of other schools of thought have received attention, and some offer a richer semantic base than the ER model. The binary relationship approach is the basis of the information analysis method called Nijssen's Information Analysis Method (NIAM) [VeVa82]. This approach, which develops normalized (fifth normal form) relations from basic semantic constructs, provides low-level primitive constructs such as lexical object type, nonlexical object type, and role. These roughly correspond to the attribute, entity, and relationship concepts, respectively, in the ER model. However, unlike the ER approach, the binary relationship model tries to avoid making entity-attribute decisions early in the conceptual modeling process. The binary relationship model also includes the semantic concepts of subtyping (generalization), relationship connectivity, and membership class (mandatory or optional existence).

One obvious difference between the binary relationship model and the ER approach is that role names in the binary relationship model are directional between two lexical object types (attributes) and between a lexical (attribute) and nonlexical object type (entity). In fact, directional role names could easily be added to the ER model, but the designer would have to consider whether or not the added role names would degrade the readability of the ER diagram.

One of the most interesting aspects of the binary relationship model is the inclusion of integrity constraints on role occurrences. Some of the NIAM constraints such as total role, exclusion, subset, and uniqueness can be easily adapted to the ER model. In the following paragraphs we illustrate how this could be done with some *nonstandard* ER notation.

Total role (relationship) constraint

The total role constraint, shown by the darkened circle in Fig. 2.7 near the entity Book, indicates that every instance of this entity must participate in the role (relationship) with the entity Publisher. Normally the role is not mandatory for every instance, so the total role constraint must be explicitly stated. This is quite different from mandatory/optional existence, where the entity instance itself may or may not exist. The term *total role* implies that if the entity exists, each instance of that entity must participate in the designated relationship type. Weak entities are implicitly considered to be "total role" at all times.

Exclusion constraint

Multiple relationships may be affected by the exclusion (disjoint or exclusive OR) constraint, which allows at most one leaf entity instance among several leaf entity types, to participate in the relationship with the root entity. For example, in Fig. 2.8, suppose the root entity is Standing_Order and the leaf entities are Journal, Publisher, and Series. At most one of the leaf entity instances could apply to an instance of the root, Standing_Order. The normal, or default, treatment of multiple relationships is the inclusive OR, which allows any or all of the leaf entities to participate.

Subset constraint

A two-relationship constraint, subset, is shown in Fig. 2.9. It requires the set of leaf entity instances in one relationship to be a subset of the leaf entity instances in the other relationship. For example, Reviewers who are employed to review articles in professional society (Prof-society) journals must

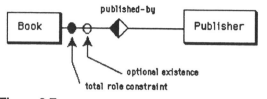

Each book must be represented by a publisher, that is, each book must participate in this relationship.

Figure 2.7
Total role constraint.

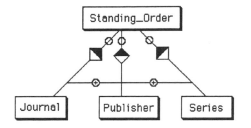

A standing order may be set up for either a journal, publisher, or series, but only one at a time.

Figure 2.8
Exclusion constraint.

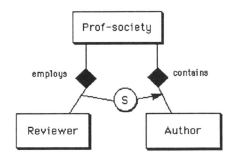

All professional societies require all reviewers to be authors, but some authors do not have to be reviewers.

Figure 2.9
Subset constraint.

be selected from Authors who publish in those journals. If the subset arrow appears closer to the root entity, then the subset relationship applies to the instances of the root entity in the two relationships. The subset constraint is not a commonly used construct.

Uniqueness constraint

The uniqueness constraint in the NIAM model combines three or more entities such that the combination of roles for the two entities in one direction uniquely determines the value of the single entity in the other direction. This, in effect, defines an FD from the composite keys of the entities in the first direction to the key of the entity in the second direction, and thus partly defines a ternary relationship. The ER constructs for ternary relationships are equivalent to the uniqueness constraint in NIAM.

2.2.3 Entity Integrity, Referential Integrity, and ID Dependency

Entity integrity, as defined in the relational model, requires that if an entity exists and it has a primary key, then its primary key must also exist. *Referential integrity* requires that for every foreign key occurrence that exists in a relation, the tuple or row (and thus the primary key occurrence) of the relation associated with that foreign key occurrence must also exist. Both of these constraints have become so common in relational systems that their implicitness need not be described in the ER model; implicitness can be stated as requirements for the resulting relational database implementation. (Chapter 4 will discuss the SQL implementation of ER constructs). *ID dependency* is a special case of existence dependency in which there is an additional constraint that the primary key of the weak entity must include the key of the associated strong (parent) entity. This could be indicated by including the letters "id" in the corner of the box for the weak entity.

2.3 Summary

The basic concepts of the entity-relationship model and their constructs are described in this chapter. An entity is a person, place, thing, or event of informational interest. Attributes are objects that provide descriptive information about entities. Attributes may be unique identifiers or nonunique descriptors. Relationships describe the connectivity between entity instances: one-to-one, one-to-many, or many-to-many. The degree of a relationship is the number of associated entities: one (unary), two (binary), three (ternary), or any n (n-ary). The role (name), or relationship name, defines the function of an entity in a relationship.

The concept of existence in a relationship determines whether an entity instance must exist (mandatory) or not (optional). So, for example, the minimum cardinality of a binary relationship—that is, the number of entity instances on one side that are associated with one instance on the other side—can either be zero if optional or one if mandatory. The concept of generalization allows for the implementation of supertype and subtype abstractions.

The more advanced concepts of ER modeling are sporadically used and have no generally accepted construct as yet. They include ternary relationships, which we define in terms of the FD concept of relational databases; constraints borrowed from the NIAM model (total role, exclusion, subset, and uniqueness); and the implicit constraints from the relational model such as referential integrity and primary key integrity.

We are now ready to apply the basic ER concepts to the life cycle database design steps.

Literature Summary

Most of the notation in this book is taken from the original ER definition by Chen [Chen76], with the total role notation taken from [Chen87], and the shaded relationship coming from the Database Design and Evaluation Workbench project at CCA [Rein85]. The concept of data abstraction was first proposed by Smith and Smith [SmSm77] and applied to the ER model by [SSW80, NaCh83, TYF86, ElNa89] among others. The application of the semantic network model to conceptual schema design was shown by [Bach77, McKi79, PoKe86, HuKi87, PeMa88], and the binary relationship model concepts, including the NIAM model, were studied by [Abri74, BPP76, NvS79, ISO82, VeVa82, Kent84, Mark87]. Other extensions to the original ER model such as the inclusion of the time dimension have also been described elsewhere [Bube77, ClWa83, LCC84, Ferg85, Aria86, Ever86, MTM89].

[Abri74]   Abrial, J. "Data Semantics," *Data Base Management, Proc. IFIP TC2 Conf.*, Cargese, Corsica, North-Holland, 1974.

[Aria86]   Ariav, G. "A Temporally Oriented Data Model," *ACM Trans. Database Systems* 11,4(Dec. 1986), pp. 499–527.

[Bach77]   Bachman, C.W. "The Role Concept in Data Models," *Proc. 3rd Int'l. Conf. on Very Large Data Bases*, Tokyo, Oct. 6–8, 1977, IEEE, New York, pp. 464–476.

[BPP76]   Bracchi, G., Paolini, P., and Pelagatti, G. "Binary Logical Associations in Data Modelling," *Modelling in Data Base Management*

Systems, Proc. IFIP TC2 Conf., Freudenstadt, North-Holland, 1976.

[Bube77]   Bubenko, J. "The Temporal Dimension in Information Modelling," *Architecture and Models in Data Base Management Systems*, G. Nijssen (editor), North-Holland, 1977.

[Chen76]   Chen, P.P. "The Entity-Relationship Model—Toward a Unified View of Data," *ACM Trans. Database Systems* 1,1(March 1976), pp. 9–36.

[Chen87]   Chen and Associates, Inc. *ER Designer* (user manual), 1987.

[ClWa83]   Clifford, J., and Warren, D. "Formal Semantics for Time in Databases," *ACM Trans. Database Systems* 8,2(1983), pp. 214–254.

[ElNa89]   Elmasri, R., and Navathe, S.B. *Fundamentals of Database Systems*, Addison-Wesley/Benjamin/Cummings, Redwood City, CA, 1989.

[Ever86]   Everest, G.C. *Database Management: Objectives, System Functions, and Administration*, McGraw-Hill, New York, 1986.

[Ferg85]   Ferg, S. "Modeling the Time Dimension in an Entity-Relationship Diagram," *Proc. 4th Int'l. Conf. on the Entity-Relationship Approach*, Chicago, IEEE Computer Society Press, Silver Spring, MD, 1985, pp. 280–286.

[HuKi87]   Hull, R., and King, R. "Semantic Database Modeling: Survey, Applications, and Research Issues," *ACM Computing Surveys* 19,3(Sept. 1987), pp. 201–260.

[ISO82]   ISO/TC97/SC5/WG3-N695 Report "Concepts and Terminology for the Conceptual Schema and the Information Base," J. van Griethuysen (editor), ANSI, New York, 1982, 180 pp.

[Kent84]   Kent, W. "Fact-Based Data Analysis and Design," *J. Systems and Software* 4(1984), pp. 99–121.

[LCC84]   Lee, R.M., Coelho, H., and Cotta, J.C. "Temporal Inferencing on Administrative Databases," *Information Systems* 10,2(1985), pp. 197–206.

[Mark87]   Mark, L. "Defining Views in the Binary Relationship Model," *Inform. Systems* 12,3(1987), pp. 281–294.

[McKi79]   McLeod, D., and King, R. "Applying a Semantic Database Model," *Proc. 1st Int'l. Conf. on the Entity-Relationship Approach to Systems Analysis and Design*, Los Angeles, North-Holland, 1979, pp. 193–210.

[MTM89]   Moyne, J.R., Teorey, T.J. and McAfee, L.C. "Time Sequencing and Ordering Extensions to the Entity Relationship Model and Their Application to the Automated Manufacturing Process," submitted to *IEEE Trans. on Data and Knowledge Engr.*

[NaCh83]   Navathe, S., and Cheng, A. "A Methodology for Database Schema Mapping from Extended Entity Relationship Models into the Hierarchical Model," *The Entity-Relationship Approach to Software Engineering*, G.C. Davis et al. (editors), Elsevier, North-Holland, 1983.

[NvS79]   Nijssen, G., van Assche, F., and Snijders, J. "End User Tools for Information Systems Requirement Definition," *Formal Models and Practical Tools for Information System Design*, H. Schneider (editor), North-Holland, 1979.

[PeMa88]   Peckham, J., and Maryanski, F. "Semantic Data Models," *ACM Computing Surveys* 20,3(Sept. 1988), pp. 153–190.

[PoKe86]   Potter, W.D., and Kerschberg, L. "A Unified Approach to Modeling Knowledge and Data," *IFIP WG 2.6 Working Conf. on Knowledge and Data*, University of South Carolina, Elsevier, North-Holland, New York, Sept. 1986, 32 pp.

[Rein85]   Reiner, D., Brodie, M., Brown, G., Friedell, M., Kramlich, D., Lehman, J., and Rosenthal, A. "The Database Design and Evaluation Workbench (DDEW) Project at CCA," *Database Engineering* 7,4(1985), 10–15.

[SSW80]   Scheuermann, P., Scheffner, G., and Weber, H. "Abstraction Capabilities and Invariant Properties Modelling within the Entity-Relationship Approach," *Entity-Relationship Approach to Systems Analysis and Design*, P. Chen (editor), Elsevier, North-Holland, 1980, pp. 121–140.

[SmSm77]   Smith, J. and Smith, D. "Database Abstractions: Aggregation and Generalization," *ACM Trans. Database Systems* 2,2(June 1977), pp. 105–133.

[TYF86]   Teorey, T.J., Yang, D. and Fry, J.P. "A Logical Design Methodol-
              ogy for Relational Databases Using the Extended Entity-Relation-
              ship Model," *ACM Computing Surveys* 18,2(June 1986),
              pp. 197–222.

[VeVa82]   Verheijen, G., and Van Bekkum, J. "NIAM: An Information
              Analysis Method," *Information Systems Design Methodologies*,
              Olle, Sol, and Verryn-Stuart (editors). North-Holland, 1982,
              pp. 537–590.

3

ER Modeling in Logical Database Design

This chapter shows how the ER approach can be applied to the database life cycle, particularly in steps I through IIb, which include the requirements analysis and conceptual modeling stages of logical database design. The case study introduced in Chapter 1 is used again to illustrate the ER modeling principles developed in this chapter.

3.1 Introduction

Logical database design is accomplished with a variety of approaches, including the top-down, bottom-up, and combined methodologies. The traditional approach has been a low-level, bottom-up activity, synthesizing individual data elements into normalized relations after careful analysis of the data element interdependencies defined by the requirements analysis. Although the traditional process is vital to the design of relational databases in particular, its complexity for large databases can be overwhelming to the point where practicing designers do not bother to use it with any regularity. In practice, a combination of the top-down and bottom-up approaches is used; in some cases, relations can be defined directly from the requirements analysis. A new form of the combined approach has recently become popular because of the introduction of the ER model into the process.

The ER model has been most successful as a tool for communication between the designer and the end-user during the requirements analysis and logical design phases. Its success is due to the fact that the model is easy to understand and convenient to represent. Another reason for its effectiveness is that it is a top-down approach using the concept of abstraction. The number of entities in a database is typically an order of magnitude less than the number of data elements, because data elements usually represent the attributes. Therefore, using entities as an abstraction for data elements and focusing on the interentity relationships greatly reduces the number of objects under consideration and simplifies the analysis. Though it is still necessary to represent data elements by attributes of entities at the conceptual level, their dependencies are normally confined to the other attributes within the entity or, in some cases, to those attributes associated with other entities that have a direct relationship to their entity.

The major interattribute dependencies are between the entity keys, the unique identifiers of different entities that are captured in the ER modeling process. Special cases such as dependencies among data elements of unrelated entities can be handled when they are identified in the ensuing data analysis.

The logical database design approach defined here uses both the ER model and the relational model in successive stages. It benefits from the simplicity and ease of use of the ER model and the structure and associated formalism of the relational model. In order to facilitate this approach, it is necessary to build a framework for transforming the variety of ER constructs into relations that are already normalized or can be normalized with the minimum of transformation. Before we do this, however, we need to first define the major steps of the relational design methodology in the context of the database life cycle.

3.2   Requirements Analysis and ER Modeling

Requirements analysis (step I of the database life cycle) has many objectives:

- to delineate the data requirements of the enterprise in terms of primitive objects

- to describe the information about the objects and the relationships among objects needed to model these data requirements

- to determine the types of transactions that are intended to be executed on the database and the interaction between the transactions and the data objects

- to define any performance, integrity, security, or administrative constraints that must be imposed on the resulting database

- to specify the hardware and software platform for the database implementation

The ER model helps the designer accurately capture the real data requirements because it requires him or her to focus on semantic detail in the data relationships, which is greater than the detail that would be provided by FDs alone. The semantics of ER allow for direct transformations of entities and relationships to at least first normal form relations. They also provide clear guidelines for integrity constraints. In addition, abstraction techniques such as generalization provide useful tools for integrating end-user views to define a global conceptual schema.

Let us now look more closely at the basic objects and relationships that should be defined during requirements analysis and conceptual design. These two life cycle steps are often done simultaneously.

Consider the substeps in step IIa, ER modeling:

- Classify entities and attributes.
- Identify the generalization hierarchies.
- Define relationships.

The remainder of this section will discuss the tasks involved in each substep.

3.2.1 Classify Entities and Attributes

Though it is easy to define entity, attribute, and relationship constructs, it is not as easy to distinguish their roles in modeling the database. What makes an object an entity, an attribute, or even a relationship? For example, publishers are located in cities. Should city be an entity or an attribute? A vita is kept for each reviewer. Is vita an entity or a relationship?

The following guidelines for classifying entities and attributes will help the designer's thoughts converge to a normalized relational database design.

- Entities should contain descriptive information.
- Classify multivalued attributes as entities.
- Attach attributes to the entities they most directly describe.
- Avoid composite identifiers.

Now we will examine each guideline in turn.

Entity Contents

Entities should contain descriptive information. If there is descriptive information about an object, the object should be classified as an entity. If an object requires only an identifier, the object should be classified as an attribute. With city, for example, if there is some descriptive information such as country and population for cities, then city should be classified as an entity. If only the city name is needed to identify a city, then city should be classified as an attribute.

Multivalued Attributes

Classify multivalued attributes as entities. If more than one value of a descriptor corresponds to one value of an identifier, the descriptor should be classified as an entity instead of an attribute, even though it does not have descriptors itself. A large publisher, for example, could have offices in several cities. In that case, city should be classified as an entity even if it needs only the city name as an identifier. If attributes are allowed to be single-valued only, the later design and implementation decisions are simplified. A corollary of this rule is to make an entity of an attribute that has a many-to-one relationship with an entity. If a descriptor in one entity has a many-to-one relationship with another entity, the descriptor should be classified as an entity, even if it does not have its own descriptors.

Attribute Attachment

Attach attributes to the entities they most directly describe. For example, attribute office-bldg should be an attribute of the entity Department instead of the entity Editor.

Composite Identifiers

Avoid composite identifiers as much as possible. If an entity has been defined with a composite identifier (that is, an identifier composed of two or more attributes) and the components of the identifier are all identifiers of other entities, then define this entity as a weak entity or as a relationship. If an entity has been defined with a composite identifier but components of the identifier are not identifiers of other entities, then there are two possible solutions. One solution is to eliminate the entity and define new entities with components of the composite identifier as entity identifiers. Then, in a subsequent step, define a relationship to represent this object. The other solution is to keep the entity with the composite identifier if it is reasonably natural.

As an example, suppose the entity Book-data has been defined, with author-name and book-name as a composite identifier. The entity Book-data could be eliminated, and two new entities—Author and Book—could be defined. Later, in a subsequent step, a relationship between Author and Book could be defined to represent the object book-data. In another example, if an entity Review-team has been defined with specialty-code and leader as a composite identifier, then it seems suitable to keep the entity, because defining an entity Specialty-code is not very natural.

The procedure of identifying entities and attaching attributes to entities is iterative: Classify some objects as entities, attach identifiers and descriptors to them, find some violation of the preceding guidelines, change some objects from entity to attribute (or from attribute to entity), attach attributes to the new entities, and so forth.

3.2.2 Identify the Generalization Hierarchies

If there is a generalization hierarchy among entities, then put the identifier and generic descriptors in the generic or supertype entity and put the same identifier and specific descriptors in the subtype entities.

For example, suppose three entities were identified in the ER model shown in Fig. 2.5:

- Individual, with identifier indiv-id and descriptors name, address, and date-of-birth
- Author, with identifier auth-id and descriptors auth-name and specialty
- Reviewer, with identifier id-no and descriptors rvr-name, topic-area, job-title, and team-leader

We determine, through our analysis, that Individual is a generalization of Author and Reviewer. Then we put identifier indiv-id and generic descriptors name, address, and date-of-birth in the generic entity Individual; put identifier indiv-id and specific descriptor specialty in the entity Author; and put identifier indiv-id and specific descriptors topic-area, job-title, and team-leader in entity Reviewer.

3.2.3 Define Relationships

We now deal with objects that were not classified as entities or attributes but represent relationships among entities. For every relationship the following should be specified: degree, connectivity, membership class, and attributes. The following are some guidelines for defining relationships:

- Redundant relationships should be carefully analyzed.
- Ternary relationships must be defined carefully.

Now we will study these guidelines.

Redundant Relationships

Analyze redundant relationships carefully. Two or more relationships that are used to represent the same concept are considered to be redundant.

Redundant relationships are more likely to result in unnormalized relations when transforming the ER model into relational schemas. Note that two or more relationships are allowed between the same two entities as long as the two relationships have different meanings. In this case they are not considered redundant.

One important case of nonredundancy is shown in Fig. 3.1a. If belongs-to is a many-to-one relationship between Author and Prof-assoc, if located-in is a many-to-one relationship between Prof-assoc and City, and if lives-in is a many-to-one relationship between Author and City, then lives-in is not redundant because the relationships are unrelated. However, consider the situation shown in Fig. 3.1b. Author rents a House located in a City, so lives-in is redundant and can be eliminated. This situation gets complicated if an author has more than one place to live, but in that case the relationships would be different and thus not redundant.

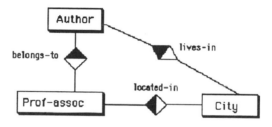

(a) Nonredundant relationships

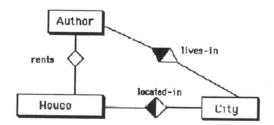

(b) Redundant relationships using transitivity

Figure 3.1
Redundant and nonredundant relationships.

Ternary Relationships

Define ternary relationships carefully. We define a ternary relationship among three entities only when the concept cannot be represented by several binary relationships among those entities. For example, let us assume there is some association among entities Author, Book, and Institution. If each author can be writing many books and is residing at the same institution as the other authors, then two binary relationships can be defined instead of one ternary relationship (see Fig. 3.2a). If, however, each author can reside at more than one institution over time, but if for every book the author resides at exactly one institution, then a ternary relationship must be defined (see Fig. 3.2b). In general, we know by our definition of ternary relationships that if the ternary relationship can be expressed by an FD involving the keys of all three entities, then it cannot be decomposed into binary relationships. If there are no FDs, then further analysis is required before attempting decomposition (see Section 5.5).

The meaning of connectivity for ternary relationships is important. Figure 3.2b shows that for a given pair of occurrences of Author and Book, there is only one corresponding occurrence of Institution; however, for a given pair of occurrences of Institution and Author, there can be many corresponding occurrences of Book.

Example: ER Modeling

We assume that analysis of the detailed requirements for data relationships in the Mathematical Reviews publication application results in the global

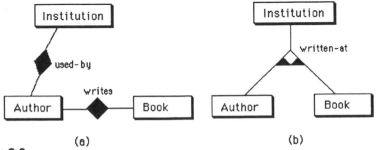

(a)   (b)

Figure 3.2
Comparison of binary and ternary relationships.

view ER diagram in Fig. 3.3, which becomes the basis for developing the normalized relations. Each relationship in Fig. 3.3 is based upon a verifiable assertion about the actual data in the enterprise. Analysis of those assertions leads to the transformation of ER constructs into candidate relations, as Chapter 4 will show.

The database design process involved expansion and redesign of an existing schema developed by the Conference of Data System Languages (CODASYL). The CODASYL schema became a relational schema. The design methodology chosen applies the ER model, which offers the following benefits:

- Use of an ER approach focuses end-user discussions on important relationships between entities. The bibliographic application is often characterized by counterexamples affecting a small number of instances, and lengthy consideration of these instances can divert attention from basic relationships.

- A diagrammatic syntax conveys a great deal of information in a compact, readily understandable form.

- Extensions to the original ER model, such as optional and mandatory membership classes, are important in many relationships. Abstraction grouping allows entities to be grouped for one functional role or to be seen as separate subtypes when other constraints are imposed.

- A complete set of rules transforms ER constructs into candidate relations, which follow easily from real-world requirements.

The material in this section is excerpted from the actual analysis. Simplifications have been made when details in the original material would have detracted from discussion of the methodology. The design work began with an initial round of user interviews, which were conducted at the departmental level and emphasized desired modifications. The departments consist of the four functional areas depicted in Fig. 3.3: the ordering area, the papers area, the author identification area, and the assigning area.

In the ordering area bibliographic data for publishers and publications is received and stored. It is also the repository for data on publication sources (booksellers and so on) and ordered items.

The data in the papers area includes complete bibliographic citations and internal processing information, such as the subject areas covered by a paper, the reviewer to whom the paper is assigned, and the internal editor

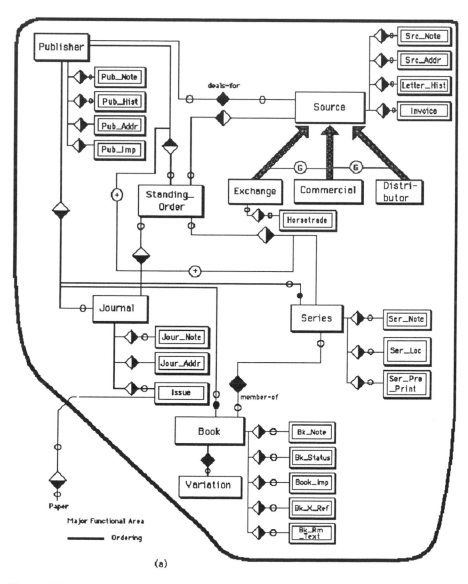

Figure 3.3
Global ER schema and functional areas.

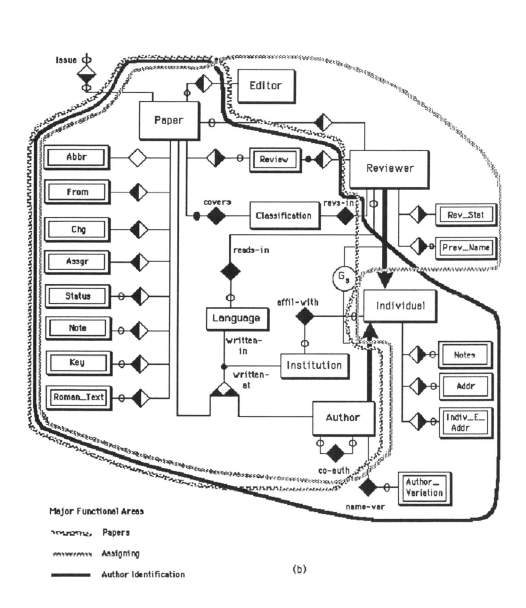

(b)

Figure 3.3, continued

making the assignment. The fact that the paper is the fundamental unit of review is reflected in its having relationships with entities from every other functional area.

Two functional areas are associated with author and reviewer data. First, the author identification area distinguishes authors who write under similar or identical names and identifies as one person an author who writes under multiple variations of one name. Second, the assigning area uses reviewer, author, and paper data to assist editors in assigning papers to reviewers.

Figure 3.3 indicates that ordering has limited contact with other departments, though the other departments overlap significantly.

During initial interviews ER diagrams and accompanying assertions depicted the entity relationships and integrity constraints; Fig. 3.4 shows the entity Book, for example. For each binary or ternary relationship, each entity alternately assumed the roles of subject or predicate of an assertion. For example, "a book may have multiple cross-references" and "a book cross-reference must have a book" shows Book as both subject and predicate of the assertion about its relationship to cross-reference. The simple declarative sentences proved very useful in that they were quickly verified or refuted by the users.

Accompanying text explained important attributes and processing concerns. For example, flag attributes that controlled processing or accommodated infrequent occurrences were noted. The text also addressed specific details important to the end-users, identified requirements too infrequent to appear in the diagrams, and served as a commentary for the applications programmer. A logical data dictionary listed each entity and its attributes along with definitions. Note that in Fig. 3.3 only the many-to-many binary relationships and the ternary relationships are labeled. In general, all relationships should be labeled, but labels are omitted here for readability.

Figure 3.3 shows a database schema resulting from this analysis. As an example of modeling simplification, we note that publication sources form a generalization hierarchy with three disjoint subtypes: Commercial, Exchange, and Distributor sources. Sources share generic data as well as relationships to orders and to the publishers for whom they vend. On the other hand, due to varying business arrangements, each subtype maintains different accounting or exchange information.

Author and reviewer processing is performed by two separate departments, each of which wants to see its data as a distinct entity. Editorial queries alternate an individual's role between that of author and reviewer;

BOOK

A book may have multiple notes, which record general information about it.

- A book may have multiple notes or none.
- A book note must have a book.

- A book may have multiple cross-references or none.
- A book cross-reference must have a book.

A book imprint consists of text, pub imprint, text.

- A book must have a book imprint and may have multiple book imprints or none.
- A book imprint must have a book.

- A book must have a current book status and may have multiple book status history records or none.
- A book status history record must have a book.

- A book may be a member of multiple series or none.
- A series may have multiple books or none.

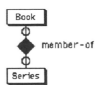

Figure 3.4
Entity development using assertion primitives.

reviewer selection is facilitated when the editor can examine the past publications an individual either wrote or reviewed. To support these queries, full information on an individual who serves as both an author and reviewer should be accessible through either role. The requirements of all three user groups can be satisfied by a subset generalization hierarchy. The entity Individual stores generic information such as notes, personal addresses, and correspondence and, through a common identifier, provides access to author-specific and reviewer-specific data. Reviewer data includes the languages and subject areas (classifications) in which the person reviews; the most important author data are the person's name variations. Views permit display of author and reviewer data as though they were separate entities.

3.3   View Integration

A most critical part of the database design process is step IIb, the integration of different user views into a unified, nonredundant conceptual schema. The individual end-user views are represented by ER conceptual models, and the integrated conceptual schema results from sufficient analysis of the end-user views to resolve all differences in perspective and terminology. Experience has shown that nearly every situation can be resolved in a meaningful way through integration techniques.

Schema diversity occurs when different users or user groups develop their own unique perspectives of the world, or at least of the enterprise to be represented in the database. For instance, marketing tends to have the whole product as a basic unit for sales, but engineering may concentrate on the individual parts of the whole product. In another case, one user may view a project in terms of its goals and progress toward meeting those goals over time; another user may view a project in terms of the resources it needs and the personnel involved. Such differences cause the conceptual models to seem to have incompatible relationships and terminology. These differences show up in ER conceptual models as different levels of abstraction; connectivity of relationships (one-to-many, many-to-many, and so on); or as the same concept being modeled as an entity, attribute, or relationship, depending on the user's perspective.

As an example of the latter case, in Fig. 3.5 we see three different perspectives of the same real-life situation, the placement of a review for a certain book. The result is a variety of schemas. The first schema (Fig. 3.5a) depicts Reviewer, Review, and Book as entities and makes-review and based-on as relationships. The second schema (Fig. 3.5b), however, defines reviews as a relationship between Reviewer and Book and omits Review as an entity altogether. Finally, in the third case (Fig. 3.5c), the relationship reviews has been replaced by another relationship, evaluates; rev-id, the key

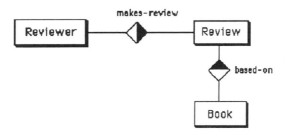

(a) The concept of review as an entity

(b) The concept of review as a relationship

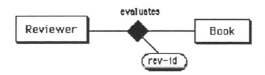

(c) The concept of review as an attribute

Figure 3.5
Entity, relationship, and attribute as three different perspectives on the concept of review.

of review, is designated as an attribute of that relationship. In other words, the concept review has been variously represented as an entity, a relationship, and an attribute, depending on perspective.

The resolution of different views is part of a view integration methodology defined by Batini, Lenzerini, and Navathe [BaLe84, BLN86]. They defined four basic steps needed for conceptual schema integration:

1. preintegration analysis
2. comparison of schemas
3. conformation of schemas
4. merging and restructuring of schemas

3.3.1   Preintegration Analysis

The first step, preintegration analysis, involves choosing an integration strategy. Typically, the choice is between a binary approach with two schemas merged at one time and an n-ary approach with n schemas merged at one time, where n is between 2 and the total number of schemas developed in the conceptual design. The binary approach is attractive because each merge involves a small number of ER constructs and is easier to conceptualize. The n-ary approach may require one grand merge only, but the number of constructs may be so large that it is not humanly possible to organize the transformations properly.

3.3.2   Comparison of Schemas

In the second step, comparison of schemas, the designer looks at how entities correspond and detects conflicts arising from schema diversity—that is, from user groups adopting different viewpoints in their respective schemas. Naming conflicts include synonyms and homonyms. *Synonyms* occur when different names are given for the same concept. These can be detected by scanning the data dictionary, if one has been established for the database. *Homonyms* occur when the same name is used for different concepts. These can only be detected by scanning the different schemas and looking for common names.

Structural conflicts occur in the schema structure itself. *Type conflicts* involve using different ER constructs to model the same concept. In Fig. 3.5, for example, an entity, a relationship, or an attribute can be used to model the concept of review in a business database. *Dependency conflicts* result when users specify different levels of connectivity for similar or even the same concepts. One resolution of such conflicts might be to use only the most general connectivity, for example, many-to-many. If that is not semantically correct, change the names of entities so that each type of connectivity has a different set of entity names. *Key conflicts* occur when different keys are assigned to the same entity in different views. For example, a key conflict occurs if an employee's full name, employee id number, and social security number are all assigned as keys. *Behavioral conflicts* result from different integrity constraints, particularly on nulls and insert/delete rules.

3.3.3   Conformation of Schemas

The resolution of conflicts often requires user and designer interaction. The basic goal is to align or conform schemas to make them compatible for integration. Not only may entities need to be renamed, but also the primary key attributes. Conversion may be required so that concepts that are modeled as entities, attributes, or relationships are conformed to only one primitive data model type. Relationships with equal degree, roles, and cardinality constraints are easy to merge. Those with differing characteristics are more difficult and, in some cases, impossible to merge. Also, relationships that are not consistent—for example, a relationship using generalization in one place and the exclusive OR in another—must be resolved. Finally, assertions may need to be modified so that integrity constraints are consistent.

Techniques used for view integration include abstraction, such as generalization and aggregation, to create new supertypes or subtypes, or even the introduction of new relationships. As an example, the generalization of Individual over different values of the descriptor attribute job-title could represent the consolidation of two views of the database, one based on an individual as the basic unit of personnel in the organization and another based on the classification of individuals by job-titles and special characteristics within those classifications. An example of a special characteristic is the allocation of personal computers to reviewers.

3.3.4   Merging and Restructuring of Schemas

Step 4 of Batini, Lenzerini, and Navathe's model consists of the merging and restructuring of schemas. This step is driven by the goals of completeness, minimality, and understandability. *Completeness* requires all component concepts to appear semantically intact in the global schema. *Minimality* requires the designer to remove all redundant concepts in the global schema. Examples of redundant concepts are entities that overlap, hierarchies that are redundant, and relationships that are truly semantically redundant. *Understandability* requires that the global schema make sense to the user.

Component schemas are first merged by superimposing the same concepts and then restructuring the resulting integrated schema for understanda-

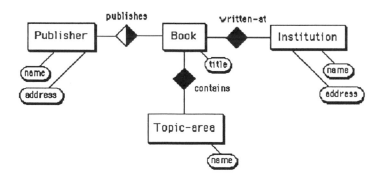

(a) Original schema 1, focused on books

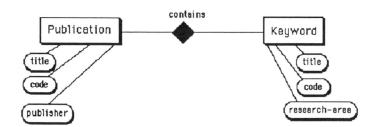

(b) Original schema 2, focused on publications

Figure 3.6
Example of two views and corresponding ER schemas.

bility. For instance, if a supertype/subtype combination is defined as a result of the merging operation, the properties of the subtype can be dropped from the schema because they are automatically provided by the supertype entity or object.

Example: View Integration

Let us look at two different views of overlapping data. The views are based on two separate interviews of end-users. We adapt the interesting example cited by Batini, Lenzerini, and Navathe [BLN86] to a hypothetical situation related to our example, Mathematical Reviews. In Fig. 3.6a we have a view

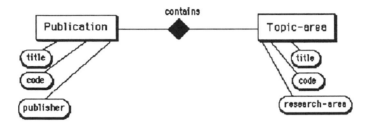

(c) Schema 2.1, in which Keyword has changed to Topic-area

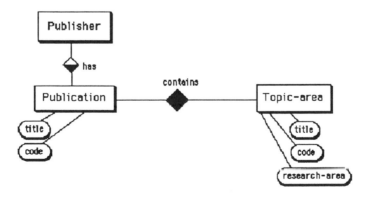

(d) Schema 2.2, in which the attribute publisher has changed to an attribute entity

Figure 3.6, continued

that focuses on books and includes data on publishers, topic areas in books, and institutions where the books are written. Figure 3.6b shows another view, with publications as the central focus and keywords on publication as the secondary data. Our objective is to find meaningful ways to integrate the two views and maintain completeness, minimality, and understandability.

We first look for synonyms and homonyms, particularly among the entities. Note that a synonym exists between the entities Topic-area in schema 1 and Keyword in schema 2, even though the attributes do not match. However, we find that the attributes are compatible and can be consolidated. This is shown in Fig. 3.6c, which presents a revised schema, schema 2.1. In schema 2.1 Keyword has been replaced by Topic-area.

Next we look for structural conflicts between schemas. A type conflict is found to exist between the entity Publisher in schema 1 and the attribute publisher in schema 2.1. The conflict is resolved by keeping the stronger entity type and moving the attribute type as an entity in schema 2.1. This transformation is seen in Fig. 3.6d, in which publisher has been deleted as an attribute of Publication and added as a separate entity with its name as an attribute.

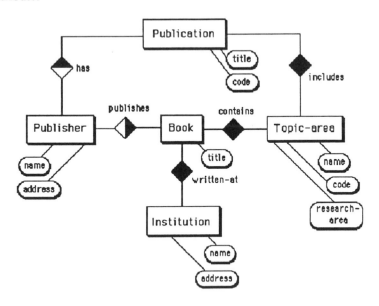

(a) Schema 3, the result of merging schema 1 and schema 2.2

Figure 3.7
View integration, stepwise refinement.

At this point we have sufficient commonality between schemas to attempt a merge. In schemas 1 and 2.2 we have common entities, Publisher and Topic-area. Other entities do not overlap and must appear intact in the superimposed, or merged, schema. The merged schema, schema 3, is shown in Fig. 3.7a. Because the common entities are truly equivalent, there are no

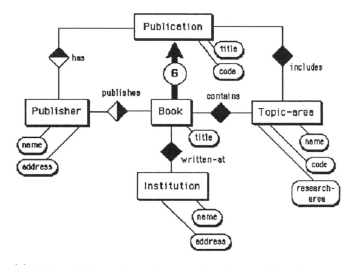

(b) **Schema 3.1: creation of a generalization relationship**

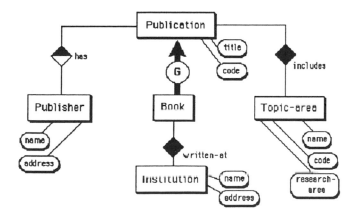

(c) **Schema 3.2: elimination of redundancy**

Figure 3.7, continued

bad side effects of the merge due to existing relationships involving those entities in one schema and not in the other. (Such a relationship exists in schema 1 between Topic-area and Book, for example.) If true equivalence cannot be established, the merge may not be possible in the existing form.

In Fig. 3.7, there is some redundancy between Publication and Book in terms of the relationships with Publisher and Topic-area. Such a redundancy can be eliminated if there is a supertype/subtype relationship between Publication and Book, which does in fact occur in this case because Publication is a generalization of Book. In schema 3.1 (Fig. 3.7b) we see the introduction of this generalization from Book to Publication. Then in schema 3.2 (Fig. 3.7c) we see that the redundant relationships between Book and Publisher and Topic-area have been dropped. The attribute title has been eliminated as an attribute of Book in Fig. 3.7c because title already appears as an attribute of Publication, at a higher level of abstraction; title is inherited by the subtype Book.

The final schema, in Fig. 3.7c, expresses completeness because all the original concepts (book, publication, topic area, publisher, and institution) are kept intact. It expresses minimality because of the transformation of publisher from attribute to entity in schema 2.2 and the merger with schema 1 to form schema 3 and also because of the elimination of title as an attribute of Book and of Book relationships with Topic-area and Publisher. Finally, it expresses understandability in that the final schema actually has more meaning than the individual original schemas. The view integration process is one of continual refinement and re-evaluation. It has therefore been difficult to automate, although some semiautomatic algorithms, with some designer interaction, can be used.

3.4   Summary

The ER approach is particularly useful in the early steps of the database life cycle, which involve requirements analysis and logical design. These two steps are often done simultaneously, particularly when requirements are determined from end-user interviews and modeled in terms of data-to-data relationships and process-to-data relationships. The ER modeling step involves the classification of entities and attributes first, then identification of generalization hierarchies and other abstractions, and finally the definition of all relationships among entities. Relationships may be binary (the most common), unary, and higher-level n-ary.

ER modeling of individual requirements typically involves creating a different view for each end-user's requirements. Then the designer must integrate those views into a global schema so that the entire database is pictured as an integrated whole. This helps to eliminate needless redundancy—such elimination is particularly important in logical design. Controlled redundancy can be created later, at the physical design level, to enhance database performance.

In the next chapter we take the global schema produced from the ER modeling and view integration steps and transform it into SQL relations. The SQL format is the end product of logical design, which is still independent of a database management system.

Literature Summary

Conceptual modeling is defined in [TsLo82, BMS84]. At the theoretical level a top-down approach to database design was investigated with regard to the universal relation assumption [BBG78; Kent81] and the combined top-down and bottom-up approach was discussed in [Date86; Swee85]. Discussion of the requirements data collection process can be found in [Mart82; TeFr82; Yao85].

Recent research has advanced view integration from a representation tool [SmSm77] to heuristic algorithms [ElWi79, NaGa82, NSE84, BaLe84, EHW85, NEL86, BLN86]. These algorithms are typically interactive, allowing the database designer to make decisions based on suggested alternative integration actions. Adopting an ER extension called the Entity-Category-Relationship model [EHW85], Navathe and others organized the different classes of objects and relationships into forms that are either compatible or incompatible for view integration [NEL86].

[BaLe84]   Batini, C., and Lenzerini, M. "A Methodology for Data Schema Integration in the Entity Relationship Model," *IEEE Trans. on Software Eng.* SE-10,6(Nov. 1984), pp. 650–664.

[BLN86]   Batini, C., Lenzerini, M., and Navathe, S.B. "A Comparative Analysis of Methodologies for Database Schema Integration," *ACM Computing Surveys* 18,4(Dec. 1986), pp. 323–364.

[BBG78]   Beeri, C., Bernstein, P., and Goodman, N. "A Sophisticate's Introduction to Database Normalization Theory," *Proc. 4th Int'l. Conf. on Very Large Data Bases*, Berlin, Sept. 13–15, 1978, IEEE, New York, 1978, pp. 113–124.

[BMS84]   Brodie, M.L., Mylopoulos, J., and Schmidt, J. (editors). *On Conceptual Modeling: Perspectives from Artificial Intelligence, Databases, and Programming Languages*, Springer-Verlag, New York, 1984.

[Date86]   Date, C.J. *An Introduction to Database Systems*, Vol. 1 (4th Ed.), Addison-Wesley, Reading, MA, 1986.

[ElWi79]   Elmasri, R., and Wiederhold, G. "Data Model Integration Using the Structural Model," *Proc. ACM SIGMOD Conf.*, Boston, 1979, ACM, New York, pp. 319–326.

[EHW85]   Elmasri, R., Hevner, A. and Weeldreyer, J. "The Category Concept: An Extension to the Entity-Relationship Model," *Data and Knowledge Engineering* 1,1(1985), pp. 75–116.

[Kent81]   Kent, W. "Consequences of Assuming a Universal Relation," *ACM Trans. Database Systems* 6,4 (1981), pp. 539–556.

[Mart82]   Martin, J. *Strategic Data-Planning Methodologies*, Prentice-Hall, Englewood Cliffs, NJ, 1982.

[NaGa82]   Navathe, S., and Gadgil, S. "A Methodology for View Integration in Logical Database Design," *Proc. 8th Int'l. Conf. on Very Large Data Bases*, Mexico City, 1982, pp. 142–152.

[NEL86]   Navathe, S., Elmasri, R., and Larson, J. "Integrating User Views in Database Design," *IEEE Computer* 19,1(1986), pp. 50–62.

[NSE84]   Navathe, S., Sashidhar, T., and Elmasri, R. "Relationship Merging in Schema Integration," *Proc. 10th Int'l. Conf. on Very Large Data Bases*, Singapore, 1984, pp. 78–90.

[SmSm77]   Smith, J., and Smith, D. "Database Abstractions: Aggregation and Generalization," *ACM Trans. Database Systems* 2,2(June 1977), pp. 105–133.

[Swee85]   Sweet, F. "Process-Driven Data Design," *Datamation* 31,16(1985), pp. 84–85, first of a series of 14 articles.

| [TeFr82] | Teorey, T., and Fry, J. *Design of Database Structures*, Prentice-Hall, Englewood Cliffs, NJ, 1982. |

[TeFr82]   Teorey, T., and Fry, J. *Design of Database Structures*, Prentice-Hall, Englewood Cliffs, NJ, 1982.

[TYF86]   Teorey, T.J., Yang, D., and Fry, J.P. "A Logical Design Methodology for Relational Databases Using the Extended Entity-Relationship Model," *ACM Computing Surveys* 18,2(June 1986), pp. 197–222.

[TsLo82]   Tsichritzis, D., and Lochovsky, F. *Data Models*, Prentice-Hall, Englewood Cliffs, NJ, 1982.

[Yao85]   Yao, S.B. (editor). *Principles of Database Design*, Prentice-Hall, Englewood Cliffs, NJ, 1985.

Exercises

Problem 3-1

An ER diagram that satisfies the following assertions is shown below. For this diagram, fill in the missing relationship connectivities, optionalities, and entities (or weak entities):

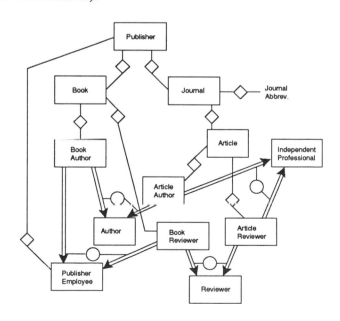

Publishers publish many different types of professional journals and books. Some publishers publish only books, some publish journals, and some publish both. No book or journal is published by more than one publisher. An author may write either books, journal articles, or both. A journal typically contains several articles, each one written by one or more authors. No article appears in more than one journal. Any journal may have one or more abbreviations or none.

Every book and article is reviewed by several professionals in the field who may or may not be authors as well. Of course, an author never reviews his or her own book or article. Each book reviewer and author works for and is paid by a single publisher. Article authors and reviewers are not paid, however. Thus article reviewers are never book reviewers. Authors and reviewers who are not paid by a publisher are known as independent professionals.

Problem 3-2

Consider the following assertions, which describe a relational database that represents the current term enrollment at a large university. Draw an ER diagram for this schema. Your diagram should take into account *all* the assertions given. There are 2000 instructors, 4000 courses, and 30,000 students. Use as many ER constructs as you can to represent the true semantics of the problem.

Assertions

a. An instructor may teach none, one, or more courses in a given term (average=2.0 courses).

b. An instructor must direct the research of at least one student (average=2.5 students).

c. A course may have none, one, or two prerequisites (average=1.5 prerequisites).

d. A course may exist even if no students are currently enrolled.

e. All courses are taught by only one instructor.

f. The average enrollment in a course is 30 students.

g. A student must select at least one course per term (average=4.0 course selections).

Problem 3-3

The following ER schema implies that students who are members of clubs sponsored by a college are *not* required to be enrolled in that same college. Using the known semantic constructs in the extended ER model, revise this ER diagram, without losing any of the original meaning, to show explicitly that students who are members of a club sponsored by a college

a. are *required* to be enrolled in that same college
b. *must not* be enrolled in that same college

Note: Do each revision separately.

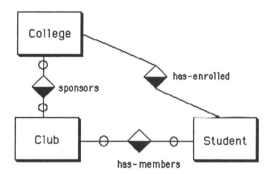

Problem 3-4

Create an ER diagram described in this problem. Your diagram should satisfy the following assertions about a general-purpose community medical facility. What questions about this enterprise's environment do these assertions leave unanswered?

A person is represented as either a patient or a medical worker. A medical worker is either a doctor, nurse, paramedic, clerk, or administrator. Medical workers work in a health facility that has a name, address, possibly a specialty area, and the name of an administrator.

A patient visits a medical facility for diagnosis of a health problem. The patient may come back for additional visits for treatment if so designated as patient may come back for additional visits for treatment if so designated as a result of the diagnosis and if the facility has the expertise to treat the problem. Each visit is called an encounter, and it must involve a patient, a medical worker, and a service. The service can be a diagnosis, treatment, checkup, or payment.

A patient may be eligible for his or her company health benefits or must pay after each encounter. Patients who are unable to pay are not turned away; they are registered as indigent citizens and are given short-term care. Patient data includes name, id number (social security number), address (street, city, state, zip), phone (day and evening), employer (company) name, employer address, type of benefits eligible for, and method of payment.

A medical worker must hold one or more credentials that are granted to work in a particular health facility. Doctors are allowed to deliver any kind of diagnosis and give treatment based on their specialty. Paramedics are allowed to give only emergency diagnoses and treatment for any type of life-threatening problem. Nurses do not deliver diagnoses, but they do participate in treatment, particularly if the patient must be prepared for surgery or remain at the facility overnight.

The facility administrator is concerned with personnel needs and assignments. Each medical worker must have at least one and possibly more assignments at a facility. Each assignment partially or completely fills an authorized slot specified by the personnel needs; thus, an authorization may involve many assignments. Medical workers have certain skills that must be recorded and accessed for a new assignment.

4

Transformation of the ER Model to SQL

This chapter focuses on the database life cycle step that is of particular interest when designing relational databases: transformation of the ER model to candidate relations (tables) and their definition in ISO and ANSI standard SQL (step IIc). We will see a natural evolution from the ER model to a relational schema. The evolution is so natural, in fact, that it supports the contention that ER modeling is an effective early step in relational database development.

4.1   Transformation Rules and SQL Constructs

We now look at each ER modeling construct in detail to see how the rules about transforming the ER model to relational schemas are defined and applied. Our example is drawn from the Mathematical Reviews ER schema illustrated in Fig. 3.3.

The basic transformations can be described in terms of the three types of tables they produce:

- *An entity relation (table) with the same information content as the original entity.* This transformation always occurs for entities with binary relationships that are many-to-many, one-to-many on the "one" (parent) side, or one-to-one on one side; entities with unary relationships that are many-to-many; and entities with any ternary or higher-degree relationship, a generalization hierarchy, or a subset hierarchy.

- *An entity relation (table) with the embedded foreign key of the parent entity.* This transformation always occurs for entities with binary relationships that are one-to-many for the entity on the "many" (child) side, for one-to-one relationships for one of the entities, and for each entity with a unary relationship that is one-to-one or one-to-many.

- *A relationship relation (table) with the foreign keys of all the entities in the relationship.* This transformation always occurs for relationships that are binary and many-to-many, relationships that are unary and many-to-many, and all relationships that are of ternary or higher degree.

The following rules apply to handling null values in these transformations:

- Nulls are allowed only for foreign keys of optional entities in an entity table.

- Nulls are not allowed for foreign keys of mandatory entities in an entity table.

- Nulls are not allowed for any key in a relationship table because only complete row entries are meaningful in the table.

In some relational systems, rules for nulls are different. These rules can be modified to be consistent with such systems.

4.1.1 SQL Constructs

Standard SQL constructs for ER models are defined within the data definition context of the create table statement [ISAN89]. A list of these constructs follows.

- *Attribute name and data type.* Character, character varying, numeric, decimal integer, smallint, float, double precision, real, date.

- *Not null.* A constraint that specifies that an attribute must have a nonnull value. This occurs when the ER diagram shows a mandatory participation in the relationship (in other words, an absence of an optionality symbol 0 next to the entity along the connection line from the relationship symbol).

- *Unique.* A constraint that specifies that the attribute is a candidate key (that is, that it has a unique value for every row in the table). Every attribute that is a candidate key must also have the constraint not null. Candidate keys are shown as underlined attributes in the ER diagram. The constraint unique is also used as a clause to designate composite candidate keys that are not the primary key. This is particularly useful when transforming ternary relationships to SQL.

- *Primary key.* A constraint that specifies which candidate key is also the primary key of the table. This may be a single attribute or a composite of several attributes. If there is only one candidate key, it becomes the primary key by default.

- *Foreign key.* The referential integrity constraint specifies that a foreign key in a referencing table column must match an existing primary key in the referenced table. The references clause specifies the name of the referenced table. An attribute may be both a primary key and a foreign key, particularly in relationship tables formed from many-to-many binary relationships or from n-ary relationships.

Foreign key constraints are defined for row deletion on the referenced table and for the update of the primary key of the referenced table. The referential trigger actions for delete and update are similar:

- on delete cascade => the delete operation on the referenced table "cascades" to all matching foreign keys.

- on delete set null => foreign keys are set to null when they match the primary key of a deleted row in the referenced table. Each foreign key must be able to accept null values for this operation to apply.

- on delete set default => foreign keys are set to a default value when they match the primary key of the deleted row(s) in the reference table. Legal default values include a literal value, "user", "system user", or "null".

- on update cascade => the update operation on the primary key(s) in the referenced table "cascades" to all matching foreign keys.

- on update set null => foreign keys are set to null when they match the old primary key value of an updated row in the referenced table. Each foreign key must be able to accept null values for this operation to apply.

- on update set default => foreign keys are set to a default value when they match the primary key of an updated row in the reference table. Legal default values include a literal value, "user", "system user", or "null".

Some systems, such as DB2 for instance, have an additional option on delete or update, called "restricted". "Delete restricted" means that the referenced table rows are deleted only if there are no matching foreign key values in the referencing table. Similarly, "update restricted" means that the referenced table rows (primary keys) are updated only if there are no matching foreign key values in the referencing table.

Other clauses in the data definition of SQL, such as the check clause, may be used in the create table statement even though they are not explicitly given in the ER diagram. This is so because they may appear in the narrative text associated with the ER model. In Figs. 4.1 through 4.5 the SQL statements needed to define each type of ER model construct are shown.

4.1.2   Binary Relationships

A one-to-one binary relationship between two entities is illustrated in Fig. 4.1, parts a through c. When both entities are mandatory (Fig. 4.1a), each entity becomes a table and the key of either entity can appear in the other entity's table as a foreign key. One of the entities in an optional relationship (see Review in Fig. 4.1b) should contain the foreign key of the other entity in its transformed table. Paper, the other entity in Fig. 4.1b, could also contain a foreign key (of Review) with nulls allowed, but this would require more storage space because of the much greater number of Paper entity occurrences than Review entity occurrences. When both entities are optional

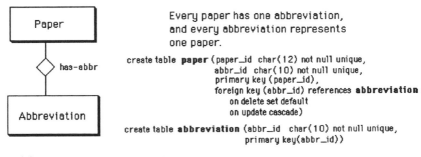

Every paper has one abbreviation, and every abbreviation represents one paper.

```
create table paper (paper_id char(12) not null unique,
                    abbr_id char(10) not null unique,
                    primary key (paper_id),
                    foreign key (abbr_id) references abbreviation
                        on delete set default
                        on update cascade)

create table abbreviation (abbr_id char(10) not null unique,
                    primary key(abbr_id))
```

(a) One-to-one, both mandatory

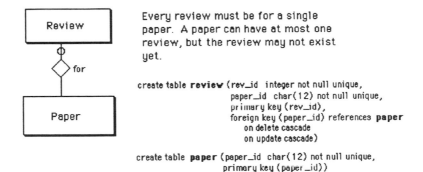

Every review must be for a single paper. A paper can have at most one review, but the review may not exist yet.

```
create table review (rev_id integer not null unique,
                    paper_id char(12) not null unique,
                    primary key (rev_id),
                    foreign key (paper_id) references paper
                        on delete cascade
                        on update cascade)

create table paper (paper_id char(12) not null unique,
                    primary key (paper_id))
```

(b) One-to-one, one entity is optional

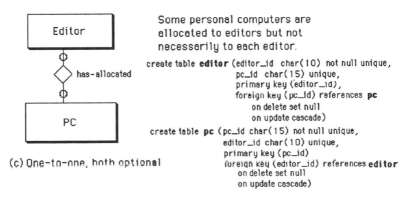

Some personal computers are allocated to editors but not necessarily to each editor.

```
create table editor (editor_id char(10) not null unique,
                    pc_id char(15) unique,
                    primary key (editor_id),
                    foreign key (pc_id) references pc
                        on delete set null
                        on update cascade)

create table pc (pc_id char(15) not null unique,
                    editor_id char(10) unique,
                    primary key (pc_id)
                    foreign key (editor_id) references editor
                        on delete set null
                        on update cascade)
```

(c) One-to-one, both optional

Figure 4.1
Binary relationship transformation rules.

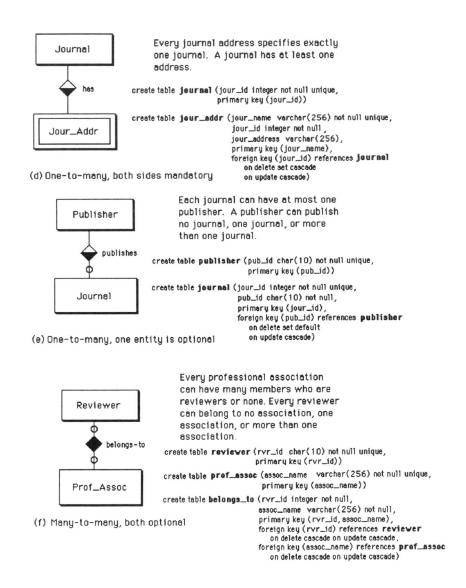

Every journal address specifies exactly one journal. A journal has at least one address.

```
create table journal (jour_id integer not null unique,
                      primary key (jour_id))

create table jour_addr (jour_name varchar(256) not null unique,
                        jour_id integer not null ,
                        jour_address varchar(256),
                        primary key (jour_name),
                        foreign key (jour_id) references journal
                          on delete set cascade
                          on update cascade)
```

(d) One-to-many, both sides mandatory

Each journal can have at most one publisher. A publisher can publish no journal, one journal, or more than one journal.

```
create table publisher (pub_id char(10) not null unique,
                        primary key (pub_id))

create table journal (jour_id integer not null unique,
                      pub_id char(10) not null,
                      primary key (jour_id),
                      foreign key (pub_id) references publisher
                        on delete set default
                        on update cascade)
```

(e) One-to-many, one entity is optional

Every professional association can have many members who are reviewers or none. Every reviewer can belong to no association, one association, or more than one association.

```
create table reviewer (rvr_id char(10) not null unique,
                       primary key (rvr_id))

create table prof_assoc (assoc_name varchar(256) not null unique,
                         primary key (assoc_name))

create table belongs_to (rvr_id integer not null,
                         assoc_name varchar(256) not null,
                         primary key (rvr_id, assoc_name),
                         foreign key (rvr_id) references reviewer
                           on delete cascade on update cascade,
                         foreign key (assoc_name) references prof_assoc
                           on delete cascade on update cascade)
```

(f) Many-to-many, both optional

Figure 4.1, continued

(Fig. 4.1c), either entity can contain the embedded foreign key of the other entity, with nulls allowed in the foreign keys.

The one-to-many relationship can be shown as either mandatory or optional on the "many" side, without affecting the transformation. On the "one" side it may be either mandatory (Fig. 4.1d) or optional (Fig. 4.1e). In all cases the foreign key must appear on the "many" side, which represents the child entity, with nulls allowed for foreign keys only in the optional "one" case. Foreign key constraints are set according to the specific meaning of the relationship and may vary from one relationship to another.

The many-to-many relationship, shown in Fig. 4.1f as completely optional, requires a relationship table with primary keys of both entities. The same transformation applies to either the optional or mandatory case, including the fact that the not null clause must appear for the foreign keys in both cases. Foreign key constraints on delete and update must always be "cascade" because each entry in the SQL table depends on the current value of, or existence of, the referenced primary key.

4.1.3   Unary Relationships

A single entity with a one-to-one relationship implies some form of entity occurrence pairing, as indicated by the relationship name. This pairing must be either completely optional or completely mandatory. In both the manda-tory case and the optional case (Fig. 4.2a), the pairing entity key appears as a foreign key in the resulting table. In both cases the two key attributes are taken from the same domain but are given different names to designate their unique use. The one-to-many relationship requires a foreign key in the entity table (Fig. 4.2b). The foreign key constraints can vary with the particular relationship.

The many-to-many relationship is shown as optional (Fig. 4.2c) and uses a relationship table; it could also be defined as mandatory (using the word *must* instead of *may*); both cases have the foreign keys defined as "not null". In many-to-many relationships, foreign key constraints on delete and update must always be "cascade" because each entry in the SQL table depends on the current value of, or existence of, the referenced primary key.

A reviewer can have one of the other reviewers as his/her spouse. (In practice this would not be allowed for a particular paper.)

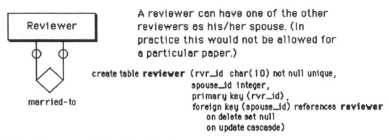

create table **reviewer** (rvr_id char(10) not null unique,
　　　　　　　　　spouse_id integer,
　　　　　　　　　primary key (rvr_id) ,
　　　　　　　　　foreign key (spouse_id) references **reviewer**
　　　　　　　　　　on delete set null
　　　　　　　　　　on update cascasde)

(a) One-to-one, with both optional

Reviewers are divided into groups for certain projects. Each group has a leader.

create table **reviewer** (rvr_id char(10) not null unique,
　　　　　　　　　leader_id integer not null,
　　　　　　　　　primary key (rvr_id) ,
　　　　　　　　　foreign key (leader_id) references **reviewer**
　　　　　　　　　　on delete set default
　　　　　　　　　　on update cascade)

is-group-leader-of

(b) One-to-many, with the "many" side optional

Author

Each author may have no coauthoar, one coauthor, or more than one coauthor.

create table **author** (auth_id char(10) not null unique,
　　　　　　　　　primary key (auth_id))

co-auth

create table **co_author** (auth_id char(10) not null,
　　　　　　　　　co_auth_id char(10) not null,
　　　　　　　　　primary key (auth_id, co_auth_id),
　　　　　　　　　foreign key (auth_id) references **author**
　　　　　　　　　　on delete cascade on update cascade,
　　　　　　　　　foreign key (co_auth_id) references **author**
　　　　　　　　　　on delete cascade on update cascade)

(c) Many-to-many, with both sides optional

Figure 4.2
Unary relationship transformation rules.

4.1.4   n-ary Relationships

An n-ary relationship has n+1 possible variations of connectivity: all n sides with connectivity "one"; n–1 sides with connectivity "one," and one side with connectivity "many"; n–2 sides with connectivity "one" and two sides with "many"; and so on until all sides are "many." The four possible varieties of a ternary relationship are shown in Fig. 4.3. All variations are transformed by creating a relationship table containing the primary keys of all entities; however, in each case the meaning of the keys is different. When all relationships are "one" (Fig. 4.3a), the relationship table consists of three possible distinct candidate keys. This represents the fact that there are three FDs needed to describe this relationship. The optionality constraint is not used here because all n entities must participate in every instance of the relationship to satisfy the FD (or multivalued dependency) constraints. (See Chapter 5 for more discussion of functional and multivalued dependencies.)

In general the number of entities with connectivity "one" determines the lower bound on the number of FDs. Thus, in Fig. 4.3b, which is one-to-one-to-many, there are two FDs; in Fig. 4.3c, which is one-to-many-to-many, there is only one FD. When all relationships are "many" (Fig. 4.3d), the relationship table is all one composite key unless the relationship has its own attributes. In that case the key is the composite of all three keys from the three associated entities.

Foreign key constraints on delete and update for ternary relationships transformed to SQL tables must always be "cascade" because each entry in the SQL table depends on the current value of, or existence of, the referenced primary key.

4.1.5   Generalization

The generalization abstraction that results in disjoint subtypes is produced by partitioning the generic entity according to different values of a common attribute—for example, src_type in Fig. 4.4. The transformation of a generalization produces a separate table for the generic or supertype entity and each of the subtypes. The supertype entity table contains the supertype entity key and all common attributes, including the common attribute used for partitioning. This, of course, assumes that such an attribute for partitioning

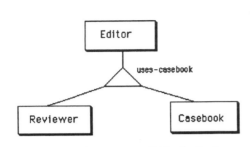

An editor uses one casebook for a given reviewer. Different editors use different casebooks for the same reviewer. No editor uses the same casebook for different reviewers, but different editors can use the same casebook for different reviewers.

```
create table editor (editor_id char(10) not null unique,
                primary key (editor_id))

create table reviewer (rvr_id char(10) not null unique,
                primary key (rvr_id))

create table casebook (book_no integer not null unique,
                primary key (book_no))

create table uses_casebook (editor_id char(10) not null,
                rvr_id  char(10) not null,
                book_no integer not null,
                primary key (editor_id, rvr_id),
                unique (editor_id, book_no),
                unique (rvr_id, book_no),
                foreign key (editor_id) references editor
                    on delete cascade on update cascade,
                foreign key (rvr_id) references reviewer
                    on delete cascade on update cascade,
                foreign key (book_no) references casebook
                    on delete cascade on update cascade )
```

uses_casebook

editor_id	rvr_id	book_no
35	101	5001
35	103	2008
42	104	1004
42	105	3005
81	103	1007
93	101	1009
93	102	5001

<u>Functional dependencies</u>

editor_id, rvr_id->book_no
editor_id, book_no->rvr_id
rvr_id, book_no->editor_id

(a) One-to-one-to-one ternary relationships

Figure 4.3
Ternary relationship transformation rules.

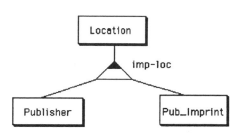

Each publisher-location pair must have
one imprint. Each publisher imprint-
location pair may refer to only one
publisher. Each publisher and publisher
imprint may occur at multiple locations.

```
create table location (loc_addr varchar(256) not null unique,
                       primary key (loc_addr))

create table publisher (pub_id char(10) not null unique,
                        primary key (pub_id))

create table pub_imprint (pub_imp_id char(10) not null unique,
                          primary key (pub_imp_id))

create table imp_loc (loc_addr varchar(256) not null,
                      pub_id char(10) not null,
                      pub_imp_id char(10) not null,
                      primary key (loc_addr, pub_id),
                      unique (loc_addr, pub_imp_id),
                      foreign key (loc_addr) references location
                          on delete cascade on update cascade,
                      foreign key (pub_id) references publisher
                          on delete cascade on update cascade,
                      foreign key (pub_imp_id) references pub_imprint
                          on delete cascade on update cascade )
```

imp_loc

loc_addr	pub_id	pub_imp_id
48101	321	B66
48101	900	E71
20702	900	A12
20702	445	D54
51266	445	G14
51266	900	A12
76323	602	B66

Functional dependencies

loc_addr, pub_id->pub_imp_id
loc_addr, pub_imp_id->pub_id

(b) One-to-one-to-many ternary relationships

Figure 4.3, continued

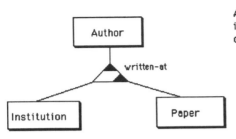

Authors can work at one or more institutions, but can credit at most one institution to a given paper.

```
create table author (auth_id char(10) not null unique,
                     primary key (auth_id))

create table paper (paper_id char(12) not null unique,
                    primary key (paper_id))

create table institution (inst_name char(20) not null unique,
                         primary key (inst_name))

create table assigned_to (auth_id char(10) not null,
                         paper_id char(12) not null,
                         inst_name char(20) not null,
                         primary key (auth_id, paper_id),
                         foreign key (auth_id) references author
                             on delete cascade on update cascade,
                         foreign key (paper_id) references paper
                             on delete cascade on update cascade,
                         foreign key (inst_name) references institution
                             on delete cascade on update cascade )
```

assigned_to

auth_id	paper_id	inst_name
305	4106	MIT
305	4200	MIT
412	7033	CalTech
412	4200	UMich
888	4106	PekingU
923	7033	UParis
923	4106	Yale

<u>Functional dependencies</u>

auth_id, paper_id -> inst_name

(c) One-to-many-to-many ternary relationships

Figure 4.3, continued

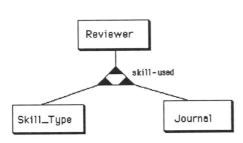

Reviewers use a wide range of skills on each journal they review for.

```
create table reviewer (rvr_id char(10) not null unique,
                       primary key (rvr_id))

create table skill_type (skill char(10) not null unique,
                         primary key (skill))

create table journal (jour_id integer not null unique,
                      primary key (jour_id))

create table skill_used (rvr_id  char(10) not null,
                         skill char(10) not null,
                         jour_id integer not null,
                         primary key (rvr_id, skill, jour_id),
                         foreign key (rvr_id) references reviewer
                           on delete cascade on update cascade,
                         foreign key (skill) references skill_type
                           on delete cascade on update cascade,
                         foreign key (jour_id) references journal
                           on delete cascade on update cascade )
```

skill_used

rvr_id	skill	jour_id
101	algebra	147
101	set-theory	147
101	algebra	316
101	geometry	316
102	algebra	147
102	set-theory	147
102	algebra	316
102	set-theory	316

Functional dependencies

None

(d) Many-to-many-to-many ternary relationships

Figure 4.3, continued

actually exists. When the attribute does not exist, it must be created.

Each subtype table contains the supertype entity key and only the attributes that are specific to that subtype. Update integrity is maintained by requiring all insertions and deletions to occur in both the supertype entity table and relevant subtype table, i.e. the foreign key constraint "cascades" must be used. If the update is to the primary key, then all subtypes as well as the supertype table must be updated. An update to a nonkey attribute affects either the supertype or one subtype table, but not both.

Overlapping subsets for subset generalization are produced by partition-

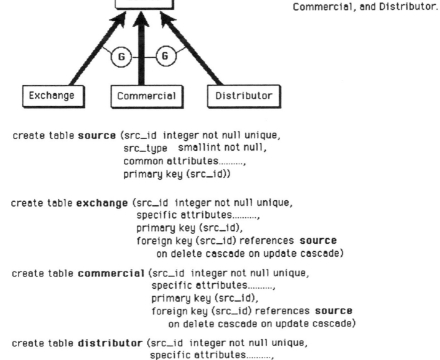

Figure 4.4
Generalization abstraction.

ing the supertype entity by values of different attributes (Fig. 4.5). The transformation of this construct produces separate tables for the supertype entity and each of the subtype entities. The key of each table is the primary key of the supertype entity; while the supertype entity table contains only common attributes, each subtype table contains attributes specific to that subtype entity. Thus, the transformation rules (and integrity rules) for the disjoint and overlapping subset generalizations are basically the same.

4.1.6 Multiple Relationships

Multiple relationships among n entities are alway considered to be completely independent. One-to-one or one-to-many unary or binary relation-

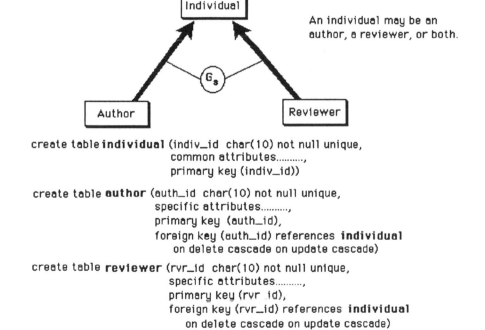

Figure 4.5
Generalization with overlapping subsets.

ships that result in entity tables that are either equivalent or differ only in the addition of a foreign key can simply be merged into a single entity table containing all the foreign keys. Many-to-many or ternary relationships that result in relationship tables that tend to be unique and cannot be merged.

4.1.7   Weak Entities

Weak entities differ from entities only in their need for keys from other entities to establish their uniqueness. Otherwise they have the same transformation properties as entities, and no special rules are needed. When a weak entity is already derived from two or more entities in the ER diagram, it can be directly transformed into an entity table without further change.

4.2   Summary of Transformation Steps

The list that follows summarizes the basic transformation steps.

- Transform each entity into a table containing the key and nonkey attributes of the entity.
- Transform every many-to-many binary or unary relationship into a relationship table with the keys of the entities and the attributes of the relationship.
- Transform every ternary or higher-level n-ary relationship into a relationship table.

Now we will study each step in turn.

4.2.1   Entity Transformation

If there is a one-to-many relationship between an entity and another entity, add the key of the entity on the "one" side (the parent) into the child table as a foreign key. If there is a one-to-one relationship between one entity and another entity, then add the key of one of the entities into the table for the other entity, thus changing it to a foreign key. The addition of a foreign key due to a one-to-one relationship can be made in either direction. One strategy is to maintain the most natural parent-child relationship by putting the parent key into the child table. Another strategy is based on efficiency: Add the foreign key to the table with fewer rows.

Every entity in a generalization hierarchy is transformed into a table. Each of these tables contains the key of the supertype entity; in reality the subtype primary keys are foreign keys as well. The supertype entity table also contains nonkey values that are common to all the relevant entities; the other tables contain nonkey values specific to each subtype entity.

SQL constructs for these transformations may include constraints for not null, unique, and foreign key. A primary key must be specified for each table, either explicitly from among the candidate keys in the ER diagram or by taking the composite of all attributes as the default superkey. Check and default clauses are optional, depending on the narrative text associated with the ER diagram.

4.2.2 Many-to-Many Binary Relationship Transformation

In this step, every many-to-many binary (or unary) relationship is transformed into a relationship table with the keys of the entities and the attributes of the relationship. A relationship table shows the correspondence between specific instances of one entity and those of another entity. Any attributes of this correspondence, such as the rating given to a paper from a reviewer, are considered intersection data and are added to the relationship table as a nonkey attribute.

SQL constructs for this transformation may include constraints for not null. The unique constraint is not used here because all candidate keys are composites of the participating primary keys of the associated entities in the relationship. The constraints for primary key and foreign key are required because of the definition of a relationship table as a composite of the primary keys of the associated entities.

4.2.3 Ternary Relationship Transformation

In this step, every ternary (or higher n-ary) relationship is transformed into a relationship table. Ternary or higher n-ary relationships are defined as a collection of the n primary keys in the associated entities in that relationship, with possibly some nonkey attributes that are dependent on the superkey formed by the composite of those n primary keys.

SQL constructs for this transformation must include constraints for not null, since optionality is not allowed. The unique constraint is not used for individual attributes, because all candidate keys are composites of the participating primary keys of the associated entities in the relationship. The constraints for primary key and foreign key are required because of the definition of a relationship table as a composite of the primary keys of the associated entities. The unique clause must also be used to define alternate candidate keys that often occur with ternary relationships. A n-ary relationship table has n foreign keys.

Example: ER to SQL Transformation

ER diagrams for our Mathematical Reviews publication database were transformed to candidate relational tables, as shown in Fig. 3.3. A summary of the transformation of all regular entities (and some of the weak entities and their relationships) to candidate tables is illustrated in the list that follows. Primary keys are underlined. Also included are some of the most typical nonkey attributes taken from the requirements analysis. The table names are in boldface.

Table 4.1 SQL tables

SQL tables transformed directly from entities

create table **abbreviation** (abbr_id char(10) not null unique,
                primary key (abbr_id))

create table **author** (auth_id char(10) not null unique,
                auth_name varchar(256),
                auth_addr varchar(256),
                auth_title varchar(256),
                primary key (auth_id))

create table **author_variation** (auth_var_id char(10) not null unique,
                      auth_var_name varchar(256),
                      primary key (auth_var_id))

create table **book** (book_id integer not null unique,
              book_title varchar(256),
              topic_area varchar(256),
              pub_id char(10) not null,
              primary key (book_id),
              foreign key (pub_id) references **publisher**
                    on delete set default
                    on update cascade)

create table **classification** (class_id integer not null unique,
              class_type char(10),
              primary key (class_id))

create table **commercial** (comm_id smallint not null unique,
              comm_name varchar(256),
              primary key (class_id))

create table **distributor** (dist_id integer not null unique,
              dist_name varchar(256),
              dist_addr varchar(256),
              primary key (dist_id))

create table **editor** (editor_id char(10) not null unique,
            editor_name varchar(256),
            editor_addr varchar(256),
            primary_topic_area char(15),
            primary key (editor_id))

create table **exchange** (exch_id integer not null unique,
              exch_type char(10),
              primary key (exch_id))

create table **individual** (indiv_id char(10) not null unique,
             primary key (indiv_id))

create table **institution** (inst_name varchar(256) not null unique,
                  inst_addr varchar(256),
                  primary key (inst_name))

create table **invoice** (inv_id integer not null unique,
                  src_id integer not null,
                  primary key (inv_id),
                  foreign key (src_id) references **source**
                          on delete set default
                          on update cascade)

create table **issue** (iss_id integer not null unique,
                  iss_date date,
                  jour_id integer not null,
                  primary key (iss_id),
                  foreign key (jour_id) references **journal**
                          on delete set default
                          on update cascade)

create table **journal** (jour_id integer not null unique,
                  pub_id char(10) not null,
                  st_ord_id integer,
                  primary key (jour_id),
                  foreign key (pub_id) references **publisher**
                          on delete set default
                          on update cascade,
                  foreign key (st_ord_id) references **standing_order**
                          on delete set null
                          on update cascade)

create table **language** (lang_name varchar(256) not null unique,
                  primary key (lang_name))

create table **paper** (paper_id char(12) not null unique,
                  paper_title varchar(256),
                  editor_id char(10) not null,
                  iss_id integer,
                  rvr_id char(10) not null,
                  abbr_id char(10) not null unique,

            primary key (paper_id),
            foreign key (editor_id) references **editor**
                 on delete set default
                 on update set default,
            foreign key (iss_id) references **issue**
                 on delete set null
                 on update cascade,
            foreign key (rvr_id) references **reviewer**
                 on delete set default
                 on update cascade,
            foreign key (abbr_id) references **abbreviation**
                 on delete set default
                 on update cascade)

create table **publisher** (pub_id char(10) not null unique,
            st_ord_id integer,
            primary key (pub_id),
            foreign key (st_ord_id) references **standing_order**
                 on delete set null
                 on update cascade)

create table **review** (rev_id char(15) not null unique,
            paper_id char(12) not null unique,
            rvr_id char(10) not null,
            primary key (rev_id),
            foreign key (paper_id) references **paper**
                 on delete cascade
                 on update cascade,
            foreign key (rvr_id) references **reviewer**
                 on delete set default
                 on update cascade)

create table **reviewer** (rvr_id char(10) not null unique,
            rvr_name varchar(256),
            rvr_addr varchar(256),
            primary key (rvr_id))

create table **series** (ser_id char(8) not null unique,
            pub_id char(10) not null,
            st_ord_id integer,

                 primary key (ser_id),
                 foreign key (pub_id) references **publisher**
                       on delete set default
                       on update cascade,
                 foreign key (st_ord_id) references **standing_order**
                       on delete set null
                       on update cascade)

create table **source** (src_id integer not null unique,
                 src_type smallint not null,
                 pub_equiv char(10),
                 primary key (src_id))

create table **standing_order** (st_ord_id integer not null unique,
                 scr_id integer not null,
                 primary key (st_ord_id),
                 foreign key (src_id) references **source**
                       on delete set default
                       on update cascade)

create table **variation** (var_id char(10) not null unique,
                 var_type integer,
                 primary key (var_id))

SQL tables transformed from many-to-many binary or unary relationships

create table **affil** (indiv_id char(10) not null,
                 inst_name varchar(256) not null,
                 primary key (indiv_id, inst_name),
                 foreign key (indiv_id) references **individual**
                       on delete cascade
                       on update cascade,
                 foreign key (inst_name) references **institution**
                       on delete cascade
                       on update cascade)

create table **co_author** (auth_id char(10) not null,
                 co_auth_id char(10) not null,

```
                primary key (auth_id, co_auth_id),
                foreign key (auth_id) references author
                        on delete cascade
                        on update cascade,
                foreign key (co_auth_id) references author
                        on delete cascade
                        on update cascade)


create table covers (paper_id char(12) not null,
                classif_id integer not null,
                primary key (paper_id, classif_id),
                foreign key (paper_id) references paper
                        on delete cascade
                        on update cascade,
                foreign key (classif_id) references classification
                        on delete cascade
                        on update cascade)


create table has (book_id integer not null,
                var_id char(10) not null,
                primary key (book_id, var_id),
                foreign key (book_id) references book
                        on delete cascade
                        on update cascade,
                foreign key (var_id) references variation
                        on delete cascade
                        on update cascade)


create table deals_for (pub_id char(10) not null,
                src_id integer not null,
                primary key (pub_id, src_id),
                foreign key (pub_id) references publisher
                        on delete cascade
                        on update cascade,
                foreign key (src_id) references source
                        on delete cascade
                        on update cascade)


create table member_of (book_id integer not null,
                ser_id char(8) not null,
```

```
                    primary key (book_id, ser_id),
                    foreign key (book_id) references book
                          on delete cascade
                          on update cascade,
                    foreign key (ser_id) references series
                          on delete cascade
                          on update cascade)


create table name_var (auth_id char(10) not null,
                    auth_var_id char(10) not null,
                    primary key (auth_id, auth_var_id),
                    foreign key (auth_id) references author
                          on delete cascade
                          on update cascade,
                    foreign key (auth_var_id) references author_variation
                          on delete cascade
                          on update cascade)


create table reads_in (rvr_id char(10) not null,
                    lang_name varchar(256) not null,
                    primary key (rvr_id, lang_name),
                    foreign key (rvr_id) references reviewer
                          on delete cascade
                          on update cascade,
                    foreign key (lang_name) references language
                          on delete cascade
                          on update cascade)


create table revs_in (rvr_id integer not null,
                    classif_id integer not null,
                    primary key (rvr_id, classif_id),
                    foreign key (rvr_id) references reviewer
                          on delete cascade
                          on update cascade,
                    foreign key (classif_id) references classification
                          on delete cascade
                          on update cascade)
```

SQL tables transformed from ternary relationships

create table **written_at** (paper_id char(12) not null,
                auth_id char(10) not null,
                inst_name varchar(256) not null,
                primary key (paper_id, auth_id),
                foreign key (paper_id) references **paper**
                        on delete cascade
                        on update cascade,
                foreign key (auth_id) references **author**
                        on delete cascade
                        on update cascade,
                foreign key (inst_name) references **institution**
                        on delete cascade
                        on update cascade)

create table **written_in** (paper_id char(12) not null,
                auth_id char(10) not null,
                lang_name varchar(256) not null,
                primary key (paper_id, auth_id),
                foreign key (paper_id) references **paper**
                        on delete cascade
                        on update cascade,
                foreign key (auth_id) references **author**
                        on delete cascade
                        on update cascade,
                foreign key (lang_name) references **language**
                        on delete cascade
                        on update cascade)

4.3   Summary

Entities, attributes, and relationships can be transformed directly into SQL relational table definitions with some simple rules. Entities are transformed into tables, with all attributes mapped one-to-one to table attributes. Tables representing entities that are the child ("many" side) of a parent-child (one-to-many or one-to-one) relationship must also include, as a foreign key, the primary key of the parent entity. A many-to-many relationship is transformed into a relationship table that contains the primary keys of the associated entities as its composite primary key; the components of that key are also designated as foreign keys in SQL.

A ternary or higher-level n-ary relationship is transformed into a relationship table that contains the primary keys of the associated entities; these keys are designated as foreign keys in SQL. A subset of those keys can be designated as the primary key, depending on the FDs associated with the relationship.

Rules for generalization require the inheritance of the primary key from the supertype to the subtype entities when transformed into SQL tables. Optionality constraints in the ER diagram translate into nulls allowed in the relational model when applied to the "one" side of a relationship. In SQL the lack of an optionality constraint determines the not null designation in the create table definition.

Literature Summary

Definition of the basic transformations from the ER model to tables is covered in [McGe74; Saka83; Mart83; Hawr84, JaNg84]. The ISO and ANSI standard is given in [ANIS89].

[Hawr84]   Hawryszkiewycz, I. *Database Analysis and Design*, SRA, Chicago, 1984.

[ISAN89]   ISO-ANSI Database Language SQL2 and SQL3, ANSI X3H2-89-110, ISO DBL CAN-3 (working draft), J. Melton (Ed.), February 1989.

[JaNg84]   Jajodia, S., and Ng, P. "Translation of Entity-Relationship Diagrams into Relational Structures," *J. Systems and Software* 4, pp. 123–133.

[Mart83]   Martin, J. *Managing the Data-Base Environment*, Prentice-Hall, Englewood Cliffs, NJ, 1983.

[McGe74]   McGee, W. "A Contribution to the Study of Data Equivalence," *Data Base Management*, J.W. Klimbie and K.L. Koffeman (editors), North-Holland, 1974, pp. 123–148.

[Saka83]   Sakai, H. "Entity-Relationship Approach to Logical Database Design," *Entity-Relationship Approach to Software Engineering*, C.G. Davis, S. Jajodia, P.A. Ng, and R.T. Yeh, (editors), Elsevier, North-Holland, New York, 1983, pp. 155–187.

[TYF86]   Teorey, T.J., Yang, D. and Fry, J.P. "A Logical Design Methodology for Relational Databases Using the Extended Entity-Relationship Model," *ACM Computing Surveys* 18,2(June 1986), pp. 197–222.

Exercises

Problem 4-1

Design a relational schema (SQL) for the ER diagram shown in Fig. 3.7c.

Problem 4-2

Continue Problem 3-2 by transforming the ER diagram into a relational (SQL) schema.

Problem 4-3

Given the following schema for a presidential database, write SQL queries (in correct syntax) for these three queries:

Queries

1. Which presidents were from the state of Ohio and also members of the Republican party?
2. Which states were admitted when President Andrew Johnson was in office?
3. Which vice-presidents (vp's) did *not* later become president? Assume that no one could be president and then vice-president, but someone could be vice-president and then president.

```
create table president
            (identifier              INTEGER NOT NULL UNIQUE,
            last_name                CHAR(16),
            first_name               CHAR(16),
            middle_init              CHAR(2),
            political_party          CHAR(16),
            state_from               CHAR(16));

create table administration
            (pres_identifier         INTEGER,
            start_date               DATE NOT NULL UNIQUE,
            end_date                 DATE,
            vp_last_name             CHAR(16),
            vp_first_name            CHAR(16),
            vp_middle_init           CHAR(2));

create table state
            (state_name              CHAR(16) NOT NULL UNIQUE,
            date_admitted            DATE NOT NULL,
            area                     INTEGER,
            population               INTEGER,
            capital_city             CHAR(16));
```

Problem 4-4

Given the ER diagram below, transform to SQL relations and define enough attributes to answer the queries and perform the updates given below.

Queries

Q1.   Who does Bill Joy manage?

Q2.   Is there a manager who manages *both* Ed Birss and Leo Horvitz? If so, who is it?

Q3.   Display employee names and room numbers who work in the "special funds" department.

Q4.   Which employees work in *either* the"engineering" or "data processing" departments.

Q5.   Display the names of project managers who are *also* department heads.

Q6. Display all projects, sorted (ascending) by project name. Specify who manages each project, which employees work on it, and show what department the project manager is in. Within a project, sort employees by employee name.

Q7. Which programmers are *not* assigned to the "new computers" project?

Q8. How much money has Mike Wilens made while working for this company?

Q9. Which employees make over $5000/month and have no project management responsibility?

Q10. Who are the first, second, and third level managers above Beverly Kahn? Use the "manager" attribute in the employee relation. Create three "views," one for the first-level manager, another for the second-level manager, and yet another for the third-level manager. Then specify three separate queries in terms of these three "views."

Updates

U1. Create a new table that has as its name-prefix, your last name and first initial, that lists employee names and three hobbies. Make up four rows for this table. (Example table name: **deppe_m_hobbies**). In this way each member of the class can add to the database without damaging the existing database. See if you can print out a nonredundant list of hobbies for those employees working in the "special funds" department.

U2. Delete one of the rows in your table.

U3. Modify one of the remaining rows to change one of the hobbies.

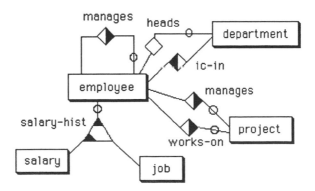

Problem 4-5

Continue Problem 3-4 by transforming the ER diagram into a relational (SQL) schema.

5

Normalization

This chapter focuses on the fundamentals of normal forms for relational databases and the database design step that normalizes the candidate relations (step IId of the database design life cycle). It also looks briefly at the equivalence between the ER model and normal forms for relations.

5.1 Fundamentals of Normalization

Relations are often defined in a form (that is, a scheme) that suffers from some rather serious problems in terms of integrity and maintainability. For example, database updates sometimes result in the elimination of useful data as an unwanted side effect. Also, when the database is defined as a single large table, it can result in a large amount of redundant data. This has the additional effect of necessitating lengthy searches for a small amount of target data. In such instances a different form of logical data organization might prevent such problems. Classes of relational database schemes, called normal forms, are defined to accomplish this goal of maintaining high integrity and maintainability. The creation of a normal form is called *normalization*. It is accomplished by analyzing the interdependencies among individual attributes associated with those relations. Let us first review the basic normal forms which have been well-established in the literature [Date86, Kent83].

5.1.1 First Normal Form

A relation is in *first normal form* (*1NF*) if and only if all underlying domains contain only atomic values, that is, there are no repeating groups (domains) within a tuple. A repeating group occurs when a multivalued attribute is allowed to have each value represented in a single tuple. When this happens, tuples must either be defined as variable length or defined with enough attribute positions to accommodate the maximum possible values. For example, for the ER diagram in Fig. 5.1a, an unnormalized relation (UNR) is shown in Fig. 5.1b with multiple attribute positions for author id, author name, and author address. Fig. 5.1c has the equivalent data defined in a 1NF relation that puts each item of author information in a separate tuple.

The advantages of 1NF over UNRs is its representational simplicity and the ease with which one can develop a query language for it. The disadvantage is the requirement for duplicate data. In this case, for instance, paper_id appears in each tuple where there are multiple authors for a particular paper. Most relational systems (but not all) require a database to be 1NF at the least.

5.1.2 Second Normal Form

A relation in 1NF often suffers from data duplication, update performance, and update integrity problems. In order to understand these issues better, however, the concept of a key needs to be defined in the context of normalized relations. A *superkey* is a set of one or more attributes, which, when taken collectively, allows us to identify uniquely an entity or relation. Any subset of the attributes of a superkey that is also a superkey and not reducible to another superkey is called a *candidate key*. A *primary key* is selected arbitrarily from the set of candidate keys to be used in an index for that relation.

As an example, in Fig. 5.1c a composite of all the attributes of the relation forms a superkey because duplicate tuples are not allowed in the relational model. Thus a trivial superkey is formed from the composite of all attributes in a relation. Assuming that each institutional address in this relation is single

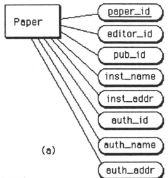

(a)

Unnormalized relation (UNR):

paper_id	inst_name	inst_addr	editor_id	pub_id	auth_id1	auth_name1	auth_addr1
4216	univ_mich	ann_arbor	woolf	14	7631	yang_d	peking_univ
5789	math_rev	providenc	bradlee	53	1126	umar_a	bellcore

auth_id2	auth_name2	auth_addr2	auth_id3	auth_name3 ....
4419	mantei_m	univ_toron	2692	koenig_j
7384	fry_j	mitre	3633	bolton_d

(b)

Normalized relation (NR):

paper_id	inst_name	inst_addr	editor_id	pub_id	auth_id	auth_name	auth_addr
4216	univ_mich	ann_arbor	woolf	14	7631	yang_d	peking_univ
4216	univ_mich	ann_arbor	woolf	14	4419	mantei_m	univ_toron
4216	univ_mich	ann_arbor	woolf	14	2692	koenig_j	math_rev
5789	math_rev	providence	bradlee	53	1126	umar_a	bellcore
5789	math_rev	providence	bradlee	53	7384	fry_j	mitre
5789	math_rev	providence	bradlee	53	3633	bolton_d	math_rev

(c)

Figure 5.1
ER diagram and transformation to unnormalized and normalized relations.

valued, we can conclude that the composite of all attributes except inst_addr is also a superkey. Looking at smaller and smaller composites of attributes and making realistic assumptions about which attributes are single valued, we find that the composite paper_id, auth_id uniquely determines all the other attributes in the relation and is therefore a superkey. However, paper_id or auth_id alone cannot determine a tuple uniquely, and the composite paper_id, auth_id cannot be reduced and still be a superkey. Thus it becomes a candidate key. Since it is the only candidate key in this relation, it also becomes the primary key.

The property of one or more attributes that uniquely determine the value of one or more other attributes is called *functional dependence (FD)*. Given a relation (R), a set of attributes (B) is functionally dependent on another set of attributes (A) if, at each instant of time, each A value is associated with only one B value. Such an FD is denoted by A->B. In the preceding example of paper_id and author_id, we have the following FDs for the relation **R**:

R: paper_id, auth_id -> auth_name   auth_id -> auth_name
       paper_id, auth_id -> auth_addr   auth_id -> auth_addr
       paper_id, auth_id -> inst_name   inst_name -> inst_addr
       paper_id, auth_id -> inst_addr   paper_id -> pub_id
       paper_id -> editor_id

These FDs can also be written in the equivalent shorthand form:

    paper_id, auth_id -> auth_name, auth_addr, inst_name, inst_addr
    auth_id -> auth_name, auth_addr
    inst_name -> inst_addr
    paper_id -> pub_id, editor_id

A relation is in *second normal form (2NF)* if and only if it is in 1NF and every nonkey attribute is fully dependent on the primary key. This means that any FD within the relation must contain all components of the primary key as the determinant (the left side of an FD), either directly or transitively.

In the preceding example, the primary key is paper_id, auth_id. However, there exist other FDs (auth_id->auth_name, auth_addr and paper_id->pub_id, editor_id) that contain one component of the primary key, but not both components. As such, relation **R** does not satisfy the conditions for 2NF.

Consider the disadvantages of 1NF as shown in relation **R**. Paper_id, pub_id, and editor_id are duplicated for each author of the paper. If the editor of the publication for the paper changes, several tuples must be updated. Finally, if a paper is withdrawn, all tuples associated with that paper must be deleted. This has the side effect of deleting the information that associates an auth_id with auth_name and auth_addr. Deletion side effects of this nature are known as the *delete anomalies*. They represent a potential loss of integrity because the only way the data can be restored is to find the data somewhere outside the database and insert it back into the database.

Most of these disadvantages can be overcome by transforming the 1NF relation into two or more 2NF relations by using the projection operator on the subset of the attributes of the 1NF relation. In the example that follows we project **R** over paper_id, auth_id, inst_name, and inst_addr to form **R1**; project **R** over auth_id, auth_name, and auth_addr to form **R2**; and project **R** over paper_id, pub_id, and editor_id to form **R3**.

> **R1**: paper_id, auth_id -> inst_name, inst_addr
> inst_name -> inst_addr
> **R2**: auth_id -> auth_name, auth_addr
> **R3**: paper_id -> pub_id, editor_id

We now have three relations that satisfy the conditions for 2NF, and we have eliminated some of the problems of 1NF. Pub_id and editor_id are no longer duplicated for each author, an editor change results in only an update to one tuple for the paper, and the deletion of the paper does not have the side effect of deleting the author information. Some performance degradation is not eliminated, however. Paper_id is still duplicated for each author and deletion of a paper requires updates to two relations instead of one.

5.1.3 Third Normal Form

The 2NF relations suffer from the same types of problems as the 1NF relations, but for different reasons. If a transitive (functional) dependency exists in a relation, then two separate facts are again represented in a single relation, one fact for each functional dependency involving a different determinant (left side). For example, in **R1**, inst_addr must be duplicated for each paper-author combination that determines a particular inst_name. Also, if we delete a paper from the database, we have the side effect of deleting the association between inst_name and inst_addr as well. If we could project relation **R1** over paper_id, auth_id, and inst_name to form relation **R11** and project **R11** over inst_name and inst_addr to form relation **R12**, we could eliminate these problems.

A relation is in *third normal form* (*3NF*) if and only if it is in 2NF and every nonkey attribute is nontransitively dependent on the primary key. In other words, a relation is in 3NF if, for every nontrivial FD X—>A, where X and A are either simple or composite attributes, one of two conditions must hold. Either

> attribute X is a superkey, or
>
> attribute A is a member of a candidate key

If attribute A is a member of a candidate key, A is called a *prime attribute*. Note: A trivial FD is of the form YZ—>Z. In the preceding example, after projecting **R1** to eliminate the transitive dependency, we have the following 3NF relations and their functional dependencies:

> **R11:** paper_id, auth_id -> inst_name
> **R12:** inst_name -> inst_addr
> **R2:** auth_id -> auth_name, auth_addr
> **R3:** paper_id -> pub_id, editor_id

5.1.4 Boyce-Codd Normal Form

A relation **R** is in *Boyce-Codd normal form* (*BCNF*) if for every nontrivial FD X—>A, X is a superkey.

BCNF is a stronger form of normalization than 3NF. BCNF eliminates the second condition for 3NF, which allowed the right side of the FD to be a prime attribute. Thus every left side of an FD in a relation must be a superkey. Every relation that is BCNF is also 3NF, 2NF, and 1NF, by the previous definitions.

The following example shows a 3NF relation that is not BCNF. Such relations have update anomalies similar to those in the lower normal forms.

Assertion 1: for each team, each reviewer is directed by only one editor. A team may be directed by more than one editor.

rvr_name, team_id -> editor_name

Assertion 2: each editor leads only one team.

editor_name -> team_id

This relation is 3NF with a composite key rvr_name, team_id, editor_name:

R: rvr_name	team_id	editor_name
Sutton	Topology	Wei
Sutton	Analysis	Bachmann
Niven	Topology	Wei
Niven	Probability	Makowski
Wilson	Probability	Chiarawongse

Relation **R** has the following delete anomaly: If Sutton drops out of the Analysis team, then we have no record of Bachmann leading the Analysis team. As shown by Date [Date86], this type of anomaly cannot have a lossless decomposition/join and preserve all FDs. (A lossless decomposition/join requires that when you decompose the relation into two smaller relations by projecting the original relation over two overlapping subsets of the scheme, the natural join of those subset relations must result in the original relation without any extra unwanted tuples.) The simplest way to avoid the delete anomaly is to create a separate relation for each of the two assertions. These two relations are partially redundant, enough so to avoid the delete anomaly. This decomposition is lossless (trivially) and preserves functional dependencies, but it also degrades update performance due to redundancy, and necessitates additional storage space.

5.2   The Design of Normalized Relations

The example in this section is based on the ER diagram in Fig. 5.2 and the following FDs:

editor_id, start_date -> editor_title, end_date

editor_id ->   editor_name, phone_no, office_no, proj_no, proj_name, dept_no

phone_no -> office_no

proj_no -> proj_name, proj_start_date, proj_end_date

dept_no -> dept_name, dept_head_id

dept_head_id -> dept_no

Our objective is to design a relational database schema that is normalized to at least 3NF and, if possible, minimize the number of relations required.

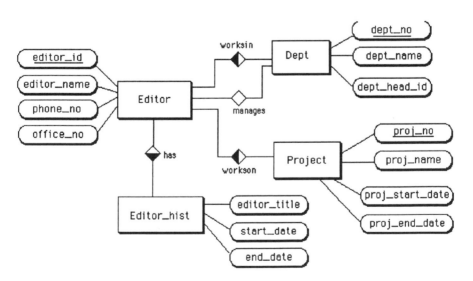

Figure 5.2
ER diagram for editor database example.

In general, the FDs can be derived from the ER diagram, explicit assertions given, or intuition (that is, from experience with the problem data). In this example we will restrict our discussion to the given FDs. Our first step is to assume that there exists initially a universal relation **R** in 1NF that contains all the attributes specified in the FDs.

> **R** (editor_id, start_date, end_date, editor_title, editor_name, phone_no, office-no, proj_no, proj_name, dept-no, dept_name, dept_head_id)

5.2.1 2NF Relations

We first look for non–fully functional dependencies and transform **R** into two or more 2NF relations. The composite attributes editor_id, start_date uniquely determine all other attribute values, are not reducible, and thus satisfy the criterion for a candidate key (and primary key).

> **R1:** editor_id, start_date->editor_title, end_date
> **R2:** editor_id ->editor_name, phone_no, office_no, proj_no,
> proj_name, dept_no
> phone_no -> office_no
> proj_no -> proj_name, proj_start_date, proj_end_date
> dept_no -> dept_name, dept_head_id
> dept_head_id -> dept_no

5.2.2 3NF Relations

We now analyze the set of FDs in **R2**, eliminating transitive dependencics. We need to eliminate all the right sides of the transitive dependencies (office_no, proj_name) from **R2** and put them into new relations, **R21** through **R25**.

> **R1:** editor_id, start_date->editor_title, end_date
> **R21:** editor_id -> editor_name, phone_no, proj_no, dept_no
> **R22:** phone_no -> office_no
> **R23:** proj_no -> proj_namc, proj_start_date, proj_end_date
> **R24:** dept_no -> dept_name, dept_head_id
> **R25:** dept_head_no -> dept_no

This solution, which is also BCNF as well as 3NF, maintains all the original FDs and avoids both the non–fully functional dependencies and transitive dependencies.

5.2.3 Minimum Set of 3NF Relations

We note that relations **R24** and **R25** have FDs that can be combined without losing 3NF because dept_no and dept_head_id are mutually dependent (a special form of transitivity that has no bad side effects for deletions). Thus we can reduce the number of 3NF relations by one:

R1: editor_id, start_date->editor_title, end_date
R21: editor_id -> editor_name, phone_no, proj_no, dept_no
R22: phone_no -> office_no
R23: proj_no -> proj_name, proj_start_date, proj_end_date
R241: dept_no -> dept_name, dept_head_id
dept_head_no -> dept_no

Alternative designs may involve splitting relations into partitions for volatile (frequently updated) and passive (rarely updated) data, consolidating relations to get better query performance, or duplicating data in different relations to get better query performance without losing integrity. In summary, the measures we use to assess the trade-offs in our design are

* query performance (time)
* update performance (time)
* storage performance (space)
* integrity (avoidance of delete anomalies)

5.3 Determining the Minimum Set of 3NF Relations

A minimum set of 3NF relations can be obtained from a given set of FDs by using the well-known synthesis algorithm developed by Bernstein [Bern76].

This process is particularly useful when you are confronted with a list of hundreds or thousands of FDs that describe the semantics of a database. In practice, the ER modeling process automatically decomposes this problem into smaller subproblems: the attributes and FDs of interest are restricted to those attributes within an entity (and its equivalent relation) and any foreign keys that might be imposed upon that relation. Thus the database designer will rarely have to deal with more than ten or twenty attributes at a time, and in fact most entities are initially defined in 3NF already. For those relations that are not yet in 3NF, only minor adjustments will be needed in most cases.

In the following we briefly describe the synthesis algorithm for those situations where the ER model is not useful for the decomposition. In order to apply the algorithm, we make use of the well-known Armstrong axioms, which define the basic relationships among FDs.

Inference rules (Armstrong axioms)

Reflexivity	If the tuples of X are a subset of the tuples of Y, then X->Y.
Augmentation	If X->Y and W is a subset of Z (that is, W->Z), then XW->YZ.
Transitivity	If X->Y and Y->Z, then X->Z.
Pseudotransitivity	If X->Y and YW->Z, then XW->Z.

(Transitivity is a special case of pseudotransitivity when W=null.)

Union	If X->Y and X->Z, then X->YZ (or equivalently, X->Y,Z).
Decomposition	If X->YZ, then X->Y and X->Z.

Before we can describe the synthesis algorithm, we must define some important concepts. Let H be a set of FDs that represents at least part of the known semantics of a database. The *closure* of H, specified by H$^+$, is the set of all FDs derivable from H using the Armstrong axioms or inference rules. For example, we can apply the transitivity rule to the following FDs in set H:

A—>B, B—>C, A—>C, and C—>D

to derive the FDs A->D and B->D. All six FDs constitute the closure H⁺. A *cover* of H, called H', is any set of FDs from which H⁺ can be derived. Possible covers for this example are:

1. A->B, B->C, C->D, A->C, A->D, B->D (trivial case where H' and H⁺ are equal)
2. A->B, B->C, C->D, A->C, A->D
3. A->B, B->C, C->D, A->C (this is the original set H)
4. A->B, B->C, C->D

A *nonredundant cover* of H is a cover of H which contains no proper subset of FDs which is also a cover. A *minimum cover* of H is a cover which minimizes the number of FDs. In the example above, cover (4) is both nonredundant and minimum. However, in many situations the minimum cover is different from a nonredundant cover, and it is much more complex to compute. Fortunately the synthesis algorithm requires only nonredundant covers.

3NF Synthesis Algorithm

Given a set of FDs, H, we determine a minimum set of relations in 3NF.

    H: AB->C   DM->NP
       A->EFGH   D->M
       E->G   L->N
       F->DJ   PQR->ST
       G->DI   PR->S
       D->KL

From this point the process of arriving at the minimum set of 3NF relations consists of six steps:

1. elimination of extraneous attributes in the determinants of the FDs
2. search for a nonredundant cover, G of H
3. partitioning of G into groups so that all FDs with the same left side are in one group

4. merge of equivalent keys
5. search for a nonredundant cover to eliminate transitive FDs
6. construction of relation schemes and FDs

Now we will discuss each step in turn, in terms of the preceding set of FDs, H.

5.3.1 Elimination of Extraneous Attributes

The first task is to get rid of extraneous attributes in the determinants of the FDs.

The following two relationships among attributes on the left side (determinant) of an FD provide the means to reduce the left side to fewer attributes.

1. XY->Z and X->Z => Y is extraneous on the left side (applying the first and third axioms).
2. XY->Z and X->Y => Y is extraneous; therefore X->Z (applying the fourth axiom).

Applying these relationships to the set of FDs in H, we get:

DM->NP and D->M => D->NP
PQR->ST and PR->S => PQR->T

5.3.2 Search for a Nonredundant Cover

We must eliminate any FD derivable from others in H using the inference rules.

Transitive FDs to be eliminated:

A->E and E->G => eliminate A->G
A->F and F->D => eliminate A->D

5.3.3 Partitioning of H'

To partition H' into groups so that all FDs with the same left side are in one group, we must separate the non–fully functional dependencies and transitive dependencies into separate relations. At this point we have a feasible solution for 3NF relations, but it is not necessarily the minimum set.

These non–fully functional dependencies must be put into separate relations:

AB->C
A->EF

Groups with the same left side:

G1: AB->C	**G6:** D->KLMNP
G2: A-> EF	**G7:** L->D
G3: E->G	**G8:** PQR->T
G4: G->DI	**G9:** PR->S
G5: F->DJ	

5.3.4 Merge of Equivalent Keys

In this step we merge groups with determinants that are equivalent (for example X—>Y and Y—>X imply that X and Y are equivalent). This step produces a minimal set, but it may lose 3NF because of new transitivities introduced by the merging process.

Groups G6 and G7 have D->L and L->D. Therefore merge these groups into a single group G67: with FDs D->KLMNP and L->D.

5.3.5 Search For a Nonredundant Cover

Find a nonredundant cover to eliminate any transitive FDs introduced in merging, then construct relation schemes (and display FDs) from the nonredundant cover.

In this case there are no further changes to the existing groups. The minimum set has been computed.

Relations and FDs: **R1:** AB->C   **R5:** F—>DJ
                  R2: A->EF   **R6:** D—>KLMNP and L—>D
                  R3: E->G   **R7:** PQR—>T
                  R4: G—>DI   **R8:** PR—>S

5.4   Normalization of Candidate Relations

Normalization of candidate relations is accomplished by analyzing the FDs associated with those relations. Further analysis is then needed to eliminate data redundancies in the normalized candidate relations.

5.4.1   Derive the Primary FDs from the ER Diagram

In this step, primary FDs represent the dependencies among the data elements that are keys of entities, that is, the inter-entity dependencies. Secondary FDs, on the other hand, represent dependencies among data elements that comprise a single entity, that is, the intra-entity dependencies. Table 5.1 shows the types of primary FDs derivable from each type of ER construct, consistent with the derivable candidate relations in Figs. 4.1 through 4.5. In fact, each primary FD is associated with exactly one candidate relation that represents a relationship among entities in the ER diagram.

      On the basis of the transformations in Table 5.1, we summarize the basic types of primary FDs derivable from ER relationship constructs:

1. key (many side) -> key (one side)
2. key (one side A) -> key (one side B)
3. key (many side A), key (many side B) -> key (one side)
4. key (one side A), key (many side) -> key (one side B)
5. key (one side A), key (one side B) -> key (one side C)
6. composite-key -> 0 (Null)

Table 5.1 Primary FDs derivable from ER relationship constructs.

Degree	Connectivity	Primary FD
Binary	1-to-1	key(one A) -> key(one B)
or Unary		key(one B) -> key(one A)
	1-to-many	key(many) -> key(one)
	many-to-many	composite-key -> 0
Ternary	1-to-1-to-1	key(A),key(B) -> key(C)
		key(A),key(C) -> key(B)
		key(B),key(C) -> key(A)
	1-to-1-to-many	key(one A),key(many) -> key(one B)
		key(one B),key(many) -> key(one A)
	1-to-many-to-many	key(many A),key(many B) -> key(one)
	many-to-many-to-many	composite-key -> 0
Generalization	(secondary FD only)	
Aggregation	(secondary FD only)	

Types (1) and (2) represent an embedded foreign key, functionally determined by the primary key, in a unary or binary relationship; types (3) through (5) apply only to ternary relationships; and type (6) applies to all degree of relationships in which the relation is represented as all key. FDs for higher degree n-ary relationships can be obtained by extending (3) through (6).

5.4.2 Examine All the Candidate Relations for Secondary FDs

Each candidate relation is examined to determine what dependencies exist among primary key, foreign key, and nonkey attributes. If the ER constructs do not include nonkey attributes, the data requirements specification or data dictionary must be consulted.

5.4.3 Normalize Candidate Relations

Normalize all candidate relations to the highest degree desired, eliminating any redundancies that occur in the normalized relations. Each candidate relation now may have some primary and secondary FDs uniquely associated with it. These dependencies determine the current degree of normalization of the relation. Any of the well-known techniques for increasing the degree of normalization can now be applied to each relation, to the desired degree stated in the requirements specification.

The elimination of data redundancy tends to minimize storage space and update cost without sacrificing data integrity. Integrity is maintained by requiring the new relation schema to include all data dependencies existing in the candidate normalized relation schema. Any relation B that is subsumed by another relation A can potentially be eliminated. Relation B is subsumed by another relation A when all the attributes in B are also contained in A, and all data dependencies in B also occur in A. As a trivial case, any relation containing only a composite key and no nonkey attributes is automatically subsumed by any other relation containing the same key attributes because the composite key is the weakest form of data dependency. If, however, relations A and B represent the supertype and subtype cases, respectively, of entities defined by the generalization or subset generalization abstraction, and A subsumes B because B has no additional specific attributes, the designer must collect and analyze additional information to decide whether or not to eliminate B.

A relation can also be subsumed by the construction of a join of two other relations (a "join" relation). When this occurs the elimination of a subsumed relation may result in the loss of retrieval efficiency, although storage and update costs will tend to be decreased. This tradeoff must be further analyzed during physical design with regard to processing requirements, to determine whether elimination of the subsumed relation is reasonable (see Chapter 6).

Example (normalization)

First we want to obtain the primary FDs by applying the rules in Table 5.1 to each relationship in the ER diagram in Fig. 3.3. The results are shown in Table 5.2.

Table 5.2 Functional dependencies derived from the ER diagram in Figure 3.3.

abbr_id—>paper_id
book_id—>pub_id
indiv_id—>auth_id, rvr_id
inv_id—>src_id
iss_id—>jour_id
jour_id—>st_ord_id, pub_id
paper_id—>iss_id, abbr_id, editor_id
paper_id, auth_id—>inst_name, lang_name
pub_id—>st_ord_id
rev_id—>paper_id, rvr_id
src_id—>exch_id, comm_id, dist_id
ser_id—>pub_id
st_ord_id—>src_id

Next we want to determine the secondary FDs from the ER diagram or requirements specification. Let us assume that the dependencies in Table 5.3 are derived from the requirements specification:

Table 5.3 Secondary functional dependencies (example).

auth_id—>auth_name, auth_addr, auth_title
auth_var_id—>auth_var_name
book_id—>book_title, topic_area
class_id—>class_type
comm_id—>comm_name
dist_id—>dist_name, dist_addr
editor_id—>editor_name, editor_addr, primary_topic_area
exch_id—>exch_type
inst_name—>inst_addr
iss_id—>iss_date
paper_id—>paper_title
rvr_id—>rvr_name, rvr_addr
src_id—>src_type, pub_equiv
var_id—>var_type

Normalization of the candidate relations is accomplished next. In Table 4.1, only the journal and series relations are not at least BCNF due to the transitive FDs jour_id—>pub_id—>st_ord_id and ser_id—>pub_id—>st_ord_id. This is easily resolved by creating the relation pub_stand_order and deleting st_ord_id from the journal and series relations (see Table 5.4). In general we observe that the candidate relations in Table 4.1 are fairly good indicators of the final schema and normally require very little refinement.

Table 5.4 Normalized relations: modifications from candidate relations in Table 4.1

```
create table pub_stand_order (pub_id char(10) not null unique,
                  st_ord_id integer,
                  primary key (pub_id)
                  foreign key (pub_id) references publisher
                        on delete set default
                        on update cascade)

create table journal (jour_id integer not null unique,
                  pub_id char(10) not null,
                  primary key (jour_id),
                  foreign key (pub_id) references publisher
                        on delete set default
                        on update cascade)

create table series (ser_id char(8) not null unique,
                  pub_id char(10) not null,
                  primary key (ser_id),
                  foreign key (pub_id) references publisher
                        on delete set default
                        on update cascade)
```

5.5 Higher Normal Forms and Equivalent ER Constructs

The following statements summarize the functional equivalence between the ER model and normalized relations:

1. within an entity—the level of normalization is totally dependent upon the interrelationships among the key and nonkey attributes. It could be any form from unnormalized to BCNF.

2. binary (or unary) one-to-one or one-to-many relationship—within the "child" entity, the foreign key (a replication of the primary key of the "parent") is functionally dependent upon the child's primary key . This is at least BCNF, assuming the entity by itself, without the foreign key, is already BCNF.

3. binary (or unary) many-to-many relationship—the intersection relation has a composite key and possibly some nonkey attributes functionally dependent upon it. This is at least BCNF.

4. ternary relationship:

   a. one-to-one-to-one => three overlapping composite keys, at least BCNF

   b. one-to-one-to-many => two overlapping composite keys, at least BCNF

   c. one-to-many-to-many => one composite key, at least BCNF

   d. many-to-many-to-many => one composite key with 3 attributes, at least BCNF. In some cases it can be also 4NF, or even 5NF.

Normal forms up to BCNF were defined solely on FDs. In this section we will look at different types of constraints on relations, multivalued dependencies and join dependencies. If these constraints do not exist in a relation, which is the most common situation, then any relation in BCNF is automatically in fourth normal form (4NF) and fifth normal form (5NF) as well. However, when these constraints do exist, there may be further update anomalies that need to be corrected. First we must define the concept of multivalued dependency.

5.5.1 Multivalued Dependencies

In a *multivalued dependency* (*MVD*) X—>>Y holds on relation **R** with relation scheme RS if, whenever a valid instance of relation **R**(X,Y,Z) contains a pair of rows that contain duplicate values of X, then the instance also contains the pair of rows obtained by interchanging the Y values in the original pair. This includes situations where only pairs of tuples exist. Note that X and Y may contain either single or composite attributes. An MVD X —>> Y is trivial if Y is a subset of X, or if X union Y=RS. Finally, an FD implies an MVD, which implies that a single row with a given value of X is also an MVD, albeit a trivial form.

The following examples show where an MVD does and does not exist in a relation. In **R1**, the first four tuples satisfy all conditions for the MVDs X—>>Y and X—>>Z. Note that MVDs appear in pairs because of the cross-product type of relationship between Y and Z=RS-Y as the two right sides of the two MVDs. The fifth and sixth tuples of **R1** (when X is 2) satisfy the row interchange conditions in the above definition. In both tuples the Y value is 2, so the interchanging of Y values is trivial. The seventh tuple (3,3,3) satisfies the definition trivially.

In relation **R2**, however, the Y values in the fifth and sixth tuples are different (1 and 2), and interchanging the 1 and 2 values for Y results in a tuple (2,2,2) that does not appear in the relation. Thus in **R2** there is no MVD between X and Y or between X and Z, even though the first four tuples satisfy the MVD definition. Note that for the MVD to exist, *all tuples* must satisfy the criterion for an MVD.

Relation **R3** contains the first three tuples that do not satisfy the criterion for an MVD, since changing Y from 1 to 2 in the second tuple results in a tuple that does not appear in the relation. Similarly, changing Z from 1 to 2 in the third tuple results in a nonappearing tuple. Thus **R3** does not have any MVDs between X and Y or between X and Z.

R1:	X	Y	Z	R2:	X	Y	Z	R3:	X	Y	Z
	1	1	1		1	1	1		1	1	1
	1	1	2		1	1	2		1	1	2
	1	2	1		1	2	1		1	2	1
	1	2	2		1	2	2		2	2	1
	2	2	1		2	2	1		2	2	2
	2	2	2		2	1	2				
	3	3	3								

By the same argument, in relation **R1** we have the MVDs Y–>> X and Y—>>Z, but none with Z on the left side. Relations **R2** and **R3** have no MVDs at all.

5.5.2 Fourth Normal Form

A relation **R** is in *fourth normal form* (*4NF*) if and only if it is in BCNF and, whenever there exists an MVD in **R** (say X ->> Y), at least one of the following holds:

The MVD is trivial

or

X is a superkey for **R**.

Applying this definition to the three relations in the example in the previous section, we see that **R1** is not in 4NF because at least one nontrivial MVD exists. In relations **R2** and **R3**, however, there are no MVDs. Thus these two relations are at least 4NF.

As an example of the transformation of a relation that is not in 4NF to two relations that are in 4NF, we observe the ternary relationship skill_required shown in Fig. 5.3. The relationship skill_required is defined as "A reviewer must have all the required skills needed for a paper to review that paper." For example, in Table 5.5 the paper with paper_id = 3 requires skills A and B by

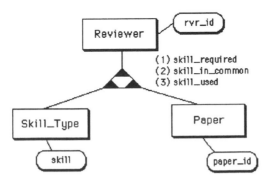

Figure 5.3
Many-to-many-to-many ternary relationship with multiple interpretations.

Table 5.5 The relation **skill_required** and its three projections.

| skill_required | | | |
rvr_id	paper_id	skill	MVDs (nontrivial)
101	3	A	paper_no—>>skill
101	3	B	paper_no—>>rvr_id
101	4	A	skill—>>paper_no
101	4	C	skill—>>rvr_id
102	3	A	
102	3	B	
102	4	A	
102	4	C	
103	5	D	

| skill_req_1 | | skill_req_2 | | skill_req_3 | |
rvr_id	paper_id	rvr_id	skill	paper_id	skill
101	3	101	A	3	A
101	4	101	B	3	B
102	3	101	C	4	A
102	4	102	A	4	C
103	5	102	B	5	D
		102	C		
		103	D		

all reviewers (see reviewers 101 and 102). The relation **skill_required** has no FDs, but it does have several MVDs and is therefore only in BCNF. In such a case it can have a lossless decomposition/join into two many-to-many binary relationships between the entities Reviewer and Paper, and Paper and Skill. Each of these two new relationships represents a relation in 4NF. It can also have a lossless decomposition/join resulting in a binary many-to-many relationship between the entities Reviewer and Skill, and Paper and Skill.

A two-way lossless decomposition/join occurs when **skill_required** is projected over {rvr_id, paper_id} to form **skill_req_1** and projected over {paper_id, skill} to form **skill_req_3**. Projection over {rvr_id, paper_id} to form **skill_req_1** and over {rvr_id, skill} to form **skill_req_2**, however, is not lossless. A 3-way lossless decomposition/join occurs when **skill_required** is projected over {rvr_id, paper_id}, {rvr_id, skill}, and {paper_id, skill}.

Relations in 4NF avoid certain update anomalies (or inefficiencies). For instance, a delete anomaly exists when two independent facts get tied together unnaturally so there may be bad side effects of certain deletes. For example, in **skill_required** the last record of a skill may be lost if an employee is temporarily not working on any projects. An update inefficiency may occur when adding a new project in **skill_required**, which requires insertions for many records (tuples) to include all the required skills for that new project. Likewise, loss of a project requires many deletions. These inefficiencies are avoided when **skill_required** is decomposed into **skill_req_1** and **skill_req_3**. In general (but not always) decomposition of a relation into 4NF relations results in less data redundancy.

5.5.3   Fifth Normal Form

A relation is in *fifth normal form* (*5NF*) if it cannot have a lossless decomposition/join by the projection operation into any number of smaller relations. As you recall, a *lossless decomposition/join* of a relation implies that it can be decomposed by two or more projections, followed by a natural join of those projections (in any order) that results in the original relation, without any spurious or missing tuples. The general lossless decomposition/join constraint, involving any number of projections, is also known as a *join dependency* (*JD*). In other words, a relation is not in 5NF if it can be lossless decomposed/joined via some n>1 projections.

A lossless decomposition/join of two projections is equivalent to an MVD, and the relation is only in BCNF. A lossless decomposition/join of three or more projections is equivalent to a JD, and the relation is only in 4NF. Thus an MVD is a special case of a JD where the number of projections is two. It is difficult to determine if a relation is in 5NF, but for ternary relations, the number of possible decompositions is small and tractable (several examples follow).

The following example demonstrates a situation with two seemingly similar relations, one that is 5NF and another that is not. A relation representing a ternary relationship may not have any two-way lossless decomposition/joins; however, it may have a three-way lossless decomposition/join, which is equivalent to three binary relationships, based on the three possible projections of this relation. This situation occurs in the relationship skill_in_common (Fig. 5.3), which is defined as "The reviewer must apply the intersection of his or her available skills with the skills needed to review certain papers." In this example skill_in_common is less restrictive than skill_required because it allows a reviewer to review a paper even if he or she does not have all the skills required for that paper. The associated relation, **skill_in_common**, is in 4NF because it has no MVDs, but it is not 5NF because it can have a lossless decomposition/join into three binary relations. In general, if the relationship can be represented as a 5NF relation, then it is truly ternary; otherwise, it can be decomposed into equivalent binary relationships.

As Table 5.6 shows, the three projections of **skill_in_common** result in a three-way lossless decomposition/join. There are no two-way lossless decomposition/joins and no MVDs; thus, the relation **skill_in_common** is in 4NF.

The ternary relationship in Fig. 5.3 can be interpreted yet another way. The meaning of the relationship skill_used is "We can selectively record different skills that each reviewer applies to reviewing individual papers." It is equivalent to a relation in 5NF that cannot be decomposed into either two or three binary relations. Note by studying Table 5.7 that the associated relation, **skill_used**, has no MVDs or JDs.

In summary, a relation may have constraints that are FDs, MVDs, and JDs. An MVD is a special case of a JD. In order to determine the level of normalization of the relation, analyze the FDs first to determine 1NF through BCNF; then analyze the MVDs to determine BCNF through 4NF; and, finally, analyze the JDs to determine 4NF through 5NF.

Returning to our discussion of the equivalence between normalized relations and ER constructs, we note that a many-to-many-to-many ternary relationship is:

1. BCNF if it can be replaced by two binary relationships,

2. 4NF if it can be replaced by three binary relationships, and

3. 5NF if it cannot be replaced in any way (and thus is a true ternary relationship).

Table 5.6   The relation **skill_in common** and its three projections.

rvr_id	skill_in_common paper_id	skill
101	3	A
101	3	B
101	4	A
101	4	B
102	3	A
102	3	B
103	3	A
103	4	A
103	5	A
103	5	C

skill_in_com_1 rvr_id	paper_id	skill_in_com_2 rvr_id	skill	skill_in_com_3 paper_id	skill
101	3	101	A	3	A
101	4	101	B	3	B
102	3	102	A	4	A
103	3	102	B	4	B
103	4	103	A	5	A
103	5	103	C	5	C

We observe the equivalence between certain ternary relationships and the higher normal form relations transformed from those relationships. Ternary relationships that have at least one "one" entity cannot be decomposed (or broken down) into binary relationships because that would destroy the one or more functional dependencies required in the definition, as shown above. A ternary relationship with all "many" entities, however, has no FDs, but in some cases may have MVDs, and thus have a lossless decomposition/join into equivalent binary relationships.

Table 5.7 The relation **skill_used**, its three projections, and natural joins of its projections.

skill_used		
rvr_id	**paper_id**	**skill**
101	3	A
101	3	B
101	4	A
101	4	C
102	3	A
102	3	B
102	4	A
102	4	B

Three projections on **skill_used** result in

skill_used_1		skill_used_2		skill_used_3	
rvr_id	**paper_id**	**paper_id**	**skill**	**rvr_id**	**skill**
101	3	3	A	101	A
101	4	3	B	101	B
102	3	4	A	101	C
102	4	4	B	102	A
		4	C	102	B

Join **skill_used_1** with **skill_used_2** to form

Join **skill_used_12** with **skill_used_3** to form

skill_used_12			skill_used_123		
rvr_id	**paper_id**	**skill**	**rvr_id**	**paper_id**	**skill**
101	3	A	101	3	A
101	3	B	101	3	B
101	4	A	101	4	A
101	4	B	**101**	**4**	**B** (spurious
101	4	C	101	4	C tuple)
102	3	A	102	3	A
102	3	B	102	3	B
102	4	A	102	4	A
102	4	B	102	4	B
102	4	C			

In summary, the three common cases that illustrate the correspondence between a lossless decomposition/join in a many-to-many-to-many ternary relationship relation and higher normal forms in the relational model are shown below:

relation name	normal form	2-way lossless decompos/ join?	3-way lossless decompos/ join?	Nontrivial MVDs
skill_required	BCNF	yes	yes	4
skill_in_common	4NF	no	yes	0
skill_used	5NF	no	no	0

5.6   Summary

In this chapter we defined the constraints imposed on relations: FDs, MVDs, and JDs. Based on these constraints, normal forms for database relations were defined: 1NF, 2NF, 3NF, and BCNF. All are based on the types of FDs present. The 4NFs and 5NFs are dependent on the type of MVDs and JDs present. In this chapter, a practical algorithm for finding the minimum set of 3NF relations was given. Finally, the equivalence between the ER model and normalized relations was demonstrated, and the application of a normalization step to our example database design case study was shown.

In the next chapter we will look at ways to refine the relational database for use by various applications. In order to make these refinements, the fundamentals of physical database design by using access methods will be presented.

Literature Summary

Effective summaries of normal forms can be found in [Date86, Kent83, DuHa89, Smit85]. Algorithms for normal form decomposition and synthesis techniques are given in [Bern76, Fagi77, Ullm88, Lien81, ZaMe81, Mart83, Maie83, Yao85]. Earlier work in normal forms was done by [Codd70, Codd74].

[Bern76]   Bernstein, P. "Synthesizing 3NF Relations from Functional Dependencies," *ACM Trans. Database Systems* 1,4(1976), pp. 272–298.

[Codd70]   Codd, E. "A Relational Model for Large Shared Data Banks," *Comm. ACM* 13,6(June 1970), pp. 377–387.

[Codd74]   Codd, E. "Recent Investigations into Relational Data Base Systems," *Proc. IFIP Congress*, North-Holland, 1974.

[Date86]   Date, C.J. *An Introduction to Database Systems*, Vol. 1 (4th Ed.), Addison-Wesley, Reading, MA, 1986.

[DuHa89]   Dutka, A.F., and Hanson, H.H. *Fundamentals of Data Normalization*, Addison-Wesley, Reading, MA, 1989.

[Fagi77]   Fagin, R. "Multivalued Dependencies and a New Normal Form for Relational Databases," *ACM Trans. Database Systems* 2,3(1977), pp. 262–278.

[Kent83]   Kent, W. "A Simple Guide to Five Normal Forms in Relational Database Theory," *Comm. ACM* 26,2(Feb. 1983), pp. 120–125.

[Lien81]   Lien, Y. "Hierarchical Schemata for Relational Databases," *ACM Trans. Database Systems* 6,1(1981), pp. 48–69.

[Maie83]   Maier, D. *Theory of Relational Databases*, Computer Science Press, Rockville, MD, 1983.

[Mart83]   Martin, J. *Managing the Data-Base Environment*, Prentice-Hall, Englewood Cliffs, NJ, 1983.

[Smit85]   Smith, H. "Database Design: Composing Fully Normalized Tables from a Rigorous Dependency Diagram," *Comm. ACM* 28,8 (1985), pp. 826–838.

[Ullm88]   Ullman, J. *Principles of Database and Knowledge-Base Systems*, Vols. 1 and 2, Computer Science Press, Rockville, MD, 1988.

[Yao 85]   Yao, S.B. (editor). *Principles of Database Design*, Prentice-Hall, Englewood Cliffs, NJ, 1985.

[ZaMe81]   Zaniolo, C., and Melkanoff, M. "On the Design of Relational Database Schemas," *ACM Trans. Database Systems* 6,1(1981), pp. 1–47.

Exercises

Problem 5-1

Answer each question "yes" or "no." Justify each answer. In each case you will be given a relation **R** with a list of attributes without the candidate keys shown.

Given R(A,B,C,D) and the FDs A->B, A->C, and A->D

1. Is A a candidate key?
2. Is this relation, **R**, in 3NF?

Given R(A,B,C,D) and the FDs A->B, B->C, and C->D

3. Does A->D?
4. Is A a candidate key?

Given R(A,B) and the FDs A->B and B->A

5. Are both A and B candidate keys?
6. Is **R** in BCNF?

Given R(A,B,C) and the FDs A->B, B->C, and C->A

7. Is A the only candidate key?
8. Is **R** only in 2NF?

Given R(A,B,C) and the FDs AB->C and C->A

9. Is AB a candidate key?
10. Is C a candidate key?
11. Is **R** in 3NF?
12. Is **R** in BCNF?

Given R(A,B,C) and the FD C->A

13. Is **R** in 3NF?
14. Is **R** in BCNF?

Given R(A,B,C,D) and the FDs A->B and C->D

15. Is A a candidate key?
16. Is C a candidate key?
17. Is **R** in 3NF?

Given R(A,B,C) and the FDs AB->C, AC->B, and BC->A

18. Is A a candidate key?
19. Is BC a candidate key?
20. Is **R** in 3NF?

Given R(A,B,C) and the FDs AB->C and AC->B

21. Is ABC a superkey?
22. Is AC a candidate key?
23. Is **R** in 3NF?
24. Is **R** in BCNF?

Given R(A,B,C) with no FDs

25. Is AB a candidate key?
26. Is ABC a superkey?
27. Is **R** in BCNF?

Given R(A,B,C,D) with the FD A->B

28. Is A a candidate key?
29. Is ACD a superkey?
30. Is **R** in 3NF?

Problem 5-2

Answer each question by writing *yes* or *no*. Justify each answer. In each case you will be given a relation, **R**, with a list of attributes, with at most one candidate key (the candidate key may be either a single attribute or composite attribute key, shown underlined).

Given R(A,B,C) and the FDs A->B and B->C

1. Is **R** in 3NF?

Given R(A,B,C) and the FD BC->A

2. Is **R** in 3NF?
3. Is **R** in BCNF?
4. Is BC a candidate key?

Given R(A,B,C) and the FD A->C

5. Is **R** in 3NF?
6. Does AB->C?

Given R(A,B,C,D) and the FD C->B

7. Is **R** in 3NF?

Problem 5-3

Given the assertions that follow, which describe the current term enrollment at a large university, do the following:

1. List the obvious functional dependencies (FDs) from the given description.
2. What level of normalization is the database implemented as a single table with no repeating columns? Justify your answer.
3. If not in BCNF already, convert the database to BCNF.

Assertions

a. An instructor may teach no course, one course, or several courses in a given term (average=2.0 courses).
b. An instructor must direct the research of at least one student (average=2.5 students).
c. A course may have no prerequisites, one prerequisite, or two prerequisites (average=1.5 prerequisites).
d. A course may exist even if no students are currently enrolled.
e. All courses are taught by only one instructor.
f. The average enrollment in a course is 30 students.
g. A student must select at least one course per term (average=4.0 course selections).

Problem 5-4

Given the following set of FDs, find the minimal set of 3NF relations. Designate the candidate key attributes of these relations.

A—>B	B—>D	E—>J
A—>C	D—>B	EG—>H
B—>C	ABE—>F	H—>G

Problem 5-5

Given the following FDs, determine the minimum set of 3NF relations. Make sure that all functional dependencies are preserved. Specify the candidate keys of each relation. Note that each letter represents a separate data element (attribute).

1. A—>B
2. AB—>DE
3. ABCDET—>GHIJKW
4. ABDET—>CGHIJKW
5. CG—>KW
6. DT—>K
7. E—>ABCMNPQRT
8. GH—>AIJKT
9. HJR—>S
10. HJS—>R
11. HRS—>J
12. J—>ABCKT
13. JRS—>H
14. KW—>M
15. KM—>W
16. M—>PQR
17. MN—>P
18. N—>T
19. T—>MN

If we eliminate the functional dependency J—>A from the above list, what effect does this have on the solution?

Problem 5-6

Answer each question by writing *true* or *false*.

A relation **R** in 2NF with FDs A—>B and B—>CDEF (where A is the only candidate key), is decomposed into two relations, **R1** (with A—>B) and **R2** (with B—>CDEF). The relations **R1** and **R2**:

1. are always a lossless decomposition of **R**
2. usually have total combined storage space less than **R**
3. have no delete anomalies
4. will always be faster to execute a query than **R**

A relation S in 3NF with FD's GH—>I and I—>H is decomposed into two relations, **S1** (with GH—>null, that is, all key) and **S2** (with I—>H). The relations **S1** and **S2**:

5. are always a lossless decomposition of S
6. are both dependency preserving
7. are both in BCNF

A relation **T** in BCNF with FDs W—>XYZ (where W is the primary key) is decomposed into two relations, **T1** (with W—>X) and **T2** (with W—>YZ). The relations **T1** and **T2**:

8. are always dependency preserving
9. usually have total combined storage space less than **T**
10. have no delete anomalies.

Note: A—>BC implies that A—>B and A—>C (one of Armstrong axioms).

Problem 5-7

Given the FDs and MVDs in the list below, what is the highest level of normalization you can claim for each of the relations, without making any further assumptions? In each case justify your answer with a single word, phrase, or sentence.

Choose from unnormalized, 1NF, 2NF, 3NF, BCNF, 4NF, and 5NF. Note that 5NF is the highest level.

	Given dependencies	Notation
Relation-1(A,B,C)	A—>B—>C	—>FD
Relation-2(D,E,F,K)	E—>K	—>>MVD
Relation-3(D,E,L)	F—>BG	
Relation-4(D,E,F,B)	B—>D	
Relation-5(F,B,G)	L—>D	
Relation-6(H,I,J)	H—>G	
Relation-7(H,I,G)	H—>>IJ	
Relation-8(H,I,K)	I—>>K	
Relation-9(A,H)		
Relation-10(All attributes A through K)		

Problem 5-8

Answer each question by writing *yes* or *no*. Justify each answer. In most cases you will be given a relation **R** with a list of attributes, with at most one candidate key (the candidate key may be either a single attribute or composite attribute key, shown <u>underlined</u>).

Given R(A,B,C,D) and the FD AB->C

1. Is **R** in 3NF?
2. Is **R** in BCNF?
3. Does the MVD AB->>C hold?
4. Does the set {**R1**(A,B,C), **R2**(A,B,D)} satisfy the lossless join property?

Given that R(A,B,C) and the set {R1(A,B), R2(B,C)} satisfy the lossless decomposition/join property

5. Does the MVD B->>C hold?
6. Is B a candidate key?
7. Is **R** in 4NF?

Assume a relation "skills_available" with attributes empno, project, and skill. The semantics of "skills_available" state that every skill an employee has must be used on every project that employee works on.

8. Is the level of normalization of "skills_available" at least 4NF?

Given relation R(A,B,C) with actual data as shown in the table that follows:

9. Does the MVD B->>C hold?
10. Is **R** in 5NF?

R:	A	B	C
	w	x	p
	w	x	q
	z	x	p
	z	x	q
	w	y	q
	z	y	p

Problem 5-9

The following FDs represent a set of airline reservation system database constraints. Design a minimum set of 3NF relations, preserving all FDs, and express your solution in terms of the code letters given below (a time-saving device for your analysis).

reservation_no-->agent_no, agent_name, airline_name, airline_name,
 flight_no, passenger_name
reservation_no-->aircraft_type, departure_date, arrival_date,
 departure_time, arrival_time
reservation_no-->departure_city, arrival_city, type_of_payment,
 seating_class, seat_no
airline_name, flight_no-->aircraft_type, departure_time, arrival_time
airline_name, flight_no-->departure_city, arrival_city, meal_type
airline_name, flight_no, aircraft_type-->meal_type
passenger_name-->home_address, home_phone, company_name
aircraft_type, seat_no-->seating_class
company_name-->company_address, company_phone
company_phone-->company_name

A: reservation_no	L: departure_city
B: agent_no	M: arrival_city
C:agent_name	N: type_of_payment

D: airline_name

E: flight_no

F: passenger_name

G: aircraft_type

H: departure_date

I: arrival_date

J: departure_time

K: arrival_time

P: seating_class

Q: seat_no

R: meal_type

S: home_address

T: home_phone

U: company_name

V: company_address

W. company_phone

6

Physical Design Fundamentals

Physical design comes last. Using some basic assumptions about the physical database environment, the designer can make refinements to the logical (global) schema that will improve performance of the database. Generally, the designer has the option to pick one of the many normalized schemas, cluster records within a table, cluster related record types together, specify primary keys for fast random access to individual records, define secondary indices to allow fast access by nonkey attributes, and specific physical parameters such as block size, buffer pool size, lock granularity, and recovery protocol.

This chapter focuses on the various access methods available and the system parameters associated with them. In order to classify access methods, we define three broad categories of database applications in terms of generic data manipulation commands:

1. random access: select one record of a given type
2. sequential access: select all records of a given type (or a large subset of those records)
3. Boolean query access: select a group of records based on some Boolean search criterion.

Each type of application, which includes both query and update requirements, implies a class of efficient access methods. The algebra used to describe the performance of each access method is typical of what a query optimizer might calculate to determine good query plans.

6.1 Access Methods and Performance Measures

The logical design of a database results in the schema definition of logical records. A *logical record* (or record) is a named collection of data items or attributes treated as a unit by an application program. In storage, a record includes the pointers and record overhead needed for identification and processing by the database management system. A *file* is a set of similarly constructed records of one or more types. For simplicity, in this chapter we will assume that a file consists of records of a single type. A *physical database* (or database) is a collection of interrelated records of different types, possibly including a collection of interrelated files. Query and update transactions (or applications) to a database are made efficient by the implementation of certain access methods as part of the database management system.

An *access method* consists of two integrated components: data structure and search mechanism. The data structure defines the framework for storing index and data blocks in memory. The search mechanism defines the access

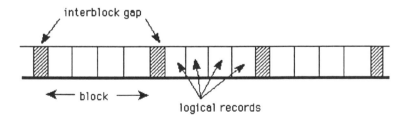

blocking factor = 4

Figure 6.1
Sequential file parameters.

path, that is, how the tables are searched. As an example, consider a sequential file. The data structure is simply a collection of contiguously stored records of a single type. The search mechanism, however, could be either a sequential search of all the records in storage order, a binary search, or some other type of random search mechanism.

Let us now look at a simple model of database access methods. We shall see that we can capture the essence of database performance by defining and analyzing just a few important parameters.

6.1.1   Basic Access Method Parameters: Sequential Files

Consider a sequential file of n records. To be stored on disk, these n records must be grouped into physical blocks as Fig. 6.1 shows. A *block* is the basic unit of input/output from disk to main memory. It can range in size from a fraction of a record to hundreds or thousands of records. Typically a block size ranges from 1 to 100 records. If a database has *normalized records*, or records of constant size, the number of records in a block is called the *blocking factor* (*bf*). For consistency and ease of programming, block sizes are usually constant for a whole system. On the other hand, almost all relational systems allow variable size records; thus we will use average record size for simplicity in our performance analysis.

Sequential Processing for an Entire File

If we have a file of n records and a blocking factor bf, the basic performance measures for a sequential search of the entire file are as follows.

$$lra=n \text{ logical record accesses} \tag{6.1}$$
$$sba=ceil(n/bf) \text{ sequential block accesses} \tag{6.2}$$
$$rba=0 \text{ random block accesses} \tag{6.3}$$
$$iotime=sba*tsba + rba*tsrba \text{ seconds} \tag{6.4}$$
where tsba is the average disk i/o service time for a sequential block access and trba is the average disk i/o service time for a random block access

Note that the ceiling function, ceil, in Eq. 6.2 is the next higher whole number (or integer) when the number of block accesses is a fraction instead of a whole number. Obviously, sequential block accesses can be minimized when the bf is maximized. However, block size is usually a function of some portion of a disk track. It is also limited by the size of buffers allowed in main memory, since block size and buffer size must be the same for efficient data transfer from disk to main memory.

If we were to access the sequential file of n records in a completely random sequence, the performance measures would be

lra=n logical record accesses	(6.5)
sba=0 sequential block accesses	(6.6)
rba=n random block accesses	(6.7)
iotime=sba*tsba + rba*trba seconds	(6.8)

These two situations, sequential and random access to a sequential file, show that a sequential search mechanism makes efficient use of the bf, but a random search mechanism does not. Thus, when random searches are required of a sequential file, a bf of 1 minimizes the search time (i/o service time), assuming that 1 is the lowest value we can use in a typical system.

Because time is a common unit for all databases, i/o service time is the most important performance measure. Response time as a performance measure is too difficult to control from the database designer perspective; that is, response time includes disk and cpu wait times which are often dependent on the rest of the computing environment workload. Response time also includes cpu service time, which unfortunately is dependent on the amount of processing a database user does with the records retrieved, and it is not a function of the access method or database implementation.

The disk service time can be estimated from this simple model:

$$tsba=rot/2+bks/tr \qquad\qquad (6.9)$$

where rot is the disk rotation time (for a full rotation),
bks is the block size in bytes (bf*record size), and
tr is the disk transfer rate in bytes per second

In other words, the average sequential block i/o service time is the average time to access the next block on disk, which is a half rotation as the average rotational delay, plus the block transfer time. The average random block i/o service time is similarly computed:

trba=seek(file)+rot/2+bks/tr (6.10)

where seek(file) is the average seek time over the extent of the file on disk

The average random block i/o service time is the average seek time over the extent of the file plus the average rotational delay plus the block transfer time. The average seek time assumption depends on the type of disk and the work load environment, dedicated or shared. In a dedicated disk environment, the disk arm is confined to the extent of the file, which we assume is in contiguous storage. In a shared disk environment, the disk arm is moved an average seek distance for each block access to your file; this assumes that other users of this disk move the disk arm away from your file some random distance.

Consequently, in a *shared disk environment*, we have

tsba=trba=seek(disk)+rot/2+bks/tr (6.11)

where seek(disk) is the average seek time over the extent of the entire disk

Equation 6.11 is the same as Eq. 6.10 except that the seek(avg) component is potentially greater in size. In this chapter we will assume that the disk environment is dedicated unless stated otherwise. Also, in the following analyses, we will compute only lra, sba, and rba and assume that the disk characteristics are known to compute the disk i/o service time, iotime.

The disk time analysis can sometimes be further simplified by noting that many systems do some sort of prefetching of multiple blocks (typically 64 KB per disk i/o, such as in DB2) to speed up the sequential processing activity. Under these conditions, dedicated disks have negligible seek times and rotational delay, while shared disks are dominated by seek times and data transfers.

Sequential Processing for a Single Record

If there are n records in a sequential file that is sorted by primary key, a sequential search for a single record, whether that record exists or not, requires approximately

$$lra=n/2 \text{ logical record accesses} \hspace{3cm} (6.12)$$
$$sba=ceiling(lra/bf) \text{ sequential block accesses} \hspace{2cm} (6.13)$$

If the file is unsorted, a sequential search for the record is lra=n/2 if the record exists and lra=n when the record does not exist.

Batch Processing of k Records

One of the advantages of a sequential database or file is the efficiency of batch processing. Let us assume a batch system with a master file and a transaction file (Fig. 6.2). Both files are sorted by primary key. The transaction file is assumed to have records of fixed size that specify what update action is to be taken on a record in the master file. Thus each transaction record includes the primary key of a master file record, but the record size of the transaction file may be quite different from the record size in the master file. The i/o service time to execute the batch of update transactions is the sum of the time to read the entire transaction file, read the entire master file, and create a new master file. In other words:

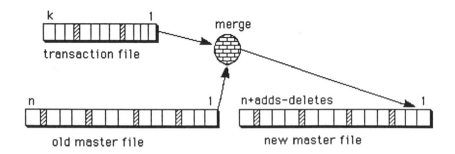

Figure 6.2
Batch processing of sequential files.

read the transaction file: lra=k where k=number of transaction records

(6.14)

sba=ceil(k/bf1) where bf1 is the transaction
file bf (6.15)

read the master file: lra=n (6.16)

sba = ceil(n/bf2) where bf2 is the master file bf

(6.17)

write a new master file: lra=n+adds–deletes (6.18)

sba=ceil((n+adds–deletes)/bf2) (6.19)

where adds is the number of records added or
inserted and
deletes is the number of records deleted

6.1.2   Random-Access Method: Hashing

Hashing is the most common form of purely random access to a file or database. The most popular form of hashing is division hashing with chained overflow, which is illustrated in Fig. 6.3. The basic mechanism is the transformation of a primary key identifier directly to a physical address, called a *bucket*, or indirectly to a bucket by first transforming it to a logical address (an integer) and letting the database management system transform it again to a physical address. Techniques that combine basic hashing with dynamic file expansion are also very popular today [ElNa89].

Address transformation is done by the central processing unit. The actual access to the target database is done using the disk. The address transformation for division hashing is typically done by dividing the primary key into partitions and applying a simple arithmetic function to those partitions (such as adding them) to get a single address value. For instance, given a primary key of a person's social security number, 527-45-6783, we can add the subset numbers: 527+45+6783=7355. Then we can transform this number into a physical disk address for a disk with 32 devices, 404 cylinders per disk, 20 tracks per cylinder, and 5 blocks per track:

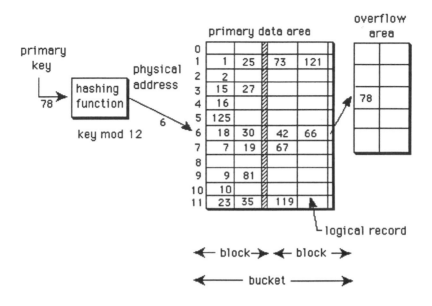

Figure 6.3
Hashing access method with separate chaining for overflow.

device address=7355 mod 32=27
cylinder address=7355 mod 404=83
track address=7355 mod 20=15   (6.20)

Access to this physical address allows us to either retrieve a record from a block on that track or store a new record in a block on that track. Collisions occur when the database user attempts to insert a record into the target (bucket) address and the bucket is filled, causing overflow. Overflow is typically handled by establishing a series of overflow blocks on each track, overflow tracks on each cylinder, and overflow cylinders on each disk. Overflow records are chained in some order, usually either FIFO (first in, first out) or LIFO (last in, first out), and the length of overflow chains is a function of the density of the database and the type of overflow data structure and search mechanism [TeFr82]. For our simple model, we compute the performance as follows.

random access to a hashed file: lra=1+overflow(avg)   (6.21)

rba=1+overflow(avg)   (6.22)

insertion into a hashed file: lra=1+overflow(avg)+rewrite   (6.23)

rba=1+overflow(avg)   (6.24)

sba=1 for the rewrite   (6.25)

Note that a *rewrite* of a block just accessed requires a single sequential block access (sba), assuming a dedicated disk. That is, a rewrite occurs after we have retrieved the block and processed the information in that block (for example, searched for the record position needed for a rewrite and then rewriting into the block in main memory). When we are ready to do the rewrite on disk, the disk rotational position is at a random distance from the beginning of the block position where we want to write, so the average delay to get to that point is rot/2. Thus a rewrite is simply a single sba. In a shared disk environment, a rewrite is always a single random block access (rba).

6.1.3   B-trees and B⁺-trees

The *B-tree* is *the* access method supported by DB2, SQL/DS, Oracle, and NonStop/SQL and is the dominant access method used by other relational database management systems such as Ingres and Sybase. It features not only fast random and sequential access, but also the dynamic maintenance that virtually eliminates the overflow problems that occur in the older hashing and indexed sequential methods (although we noted above that the more recent dynamic hashing methods make use of the dynamic maintenance capability as well).

The data structure of a B-tree has evolved considerably since its inception in 1972 [BaMc72, ElNa89]. Originally, each node in the tree consisted of p–1 records and p tree pointers to the next level in the tree, consisting of p nodes (see Fig. 6.4a). The value p is known as the *order* of the B-tree. More recently, the structure of each node has been modified to become p pointers and p–1 sets of pairs: a search key value for a data record and a pointer to that data record, called a data pointer (Fig. 6.4b). The actual record is stored elsewhere, not in the path of the B-tree search. Because the search key value and data-pointer pair is usually much smaller than the entire logical record,

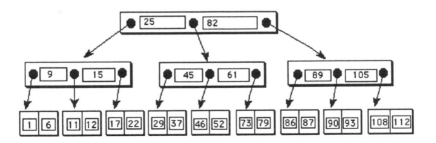

(a) B-tree with embedded records at each node

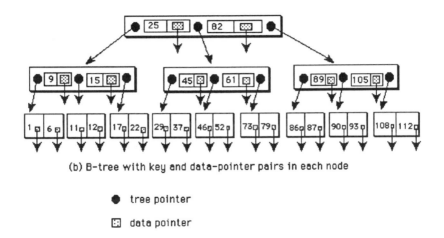

(b) B-tree with key and data-pointer pairs in each node

● tree pointer

▣ data pointer

Figure 6.4
B-tree configurations with order 3(p=3).

the order of a B-tree is potentially much larger than originally defined, given a physical limit on node size (similar to the limit on block size). Thus the search time to a random record in the file or database can be greatly decreased.

The most often used implementation of the B-tree is the B+-tree (or B*-tree). This variation eliminates the data pointers from all nodes but the leaf nodes in the B+-tree index (see Fig. 6.5). Therefore the tree index search is very efficient. Each nonleaf node consists of p tree pointers and p–1 key

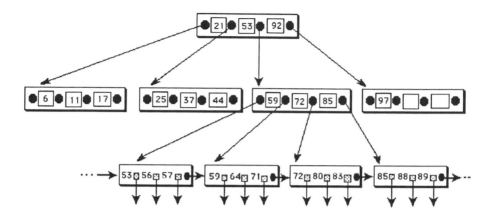

Figure 6.5
B$^+$-tree configuration with order 4(p=4) and height 3.

values. The key values denote where to search to find records that have either smaller key values (by taking the tree pointer to the left of the key) or greater or equal key values (by taking the tree pointer to the right of the key). Each leaf node consists of a series of key and data-pointer combinations that point to each record. The leaf nodes are connected logically by block pointers so that an ordered sequence of records can be found quickly.

Example: B$^+$-tree

To determine the order of a B$^+$-tree, let us assume that the database has 500,000 records of 200 bytes each, the search key is 15 bytes, the tree and data pointers are 5 bytes, and the node (and data block size) is 1024 bytes. For this configuration we have

nonleaf node size=1024 bytes=p*5+(p–1)*15 bytes

$$p = floor((1024-15)/20) = floor(50.45) = 50 \tag{6.26}$$

where the floor function is the next lower whole number, found by truncating the actual value to the next lower integer. Therefore we can have up to 50 entries in each nonleaf node. In the leaf nodes each entry has 15 bytes for the search key value and 5 bytes for the data pointer. Each node has a single pointer to the next leaf node to make a sequential search of the data records possible without going through the index-level nodes. In this example the number of entries in the leaf nodes is floor ((1024–5)/(15+5))=50.

The *height* h of the B⁺-tree is the number of index levels, including the leaf nodes. It is computed by noting that the root node (ith level) has p pointers, the i-1st level has p^2 tree pointers, i-2nd level has p^3 tree pointers, and so on. At the leaf level the number of pointers must be greater than or equal to the number of records in the database, n.

Therefore

$$p^h \geq n$$
$$h \log p \geq \log n$$
$$h \geq \log n / \log p \tag{6.27}$$

In this example, therefore,

$$h \geq \log 500{,}000 / \log 50 = 5.69897/1.69897 = 3.35$$
$$h = 4 \tag{6.28}$$

Query of a single record in a B⁺-tree is simply the time required to access all h levels of the tree index plus the access to the data record. All accesses to different levels of index and data are assumed to be random block accesses, but a rewrite of a record just read is always a sequential block access in a dedicated disk environment and a random block access in a shared disk environment.

$$\text{read a single record (B⁺-tree)} = h+1 \text{ rba} \tag{6.29}$$

Updates of records in a B⁺-tree can be accomplished with a simple query and rewrite unless the update involves an insertion that overflows a node or a deletion that empties a node. Consider the simple case of updating data values in a record, assuming that each node is implemented as a block.

$$\text{update a single record (B⁺-tree)} = \text{search cost} + \text{rewrite data block}$$
$$= (h+1) \text{ rba} + 1 \text{ sba} \tag{6.30}$$

If the update is an insertion and the insertion causes overflow of a leaf node, additional accesses are needed to split the saturated node into two nodes that are half filled (using the basic splitting algorithm) and to rewrite the next higher nonleaf node with a new pointer to the new leaf node (see Fig. 6.6). The need for a split is recognized after the initial search for the record has been done. A split of a leaf node requires a rewrite of the saturated leaf

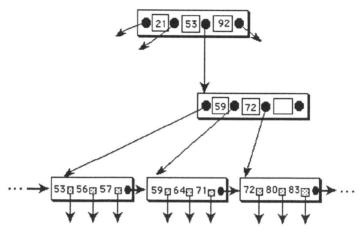

(a) B⁺-tree before the insertion of record with key value 77

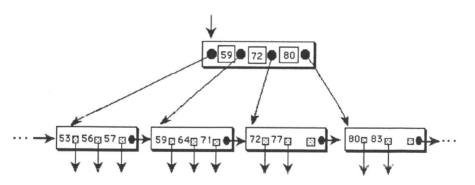

(b) B⁺-tree after the insertion and split block operation

Figure 6.6
Dynamic maintenance in a B⁺ tree for record insertion.

node, half filled with data; a random write of a new leaf node also half filled; and a rewrite of the nonleaf node with a new pointer value to the new leaf node. When multiple rewrites are required, only one can be a sequential block access; all others must be random block accesses since only one can take advantage of the disk arm position being unmoved.

Occasionally, the split operation of a leaf node necessitates a split of the next higher nonleaf node as well. In the worst case the split operations may cascade all the way up to the root node. The probability of additional splits depends on the type of splitting algorithm and the dynamics of insertions and deletions in the work load—a topic beyond the scope of this text. However, we can estimate the cost of each additional split in terms of block accesses required, as follows.

general update cost for insertion (B^+-tree)

=search cost+simple rewrite of data block+nos*(rewrite of existing
    leaf node
  +random write of new leaf node
  +rewrite of the nonleaf node pointer to the new leaf node)

$$=(h+1) \text{ rba}+1 \text{ sba}+\text{nos}*(3 \text{ rba}) \qquad \text{for nos}>0 \qquad (6.31a)$$
$$=(h+1) \text{ rba}+1 \text{ sba}+1 \text{ rba} \qquad \text{for nos}=0 \qquad (6.31b)$$

where nos is the number of split node operations required.

When nos=0 we need only to search for the data block, rewrite the data block, and rewrite the leaf node block with a new data pointer. A more detailed treatment of B-tree splitting can be found in [ElNa89].

Deletions may result in emptying a node, which necessitates the consolidation of two nodes into one. This requires a rewrite of the nonleaf node to reset its pointers. The empty node can be either left alone or rewritten with nulls, depending on the implementation. We will assume that the node where data is deleted must be rewritten, empty or not. Occasionally the nonleaf nodes become empty and need consolidation as well. Thus we obtain the cost of deletion:

general update cost for deletion (B^+-tree)
=search cost+noc*(rewrite of the leaf node pointer to the data block
    +rewrite of the nonleaf node pointer for an empty leaf node)

$$=(h+1)\text{ rba}+\text{noc}*(1\text{ sba}+1\text{ rba}) \qquad \text{for noc}>0 \qquad (6.32a)$$
$$=(h+1)\text{ rba}+1\text{ sba} \qquad \text{for noc}=0 \qquad (6.32b)$$

where noc is the number of consolidations of nodes required.

When noc=0 we need only to search for the data block's leaf node and rewrite it with the data block pointer deleted. As an example, consider the insertion of a node (with key value 77) to the B$^+$-tree shown in Fig. 6.6. This insertion requires a search (query) phase and an insertion phase with one split node. The total insertion cost for height 3 is

$$\text{insertion cost}=(3+1)\text{ rba search cost}+1\text{ split }*(1\text{ sba}+2\text{ rba})$$
$$=6\text{ rba}+1\text{ sba} \qquad (6.33)$$

6.1.4 Secondary Indices

A *secondary index* is an access method that efficiently searches a base table, given a Boolean search criterion. Secondary indices are tables that replicate secondary key data from the base table to allow quick lookup of the primary key, given secondary key values. Boolean search criteria such as "find all employee records where the job title is 'database administrator' and location is 'chicago'" result in the access to a set of target records that is typically a small subset of the entire population of records, but usually significantly more than a single record. Using access methods based on the primary key will not work here, and frequent exhaustive scans of the entire base table is usually prohibitively expensive.

Conceptually, the basic components of a secondary index (Fig. 6.7) are the attribute type index, attribute value index, an accession list, and the data blocks which house the base table. The attribute type index is a simple index that lists all the attributes you wish to build secondary indexes on; each entry consists of the attribute name and a pointer to the appropriate attribute value index for that name. The attribute value index, in turn, has entries for each possible attribute value for each attribute type, and a pointer to an accession list for that value. Attribute type and value indexes are usually quite small and are usually permanently stored in main memory while the database is active.

An *accession list* is an ordered list of pointers to records that contain the appropriate attribute value specified in the attribute value index that points

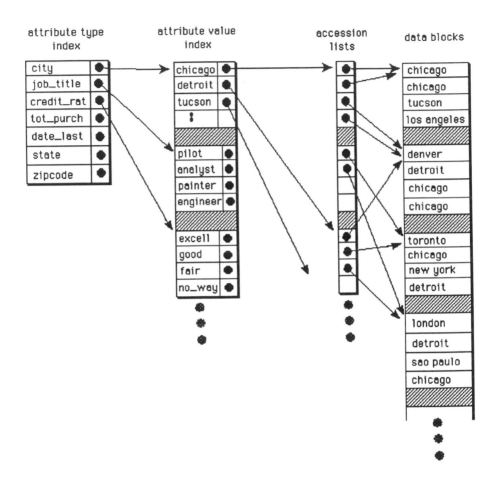

attribute type index · attribute value index · accession lists · data blocks

Figure 6.7
Secondary index structure.

to the accession list. Each pointer consists of a block address plus a record offset that ensures that each pointer is unique in the file or database.

Each attribute value has its own individual accession list. The pointers are ordered by record address (block address and record offset) so that multiple accession lists representing a complex AND condition in a query can be merged in a single pass. For example, in our query "Find all employee records where the job title is 'database administrator' and location is 'chicago'", an accession list for job_title='database administrator' and an accession list for location='chicago' must be searched to find the intersection of records that satisfy both conditions. The result of this merge is a new target accession list, held in a buffer in main memory unless larger than the block size. This list points to the target records that satisfy the conjunctive AND (condition AND condition AND condition AND . . . .) query. A query that contains disjunctive OR conditions involves searching target records for each condition separately and appending the results to each other at the completion of each search. Queries that combine AND and OR conditions use a combination of the individual approaches, with the AND conditions within each OR condition executed first.

Assuming that the attribute type and attribute value indexes are stored in main memory, no disk access analysis is needed. However, we do need to analyze the access cost to the accession list and the target data blocks. The accession lists can be assumed to be small sequential files, and the merge operation is similar to the merge required for a sequential file batch processing operation. Access to the data blocks is assumed to be strictly random via hashing or B-tree search. Each record pointer is treated as a random access, since the data is rarely ordered by secondary key value.

Boolean query cost (secondary index)
=search attribute type index+search attribute value index
    +search and merge m accession lists+access t target records

= 0+0+sum of m accession list accesses+t rba

= sum of m accession list cost+t rba   (6.34)

where m is the number of accession lists to be merged and t is the number of target records to be accessed after the merge operation

accession list cost (for accession list j)=ceil(p_j/bfac)sba   (6.35)

where p_j is the number of pointer entries in the jth accession list and bfac is the blocking factor for all accession lists

bfac=block_size/pointer_size   (6.36)

We assume that all accesses to the accession list are sequential and ignore the error incurred by assuming that the first block access is sequential. In practice it is often random. Generally we ignore errors of 1% or less in this type of analysis, because of the simplifying assumptions we often make.

Example: Mail Order Business

Assume we have a file of 10,000,000 records of mail order customers for a large commercial business. Customer records have attributes for customer name, customer number, street address, city, state, zip code, phone number, employer, job title, credit rating, date of last purchase, and total amount of purchases. Assume that the record size is 250 bytes; block size is 5000 bytes (bf=20); and pointer size, including record offset, is 5 bytes (bfac=1000). The query to be analyzed is "Find all customers whose job title is 'engineer', city is 'chicago', and total amount of purchases is greater than $1,000." For each AND condition we have the following hit rates, that is, records that satisfy each condition:

> job title is 'engineer': 84,000 records
> city is 'chicago': 210,000 records
> total amount of purchases>$1000: 350,000 records

> total number of target records that satisfy all three conditions=750

Applying Eqs. 6.34 through 6.36, we estimate the query access cost to be

> query cost (inverted file)=merge of 3 accession lists+access 750 target records

> =[ceil(n1/bfac)+ceil(n2/bfac)+ceil(n3/bfac)] sba+750 rba

> =[ceil(84,000/1000)+ceil(210,000/1000) + ceil(350,000/1000] sba + 750 rba

> =(84+210+350) sba+750 rba

> =644 sba+750 rba   (6.37)

If we assume tsba is 10 milliseconds and trba is 25 milliseconds, we obtain

query iotime (secondary index)=644 sba*10 ms+750 rba*25 ms
$$=25190 \text{ ms}$$
$$=25.19 \text{ sec} \qquad (6.38)$$

query iotime (sequential scan) =ceil(n/bf) sba *tsba
$$=\text{ceil}(10,000,000/20)*10 \text{ ms}$$
$$=5,000,000 \text{ ms}$$
$$=5000 \text{ sec} \qquad (6.39)$$

Thus we see that the secondary index time reduces the exhaustive scan time by a factor of almost 200. In Fig. 6.6 we see that at approximately 200,000 target records that sequential becomes the more efficient method.

There is an inherent inefficiency in secondary indices with large numbers of target records in that each target record in a given data block has a separate (redundant) pointer to it from each accession list, and from the target accession list. Variants of secondary indices exist in which these redundant pointers are eliminated so that each accession list pointer references a data block that contains at least one target record for that Boolean condition, and it has a target accession list pointer that references a data block that contains at least one target record for all the Boolean conditions in the query. This reduces the lengths of the accession lists as well as the number of accesses to the target records, since an access to a data block containing at least one target record will result in accesses to all target records in that block.

6.2   Usage Refinement of Logical Databases

Database designers for network systems (CODASYL systems, for example) and hierarchical systems often used processing requirements to refine the DBMS schema before or during the physical design phase, if there were obvious efficiency gains to be made. If it would produce more efficient database schemas without loss of data integrity, a similar technique could be applied to relational databases, and it would be relatively easy to implement. Let us look at a relational schema refinement algorithm based on a process-oriented, or usage view, that increases database efficiency for current processing requirements and yet retains all the information content of the natural view of data.

The application of a usage refinement algorithm is the logical next step in practical database design methodologies. Usage refinement is often used to analyze alternative logical structures during physical design and thus provide the designers with other feasible solutions to choose from. More efficient databases are the likely outcome of evaluating alternative structures.

The process of usage refinement is referred to as *denormalization* in real-world databases [Rodg89] because the transformation can cause the degree of normalization in the resulting table to be less than the degree of at least one of the original tables. Five basic types of denormalization are defined as:

1. *Two entities in a many-to-many relationship.* The relationship table resulting from this construct is composed of the primary keys of each of the associated entities. If we implement the join of this table with one of the entity tables as a single table instead of the original tables, we can avoid certain frequent joins that are based on both keys, but only the nonkey data from one of the original entities. This is similar to the so-called semi-join operation [CePe84]. This type is illustrated in the examples to follow.

2. *Two entities in a one-to-one relationship.* The tables for these entities could be implemented as a single table, thus avoiding frequent joins required by certain applications.

3. *Reference data in a one-to-many relationship.* When artificial primary keys are introduced to tables that either have no primary keys or have keys that are very large composites, they can be added to the child entity in a one-to-many relationship as a foreign key and avoid certain joins in current applications.

4. *Entities with the most detailed data.* Multivalued attributes (such as dependents or months in a year) are usually implemented as entities, and

are thus represented as separate records in a table. Sometimes it is more efficient to implement them as individually named columns as an extension of the parent entity (table) when the number of replications is a small fixed number for all instances of the parent entity.

5. *Derived attributes.* If one attribute is derived from another at execution time, then in some cases it is more efficient to store both the original value and the derived value directly in the database. This adds at least one extra column to the original table and avoids repetitive computation.

Let us look at the first type of denormalization described above. We assume that all attributes are initially assigned to tables based on FDs, and that the tables are at least 3NF. This establishes the requirement of an accurate representation of reality and of flexibility of the design for future processing requirements. Efficiency of the current query requirements can be increased by redundantly adding attributes, used together in a query, to an existing table so that all attributes needed for that query reside in a new table, called a *join table.* Access time will now be greatly reduced because fewer joins will be needed. However, the side effects of this redundant extension include an increase in required storage space, an increase in the update cost, potential denormalization and loss of integrity, and the necessity for program transformations for all relevant queries. These effects require careful consideration.

To illustrate some of these effects, let us assume that the table **paper** is associated with the tables **editor** and **reviewer** as the table that follows shows. The extension of the **paper** table, **ext_paper**, is shown as a means of reducing the number of joins required in the query. This extension results in a real denormalization, that is, paper_id->editor_id->editor_addr with the side effects of add and update anomalies. However, the delete anomaly cannot occur because the original data is redundant in the extended schema.

Original Tables and Process (Query)		
Table	**Primary Key**	**Nonkeys**
editor	editor_id	editor_name, editor_addr, primary_topic_area
reviewer	rvr_id	rvr_name, rvr_addr
paper	paper_id	paper_title, editor_id, iss_id, rvr_id, abbr_id

Query: For a given paper id number, display the editor name and address.

> select e.editor_name, e.editor_addr
> from **editor** e, **paper** p
> where p.paper_id = 'xxxx'

Extended table ext_paper in 2NF

> create table **ext_paper** (paper_id char(12) not null unique,
>   paper_title   varchar(256),
>   editor_id   char(10) not null,
>   iss_id   integer,
>   rvr_id   char(10) not null,
>   abbr_id   char(10) not null,
>   editor_addr   varchar(256),
>   primary key (paper_id),
>   foreign key (editor_id) references **editor**
>   on delete set default
>   on update set default,
>   foreign key (iss_id) references **issue**
>   on delete set null
>   on update cascade,
>   foreign key (rvr_id) references **reviewer**
>   on delete set default
>   on update cascade,
>   foreign key (abbr_id) references **abbreviation**
>   on delete set default
>   on update cascade)

The storage and processing cost of a logical relational database is to be computed for both the existing and new join tables. The formula for the computation follows.

$$\text{total cost} = [\text{iotime}(q) + \text{iotime}(u)]*\text{cost}(q) + \text{volume}(s)*\text{cost}(s) \qquad (6.40)$$

where cost(q)=unit cost per i/o second for query or update processes
       cost(s)=unit cost per byte for stored data
       iotime(q)=i/o service time for query processes (sec)
       iotime(u)=i/o service time for update processes (sec)
       volume(s)=total volume in bytes for stored data

Unit costs are selected based on the computing environment defined in the requirements specification. The i/o service time for query and update can be determined from the processing operations, their frequencies, and the hardware device characteristics; stored data volume can be obtained from the size of the tables defined. Each query process must be expressed in terms of basic relational algebra—operations such as selection, projection, and join. At this point some initial assumptions must be made about sequential and random accesses needed to efficiently accomplish the query or update, but the actual use of indexes, sorting, and the like is deferred to physical design, when the final configuration decisions are made.

6.2.1 Table Usage Algorithm

The strategy for table usage is to select only the most dominant processes to determine those modifications that will most likely improve performance. The basic modification is to add attributes to existing tables to reduce join operations. The steps of the strategy follow.

1. Select the dominant processes based on such criteria as high frequency of execution, high volume of data accessed, response time constraints, or explicit high priority. Remember this rule of thumb: Any process whose frequency of execution or data volume accessed is 10 times that of another process is considered to be dominant.

2. Define join tables, when appropriate, for the dominant processes.

3. Evaluate total cost for storage, query, and update for the database schema, with and without the extended table, and determine which configuration minimizes total cost.

4. Consider also the possibility of denormalization due to a join table and its side effects. If a join table schema appears to have lower storage and processing cost and insignificant side effects, then consider using that schema for physical design in addition to the original candidate table schema. Otherwise use only the original schema.

In general, avoid joins based on nonkeys. They are likely to produce very large tables, thus greatly increasing storage and update costs. For example, if two tables have 100 and 200 records, respectively, then a join based on the key of either one results in a maximum of 200 records, but a join based on a nonkey of either one can result in a maximum of 100*200, or 20,000 records. Null values are also restricted to nonkey attributes so that they will not be used inadvertently in join operations.

6.2.2   Usage Applications

The following examples will extend the Mathematical Reviews database design illustrated in Fig. 3.3. They will show the extremes of applicability and nonapplicability of the table usage algorithm. In each case we will apply the algorithm to a given relational schema and given processing requirements. Cost trade-offs are then evaluated to determine if schema refinement is justifiable.

Example: Usage Refinement, Favorable Case

This example, which extends slightly the relational schema in Chapter 4, illustrates favorable conditions for improving efficiency with the table usage algorithm. The query (shown later this example in both natural language and standard SQL) is executed by a join of **reviewer** and **assigned_to** over rvr_name, followed by 20,000 random accesses to **project** (based on proj_name) to match hq_city with each rvr_city in the temporary table resulting from the join. To simplify the computation of query time, the tables are assumed to be accessed as **reviewer** (sequential, ordered on rvr_id), **project** (indexed on proj_name), and **assigned_to** (sequential, ordered on rvr_id).

Table	Primary Key	Nonkey	Bytes /Record	Records	Blocking Factor
reviewer	rvr_name	rvr_city	120	10,000	34
project	proj_name	hq_city	200	500	20
assigned_to	rvr_name,proj_name		20	20,000	204

Query: Display each reviewer name and project name in which the project headquarters is located in the same city where the reviewer lives. Frequency=100/day.

select r.rvr_name, p.proj_name
   from **reviewer** r, **project** p, **assigned_to** a
   where r.rvr_name=a.rvr_name
   and   p.proj_name=a.proj_name
   and   r.rvr_city=p.hq_city

Update: Delete a given reviewer from all associated projects. Frequency=100/day.

delete **assigned_to**
   where   rvr_name='xxxx'

Using a typical hardware configuration, we assume the following timing and cost characteristics:

   Page transfer time (at 4096 bytes per page): 3.4 ms

   Average disk rotation time (half rotation): 8.3 ms

   Average disk seek time: 16.0 ms

   Average sequential page access: 11.7 ms (tsba)

   Average random page access: 27.7 ms (trba)

   cost(q)=9.00 dollars per i/o hour

   cost(s)=.0031 dollars per page-day

Given the number of bytes in each of the tables and the searching required for the query, we can calculate the i/o service time (iotime(q)) for the query, and thus the total cost (see Eq. 6.40). The rest of the example shows how to determine the number of pages for query and update operations and storage space and how to calculate total cost. Typical join algorithms include the nested loop, sort/merge, and hash/join methods [Seli79]. In this case we assume the hash/join method first, then try the sort/merge method as an alternative.

iotime(q) −scan **reviewer**+scan **assigned_to**+20000 random accesses to
     project
     =ceiling(10,000/34)*11.7
        +ceiling(20,000/204)*11.7+20000*27.7 ms
     =558.6 sec
     =.16 hour   (6.41)

i/o cost (query) =iotime(q)*cost(q)

$$=.16*9.0$$

$$= 1.440 \tag{6.42}$$

i/o cost (at 100 queries per day)=144.0 (6.43)

Significant improvements in performance for this query can be obtained by the following sort/merge method optimization: first sort the temporary table from the first join on rvr_city and then sort the **project** table on hq_city; then proceed with the join as a single pass of both tables. We assume that the sort operation is complexity n $\log_2$ n logical record accesses, where n is the number of records in a table. We also assume that the width of the temporary table is 130 bytes and thus the blocking factor is floor(4096/130)=31.

iotime(q) =scan **reviewer**+scan **assigned_to**+sort temporary table+sort **project**

+ scan temporary table+scan **project**

=[ceiling(10,000/34)+ceiling(20,000/204)+ceiling ((20,000 $\log_2$ 20,000)/31)+ceiling ((500 $\log_2$ 500)/20)+ceiling(20,000/ 31)+ceiling(500/20)]*11.7 ms

=10,968 sba*11.7 ms

=128.33 sec

=.0356 hour (6.44)

i/o cost (query)= iotime(q)*cost(q)

$$=.00356*9.0$$

$$=.320 \tag{6.45}$$

i/o cost (at 100 queries per day)=32.0 (6.46)

The update operation "delete a given reviewer from all associated projects" requires random access to **assigned_to** based on rvr_id and a scan of an additional page to delete all records with a given rvr_id.

iotime(u) =27.7 ms +11.7 ms

$$=.039 \text{ sec} \tag{6.47}$$

i/o cost (update)=iotime(u)*cost(q)

$$=.039/3600*9.0$$

$$=.0001 \tag{6.48}$$

i/o cost (at 100 updates per day)=.01 (6.49)

storage cost =volume(s)*cost(s)
      = (ceiling(1,200,000/4096)+ ceiling(100,000/4096)
        + ceiling(400,000/4096))*(.0031 per page day)
      = 416 pages*.0031
      = 1.29 (6.50)

total cost=144.0+.01+1.29=145.3 (6.51)

Now we can look at the affect of applying the table usage algorithm. The attributes rvr_city and hq_city are appended to **assigned_to** so that only a single scan of the new table, which we will call **ext_assigned_to**, is needed to satisfy the query. The table **ext_assigned_to** now has 40 bytes per record; therefore, at 20,000 records it has a total of 800,000 bytes and is double the size of **assigned_to**. Redoing the calculations for query, update, and storage with **ext_assigned_to**, we obtain the cost figures shown in Table 6.1. We see that a dramatic reduction in cost results from using the extended join table and thus avoiding the join operation and random indexing in the original solution.

Example: Usage Refinement, Unfavorable Case

This example, which assumes minor modifications to the relational schema in Chapter 4, illustrates very unfavorable conditions for efficiency improvement with the table usage algorithm. The query in this example is executed by a join on the tables **journal** and **publisher** over the common attribute pub_id. This is accomplished by a scan of **journal** and **publisher**. These two tables **publisher** and **journal** are assumed to be accessed sequentially based on pub_id.

Table	Primary Key	Nonkey	Bytes /Record	Records	Blocking Factor
journal	jour_id	jour_name, topic_area, pub_id	200	10,000	20
publisher	pub_id	pub_name, pub_addr	250	60	16

Query: Display the journal id number, name, topic area, and publisher name for all journals with a given topic area. Frequency=100/day.

select j.jour_id, j.jour_name, j.topic_area, p.pub_name
from   **journal** j, **publisher** p
where p.pub_id=j.pub_id

Update: Scan the **journal** table and change the topic area from theoretical mathematics to applied mathematics. Frequency=100/day.

update **journal**
        set   topic area='applied mathematics'
        where   topic area='theoretical mathematics'

iotime(q) =scan of **journal**+scan of **publisher**
        =ceiling(10,000/20)*11.7 ms+ ceiling(60/16)*11.7 ms
        =5850 ms+35 ms
        =5885 ms   (6.52)

i/o cost (query)=9.00*5.885 sec/3600=.015   (6.53)

i/o cost (query at frequency of 100 per day)=1.5   (6.54)

The update of publisher id of every journal is accomplished with a scan (read) and rewrite of **journal**:

iotime(u) =scan and rewrite of **journal**
        =[ceiling(10,000/20)*11.7 ms]*2
        =11,700 ms   (6.55)

i/o cost (update)=9.00*11.7 sec /3600=.029   (6.56)

i/o cost (update at frequency of 100 per day)=2.9   (6.57)

Storage cost = ceiling(10,000/20)*.0031+ ceiling(60/16)*.0031
        = 1.6 per day   (6.58)

The extended join table solution is to add the attributes pub_name and pub_addr to table **journal**, thus increasing the record size from 200 to 250 bytes. The size of the entire table **ext_journal** is 2.5 megabytes, compared to 2 megabytes for **journal**. The cost for query, update, and storage space for the extended table is shown in Table 6.2. The results show higher cost in all three areas due to the extended join table, mainly because the table **journal** is much larger than the table **publisher** and the extension **ext_journal** is larger than **journal** and **publisher** combined. Thus, the join table schema is not a candidate for physical design in this case.

To summarize, the extended join table tends to significantly lower the storage and processing cost for one or more joins if:

- either of the joined tables are of comparable size
- only the smaller table is extended, or
- it can avoid a large number of random accesses to at least one of the tables

Table 6.1   Summary of total cost per day, favorable case.

	Original Table	Orig. Table (optimized)		Join Table
cost(q)*iotime(q)	144.0	32.0	.58	Query cost
cost(q)*iotime(u)	.01	.01	.01	Update cost
cost(s)*volume(s)	1.29	1.29	1.59	Storage cost
	145.3	33.3	2.18	Total cost

Table 6.2   Summary of total cost per day, unfavorable case.

	Original Table	Join Table	
cost(q)*iotime(q)	1.5	1.8	Query cost
cost(q)*iotime(u)	2.9	3.6	Update cost
cost(s)*volume(s)	1.6	1.9	Storage cost
	6.0	7.3	Total cost

6.3   Summary

This chapter discussed the basic principles of physical database design in terms of the types of processing of data typically done in database applications and the access methods needed to do each type of processing efficiently. Database performance is defined at three levels of detail: logical record access, sequential and random block access, and disk i/o service time. The i/o time computation applies to a dedicated or shared disk environment.

Sequential processing uses sequential data structures and search mechanisms that range from sequential scans to binary searches. Random processing of individual records is best done by hashing. The B-tree, and in particular the B^+-tree, is the dominant sequential and random-access method used today, and it has the added advantage of dynamically maintaining the database and avoiding the severe performance degradation due to long overflow chains, such as in indexed sequential files. Hashing methods that use the dynamic maintenance facilities found in B-trees are rapidly replacing the older implementations.

Database applications involving complex Boolean queries are used effectively only with systems that have some form of secondary index capability. Secondary indices are implemented using accession lists of pointers to target records and can be merged easily for complex query conditions. Cellular secondary indices are variants of secondary indices that enhance performance, particularly when target records are clustered in data blocks.

Usage refinement of relational databases is seen as a method to decrease query time for certain queries requiring multiple table joins. Analysis of the effectiveness of a pre-join strategy is done using the block access and i/o time approach defined earlier in the chapter.

Literature Summary

The idea for extending a table for usage efficiency came from [ScSo80], and practical advice on denormalization is given in [Rodg89]. Comprehensive surveys of access methods can be found in [Harb88, Gros86, Loom83, TeFr82, Wied87], and brief surveys are given in [Card85, ElNa89].

[BaMc72]   Bayer, R., and McCreight, E. "Organization and Maintenance of Large Ordered Indexes," *ACTA. Inf.* 1,3(1972), pp. 173–189.

[Card85]   Cardenas, A.F. *Data Base Management Systems*, 2nd ed., Allyn and Bacon, Boston, 1985.

[ElNa89]   Elmasri, R., and Navathe, S.B. *Fundamentals of Database Systems*, Addison-Wesley, Benjamin/Cummings, Redwood City, CA, 1989.

[Gros86]   Grosshans, D. *File Systems Design and Implementation*, Prentice-Hall, Englewood Cliffs, NJ, 1986.

[Harb88]   Harbron, T.R. *File Systems Structures and Algorithms*, Prentice-Hall, Englewood Cliffs, NJ, 1988.

[Loom83]   Loomis, M.E.S. *Data Management and File Processing*, Prentice-Hall, Englewood Cliffs, NJ, 1983.

[Rodg89]   Rodgers, U. "Denormalization: Why, What, and How?" *Database Programming and Design* 2,12(Dec. 1989), pp. 46–53.

[ScSo80]   Schkolnick, M., and Sorenson, P. "Denormalization: A Performance Oriented Database Design Technique," *Proc. AICA 1980 Congress*, Bologna, Italy, AICA, Brussels, 1980, pp. 363–377.

[TeFr82]   Teorey, T., and Fry, J. *Design of Database Structures*, Prentice-Hall, Englewood Cliffs, NJ, 1982.

[Wied87]   Wiederhold, G. *File Organization for Database Design*, McGraw-Hill, New York, 1987.

Exercises

Problem 6-1

Given the relations and applications (queries with equal frequency) specified below, state one argument in favor of and one argument against each of the two proposed schema refinements, taking into consideration usage and integrity.

Proposal 1:   Split table **employee** into two tables, with only the employee's name and address in one table, and the other table containing everything except the address.

Proposal 2:   Add the foreign key dept_no to table **office**.

Query A. Which office numbers are associated with each department?

Query B. List all employee names and their addresses.

Query C. Which employees currently work on the clean air project?

Table	Primary Key	Foreign Key(s)	Other Attributes
employee	emp_no	dept_no; proj_no; office_no	emp_name, address, phone_no, office_no
emp_job	emp_no, start_date	emp_no	job_title, salary_level
department	dept_no	-	dept_name, manager_no
office	office_no	-	office_size, office_type
project	proj_no	-	proj_name, proj_manager_no

Problem 6-2

The lists that follow describe a single-record type database (that is, a file) stored on disk and typical queries on that database. Attribute sizes are given in bytes.

Database: Number of employees=150,000 (id-no=10 bytes (key), name=25 bytes, addr=30 bytes)
Number of departments=80 (dept-no=2 bytes, dept-name=12 B)
Number of degree types=6 (degree=3 bytes)
Number of job titles=150 (job-title=18 bytes)
Other attributes total 300 bytes (Note: total of 20 attibutes)
Total logical records (tuples)=150,000 (size of each record is 400 bytes)

Block size (data and index blocks) is 6000 bytes
Pointer size is 5 bytes

Average i/o time for a sequential block access=
15 milliseconds
Average i/o time for a random block access=
30 milliseconds over the entire file or disk

We also assume the following:

a. The database is new and has no overflow or other degradation.

b. Dedicated disk environment.

c. The pointers in B⁺-tree data blocks can be ignored.

d. Any level of an index that fits into a single index block can be considered to reside in main memory and does not need a disk access.

Query A: List all employee information in id-no order.

Query B: Display all employee data for id-no=zzzzzzzzzz.

Query C: Display the name and department name of employees with job title x and holding degree y. Average number of target records=600.

1. Given that B⁺-tree is to be used for some of these queries, how many levels of indexing would be required for an order-14 B⁺-tree index? How many index nodes could fit into a single index block?

2. Compute the time for sequential access for Query A.

3. Compute the i/o service time for sequential and B+-tree access for Query B.

4. Analyze the tradeoffs between sequential access and secondary index for Query C, given that the number of target records is 600.

Problem 6-3

Given the relational schema and physical characteristics shown in this problem, evaluate the total i/o time for the following access methods to obtain the names of all students whose research is directed by John Smith. State all the assumptions that you must make.

1. Sequential search of the student records (tuples), testing for the foreign key for the research instructor.
2. Secondary index access to student records (tuples).

Each instructor directs the research of an average of 10 students. Not all students conduct research, only seniors and graduate students.

Each instructor teaches an average of three course sections per term.

Each student takes an average of five courses per term.

Courses contain an average of 25 students.

Relational schema (SQL):

create table **instructor** (instr_id char(9) not null unique,
                    instr_name char(20),
                    instr_room_no char(6),
                    primary key (instr_id))

create table **course** (course_no char(6) not null unique,
                    course_name char(15),
                    course_instr_name char(20),
                    day char(5),
                    hour char(2),
                    primary key (course_no),
                    foreign key (course_instr_name))

create table **student** (student_id char(10) not null unique,
                    student_name char(20),
                    student_addr char(25),
                    research_instr_id char(9),
                    primary key (student_id),
                    foreign key (research_instr_id))

create table **enrollment** (student_id char(10) not null,
                    course_no char(6) not null,
                    primary key (student_id, course_no),
                    foreign key (student_id) references **student**,
                    foreign key (course_no) references **course**)

Number of instructor records=2500
Number of course records=4000
Number of student records=20,000
Number of enrollment records=100,000
Blocksize=1000 bytes
Disk seek time=40 milliseconds (average)
Disk full rotation time=20 milliseconds
Disk transfer rate=200 kilobytes/second

7

An Example of Relational Database Design

The following example illustrates how to proceed through the database life cycle, in a practical way, for a centralized relational database. We will see how physical design for usage refinement and index selection extends a logical design methodology to attain significant improvements in performance, given that the available access methods are known.

7.1   Requirement Specification

The management of a large retail store would like a database to keep track of sales activities The requirements for this database leads to the following six entities and their unique identifiers:

Entity	Entity Id	Id length(avg) in characters	Cardinality
Customer	cust_no	6	80,000
Job	job_title	24	80
Order	order_no	9	200,000
Salesperson	sales_name	20	150
Department	dept_no	2	10
Item	item_no	6	5,000

The following assertions describe the data relationships:

- Each customer has one job_title, but different customers may have the same job_title.

- Each customer may place many orders, but only one customer may place a particular order.

- Each department has many salespeople, but each salesperson must work in only one department.

- Each department has many items for sale, but each item is sold in only one department. (*Item* means item type, like IBM PC).

- For each order, items ordered in different departments must involve different salespeople, but all items ordered within one department must be handled by exactly one salesperson. In other words, for each order, each item has exactly one salesperson; and for each order, each department has exactly one salesperson.

Design Problems

1. Using the information given and, in particular, the six assertions, derive an ER diagram and a set of FDs that represent all the data relationships.

2. Transform the ER diagram into a set of candidate tables. List the relations (tables), their primary keys, and other attributes.

3. Find the minimum set of 3NF tables that are functionally equivalent to the candidate tables. Analyze performance and integrity trade-offs resulting from the definition of this minimum set.

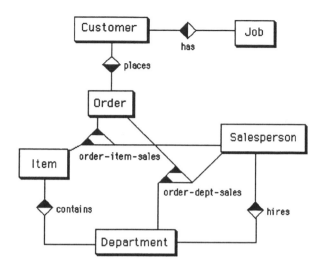

Figure 7.1
Extended ER diagram for the retail store database.

4. Given the transactions "Select all order numbers assigned to customers
    who are computer engineers" and "Add a new customer and the
    customer's order to the database," analyze the performance and data
    integrity trade-offs for strategies to execute these transactions by using
    both the minimum set 3NF schema and a refined schema designed to
    reduce the number of joins needed for data retrieval.

7.2   Logical Design

Our first step is to develop an ER diagram and a set of FDs to correspond to
each of the assertions given. Figure 7.1 presents the diagram. Normally the
ER diagram is developed without knowing all the FDs, but in this example
the nonkey attributes are omitted so that the entire database can be represented with only a few statements and FDs. The result of this analysis, relative
to each of the assertions given, follows.

ER Construct	FDs
Customer(many):Job(one)	cust_no -> job_title
Order(many): Customer(one)	order_no -> cust_no
Salesperson(many): Department(one)	sales_name -> dept_no
Item(many): Department(one)	item_no -> dept_no
Order(many): Item(many): Salesperson(one)	order_no,item_no->sales_name
Order(many): Department(many): Salesperson(one)	order_no,dept_no->sales_name

The candidate tables needed to represent the semantics of this problem can be easily derived from the constructs for entities and relationships. Primary keys and foreign keys are explicitly defined.

```
create table customer (cust_no   char(6) not null unique,
                job_title  varchar(256),
                primary key (cust_no),
                foreign key (job_title) references job
                        on delete set null
                        on update cascade)
```

```
create table job (job_title varchar(256) not null unique,
                primary key (job_title))
```

```
create table order (order_no      char(9) not null unique,
                cust_no        char(6) not null,
                primary key (order_no),
                foreign key (cust_no) references customer
                        on delete cascade
                        on update cascade)
```

```
create table salesperson (sales_name  varchar(256) not null unique,
                dept_no      char(2),
                primary key (sales_name),
                foreign key (dept_no) references department
                        on delete set null
                        on update cascade)
```

create table **department** (dept_no char(2) not null unique,
    primary key (dept_no))

create table **item** (item_no char(6) not null unique,
    dept_no char(2),
    primary key (item_no),
    foreign key (dept_no) references **department**
        on delete set null
        on update cascade)

create table **order_item_sales** (order_no   char(9) not null,
    item_no   char(6) not null,
    sales_name   varchar(256) not null,
    primary key (order_no, item_no),
    foreign key (order_no) references **order**
        on delete cascade
        on update cascade,
    foreign key (item_no) references **item**
        on delete cascade
        on update cascade,
    foreign key (sales_name) references **salesperson**
        on delete cascade
        on update cascade)

create table **order_dept_sales** (order_no   char(9) not null,
    dept_no   char(2) not null,
    sales_name   varchar(256) not null,
    primary key (order_no, dept_no),
    foreign key (order_no) references **order**
        on delete cascade
        on update cascade,
    foreign key (dept_no) references **department**
        on delete cascade
        on update cascade,
    foreign key (sales_name) references **salesperson**
        on delete cascade
        on update cascade)

This process of decomposition and reduction of tables moves us closer to a minimum set of 3NF tables. Additionally, we must consider the tables **job** and **department**. Because we have not defined other attributes in these tables, **job** and **department** are simple tables consisting of a single key attribute. When this occurs and the key attribute appears in other tables as a nonkey, we can consider the elimination of the simple table. The trade-off is between the decrease in storage space and update cost when we eliminate a table and the possible loss of data integrity as a side effect of deletions on another table in which the key of the eliminated table has become a nonkey. In our example, if we can justify this trade-off and eliminate the simple tables, we have the following minimum set of 3NF tables:

Table	Primary key	Nonkey
customer	cust_no	job_title
order	order_no	cust_no
salesperson	sales_name	dept_no
item	item_no	dept_no
order_item_sales	order_no,item_no	sales_name
order_dept_sales	order_no,dept_no	sales_name

In summary, the reductions shown in this section have decreased storage space and update cost and have maintained the normalization at a minimum of 3NF. But we have potentially higher retrieval cost—given the transaction "list all job_titles", for example—and have increased the potential for loss of integrity because we have eliminated simple tables with only key attributes.

7.3　Physical Design

7.3.1　Schema Refinement Based on Usage

Let us now look at the quantitative trade-offs of further refinement of tables to improve processing efficiency. Assume that each of the following transactions are to be executed once per fixed time unit.

Query: Select all order numbers assigned to customers who are computer engineers.

select o.order_no, c.cust_no, c.job_title
   from   **order** o, **customer** c
   where c.cust_no=o.cust_no
   and   c.job_title='computer engineer'

Update: Add a new customer, a painter, with number 423378 and the customer's order number, 763521601, to the database.

insert into customer (cust_no, job_title)
   values ('423378','painter')
insert into order (order_no, cust_no)
   values ('763521601','423378')

Using the minimum set 3NF schema, the system query optimizer can choose from a number of different ways to execute the transaction. Let us first assume that the tables are all ordered physically by their primary keys. We use the sort/merge join strategy for the first transaction: Sort the **order** table by cust_no, then join tables **order** and **customer** with a single scan of each, and select only tuples that have job_title of computer engineer. We then project on order_no to answer the query. To simplify the analysis we assume that a sort of n tuples takes n $\log_2$ n tuple (logical record, lra) accesses and that computer engineers make up 5% of the customers and orders in the database.

lra =sort **order**+scan **order**+scan **customer**+create **order_cust**
     +scan **order_cust**+create **comp_engr**+project **comp_engr**

=(200,000 $\log_2$ 200,000)+200,000+80,000
    +200,000+200,000+200,000*.05+200,000*.05

=200,000*(17.61+3.10)+80,000
=4,222,000 tuple accesses

All tuple accesses are sequential in this strategy. We also assume 30 milliseconds for a sequential block access, 60 milliseconds for a random block access, a block size of 4 Kb (4096 bytes) and a prefetch buffer size of 64 Kb (as done in DB2). We can estimate the i/o service time by first computing the effective prefetch blocking factors for the tables **order,**

customer, order_cust, and **comp_engr**: 4368, 2176, 1680, and 1680, respectively. We compute the sequential block accesses as follows.

sba =ceiling(200,000*(17.61 +1)/4368)+ceiling(80,000/2176)
    +ceiling(420,000/1680)
    =1,140

iotime=1,140*30 ms=34.2 sec

The strategy to execute the second transaction, using the same schema, is to scan each table (**order** and **customer**) and rewrite both tables in the new order.

sba =ceiling(200,000/4368)*2 +ceiling(80,000/2176)*2
    =166

iotime=166*30 ms=5.0 sec

If we refine the minimum set 3NF schema to avoid the join in the first transaction, the resulting schema will have a single table **order_cust,** with primary key order_no and nonkey attributes cust_no and job_title, instead of separate tables **order** and **customer**. This not only avoids the join, but also the sort needed to get both tables ordered by cust_no. The strategy for the first transaction is now to scan **order_cust** once to find the computer engineers, write the resulting data on disk, and then read back from disk to project the resulting temporary table, **comp_engr**, to answer the query.

sba =ceiling(200,000/1680)+[ceiling(200,000*.05/1680)]*2
    =132

iotime=132*30 ms=4.0 sec

The strategy for the second transaction, using this refined schema, is to scan **order_cust** once to find the point of insertion and then to scan again to reorder the table.

sba=ceiling(200,000/1680)*2=240

iotime=240*30 ms=7.2 sec

Common to both strategies is the addition of an order record to the tables **order_item_sales** and **order_dept_sales**. For the sake of simplicity, we will assume these tables to be unsorted, so the addition of a new order will require only one record access at the end of the table and, thus, negligible i/o time.

The basic performance and normalization data for these two schemas and the two transactions given previously are summarized in Table 7.1.

The refined schema dramatically reduces the i/o time for the query transaction, but the cost is the loss of performance for the update, more storage space, and significant reduction in the degree of normalization. The normalization is reduced because we now have a transitive FD: order_no ->cust_no->job_title in table **order_cust**. The implication of this is, of course, that there is a delete anomaly for job_title when a customer deletes an order or the order is filled.

The significance of these performance and data integrity differences depends upon the overall objectives as well as the computing environment for the database, and it must be analyzed in that context. For instance, the performance differences must be evaluated for all relevant transactions, present and projected. Storage space differences may or may not be significant in the computing environment. Integrity problems with the deletion commands need to be evaluated on a case-by-case basis to determine whether the side effects of certain record deletions are destructive to the objectives of the database. In summary, the database designer now has the ability to evaluate the trade-offs among query and update requirements, storage space, and integrity associated with normalization. This knowledge can be applied to a variety of database design problems.

Table 7.1. Comparison of performance and integrity of original tables and join table.

	Minimum Set 3NF Schema (order and customer)	Refined Schema (order_cust)
Query	34.2 sec	4.0 sec
Update	5.0 sec	7.2 sec
Storage space (relevant tables)	5.4 MB	7.8 MB
Normalization	3NF	2NF

7.3.2   Index Selection Problem

The usage refinement solution can be further improved by a careful selection of indices. If we create a secondary index to access the **order_cust** table for the 5% of customers with orders who are computer engineers, we then will have 5% of 200,000 records or 10,000 records to randomly access at 60 ms each. This will take 600 seconds, which is clearly unacceptable compared to the previously mentioned solutions (Table 7.1). Building a secondary index on job-title to the customer table is similarly poor in performance.

On the other hand, the performance of the update to **customer** and **order** would significantly improve with a primary index to each table. In each case, access via hashing is typically one random block access to each table plus a sequential rewrite, while access via B+-tree is one to two random block accesses plus a sequential rewrite. In either case, the total time to perform the update is well under one second. Similarly, with the join table order_cust, a primary index can be built for the composite key order_no, cust_no which results in less than one second update time. Thus creation of two primary indices clearly improves update performance, and hence improves overall performance.

7.4   Summary

In this chapter we developed a global (logical) schema for a centralized relational database, given the requirements specification for a retail store database. The example illustrates the life cycle steps of ER modeling, global schema design, normalization, and schema refinement based on processing efficiency. It summarizes the techniques presented in Chapters 1 through 6. Next we turn to distributed databases as the next part of our analysis of database design.

8

Distributed Database Design Concepts

Distributed database design is an integral part of the distributed database life cycle. Design components that are unique to distributed databases include data fragmentation, data distribution strategies, and data allocation methods. In this chapter we look at each of these components briefly and then examine two data allocation methods in detail, one in which no data redundancy is allowed and another with data redundancy. These methods are easily computable by hand for small to medium configurations or implementable in software for large configurations.

8.1   Introduction

Advances in the computer and communications technologies have led to distributed computer systems, which interconnect mainframes, minicomputers, and workstations through various communications media. This was accompanied by the development of distributed operating systems, distributed languages, and distributed database management systems. A *distributed database management system* (*DDBMS*) is a software system that supports the transparent creation, access, and manipulation of interrelated data located at the different sites of a computer network. Each site of the network has autonomous processing capability and can perform local applications. Each site also participates in the execution of at least one global application, which requires network communication [Chu84, CePe84]. The goal of a DDBMS is to improve the accessibility, sharability, and performance of a DBMS while preserving the appearance of a centralized DBMS.

Because of the nature of the loosely coupled network of computers, the database design issues encountered in distributed database systems differ from those encountered in centralized database systems [Heba77, FHS80]. In centralized databases, access efficiency is achieved through local optimization by using complex physical structures. In distributed databases, the global optimization of processing, including network communication cost and local processing cost, is of major concern. Total cost is a function of the network configuration, the user work load, the data allocation strategy, and the query optimization algorithm.

We will first look at basic data allocation strategies common to DDBMSs and then illustrate two easily computable methods, or strategies, for allocating data (files, tables, or fragments of tables) in a distributed database system.

8.2   Distributed Database Design

Once a DDBMS has been developed or purchased, the database designers or administrators need to know how to design and allocate the distributed database. This is significantly influenced by the architecture and the facilities of the DDBMS; it, in turn, significantly impacts the query processing, concurrency control, and availability of the database.

The three most common objectives of distributed database design are the

- separation of data fragmentation from data allocation
- control of data redundancy
- independence from local DBMSs

The distinction between designing the fragmentation and allocation schema is conceptually relevant: The first is a *logical* mapping but the second is a *physical* mapping. In general, it is not possible to determine the optimal fragmentation and allocation by solving the two problems independently; they are interrelated.

8.2.1   Fragmentation

A table r is fragmented by partitioning it into a minimal number of disjoint subtables (fragments) $r_1, r_2, ..., r_n$. These fragments contain sufficient information to reconstruct the original table r. Basically, there are two different schemes for fragmenting a table: *horizontal* and *vertical*.

Horizontal fragmentation partitions the records of a global table into subsets. A fragment, r_i, is a *selection* on the global table r using a predicate P_i, its *qualification*. The reconstruction of r is obtained by taking the union of all fragments.

Vertical fragmentation subdivides the attributes of the global table into groups. The simplest form of vertical fragmentation is decomposition. A unique *record-id* may be included in each fragment to guarantee that reconstruction through a join operation is possible. Note that mixed fragmentation is the result of the successive application of both fragmentation techniques.

Rules for Fragmentation

* Fragments are formed by the select predicates associated with dominant database transactions. The predicates specify attribute values used in the conjunctive (AND) and disjunctive (OR) form of select commands and in records containing the same values form fragments.

* Fragments must be disjoint and their union must become the whole table. Overlapping fragments are too difficult to analyze and implement.

* The largest fragment is the whole table. The smallest fragment is a single record. Fragments should be designed to maintain a balance between these extremes. The whole table as a fragment disallows the potential efficiency of partitioning the table across local sites by usage. Single records as fragments, on the other hand, introduce undue complexity into

the data allocation problem, extreme sensitivity to changing applications, and potentially too much overhead to execute joins between tables.

8.2.2 Data Allocation

The constraints under which data allocation strategies may operate are determined by the system architecture and the available network database management software. The four basic approaches are

- the centralized approach
- the partitioned approach
- the replicated data approach
- the selective replication approach

In the *centralized approach*, all the data are located at a single site. The implementation of this approach is simple. However, the size of the database is limited by the availability of the secondary storage at the central site. Furthermore, the database may become unavailable from any of the remote sites when communication failures occur, and the database system fails totally when the central site fails.

In the *partitioned approach*, the database is partitioned into disjoint fragments, and each fragment is assigned to a particular site. This strategy is particularly appropriate where local secondary storage is limited compared to the database size, the reliability of the centralized database is not sufficient, or operating efficiencies can be gained through the exploitation of the locality of references in database accesses.

The *completely replicated data approach* allocates a full copy of the database to each site in the network. This completely redundant distributed data strategy is only appropriate when reliability is critical, the database is small, and update inefficiency can be tolerated. It is much less commonly used than selective replication.

The *selective replication approach* partitions the database into critical and noncritical fragments. Noncritical fragments need only be stored once, while critical fragments are replicated as desired to meet the required level of availability and performance. This is the most commonly used strategy because of its great flexibility.

The cost/benefit of the replicated database allocation strategy can be estimated in terms of storage cost, communication costs (query and update time), and data availability. Figure 8.1 briefly illustrates the trade-off by showing the data replication on the horizontal axis and costs on the vertical axis. It can be seen from Fig. 8.1 that

- The read communication cost decreases as the number of copies increases because most data can be found at local sites, thus eliminating the need for communication calls.
- The update communication cost increases with the number of copies because duplicated data will need to be updated.
- The storage cost and local processing cost increase as the number of copies increases.
- The availability of data increases with the number of copies in the system.

An optimal data allocation can be theoretically determined to minimize the total cost (storage+communication+local processing) subject to some

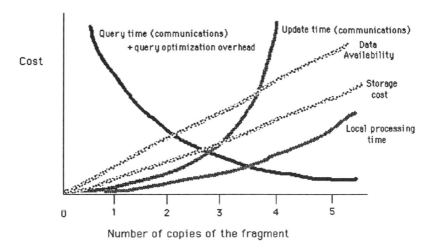

Figure 8.1
Trade-off in database distribution due to data replication.

response time and availability constraints. This problem, traditionally referred to as the File Allocation Problem (FAP) in computing networks, was first addressed by Wesley Chu [Chu69]. Since then many different file allocation algorithms have appeared in the literature [Case72, MaRi76, MoLe77, CoGe80, FiHo80]. Earlier allocation resolutions were simple, but more recent methods are actual design methodologies that utilize the allocation techniques for one of the decisions [CPW87]. Application of the FAP problem depends on the nature of the problem, the availability of information needed to reach an exact solution, and the need to determine optimal versus approximate solutions in real life. It has often been found that, for real-life situations, sophisticated FAP solutions are rarely needed. In most cases, data allocation decisions can be made by exercising judgment and using real-life constraints of security and management. However, it is preferable to use simple analytical models to support the decisions and improve insights.

8.3   The General Data Allocation Problem

Assume knowledge of application system specifications and distributed system configuration as outlined in the list that follows.

*   Application system specifications:

    A database global schema and fragmentation schema

    A set of user transactions and their frequencies

    Security: data ownership (who can update) and access authorization (who can query) for each transaction

    Recovery: estimated frequency and volume of backup operations

    Integrity: referential integrity, boundary value integrity rules, journaling overhead

*   Distributed system configuration and software:

    The network topology, network channel capacities, and network control mechanism

The site locations and their processing capacity (cpu and i/o processing)

Sources of data (where data can be located), and sinks of data (where user transactions can be initiated and data transferred)

The transaction processing options and synchronization algorithms

The unit costs for data storage, local site processing, and communications

Find the allocation of programs and database fragments to sites that minimizes C, the total cost. Keep in mind that

$$C = C_{comm} + C_{proc} + C_{stor}$$

where

C_{comm}=communications cost for message and data
C_{proc}=site processing cost (cpu and i/o)
C_{stor}=storage cost for data and programs at sites

are subject to possible additional constraints on

- transaction response time, which is the sum of communication delays, local processing, and all resource queuing delays
- transaction availability, which is the percentage of time the transaction executes with all components available

In some cases, the total cost (possibly including equipment cost) could be considered a constraint and minimum response time the objective. In other cases, the network topology and/or local site processing capacity is to be analyzed as well as the data distribution.

8.4 Data Allocation Strategies

A general rule for data allocation states that data should be placed as close as possible to where it will be used, and then load balancing should be considered to find a global optimization of system performance. In the following sections we describe two methods originally defined by Ceri and Pelagatti [CePe84] and extend the discussion by adding illustrative examples and practical interpretation of the important parameters.

8.4.1   The Nonredundant "Best Fit" Method

The *nonredundant "bestfit" method* determines the single most likely site to allocate a fragment (which may be a file, table, or subset of a table) based on maximum benefit, where benefit is interpreted to mean total query and update references. In particular, place fragment r_i at the site s^*, where the number of local query and update references by all the user transactions is maximized.

Let us illustrate the application of this method with a simple example of a global schema and its processing characteristics. In this example each fragment to be allocated is an entire table. The average disk i/o service times are given for a query or update originating from the same site in the network (local) or combined disk and network service times from different sites (remote).

System Parameters

Table	Size	Avg Local Query(Update) Time (Milliseconds)	Avg Remote Query(Update) Time (Milliseconds)
R1	300 Kb	100 (150)	500 (600)
R2	500 Kb	150 (200)	650 (700)
R3	1.0 Mb	200 (250)	1000 (1100)

User transactions are described in terms of their frequency of occurrence, which tables they access, and whether the accesses are reads or writes.

Transaction	Site(s)	Frequency	Table Accesses (Reads,Writes)
T1	S1, S4, S5	1	four to **R1** (3 reads, 1 write), two to **R2** (2 reads)
T2	S2, S4	2	two to **R1** (2 reads), four to **R3** (3 reads, 1 write)
T3	S3, S5	3	four to **R2** (3 reads, 1 write), two to **R3** (2 reads)

Security: User transactions T1, T2, and T3 can either query or update (no restrictions)

Sources of data: All sites—S1, S2, S3, S4, S5

Sinks of data (possible locations of transactions): All sites S1, S2, S3, S4, S5

Local Reference Computations

Our goal is to compute the number of local references to each table residing at each site, one by one. The site that maximizes the local references to a given table is chosen as the site where that table should reside.

The preceding tables tell us that table **R1** has the following local references: at site S1 it has only transaction T1 with four references at a frequency of one, and thus four total references; at site S2 it has transaction T2 with two references at a frequency of two, and thus four total references; at site S3 it has no transaction references; at site S4 it has both transactions T1 and T2 for a total of eight references; and at site S5 it has transaction T1 for a total of four references. A maximum of eight local references to table **R1** occurs at site S4 (see Table 8.1).

Table **R2** has the following local references: at site S1 it has only transaction T1 for a total of two references; at site S2 it has no references by any transaction; at site S3 it has four references by transaction T3 and a frequency of three, thus 12 total references; at site S4 it has only transaction T1 for a total of two references; at site S5 it has transactions T1 and T3 for a total of 14 references. A maximum of 14 local references to table **R2** occur at site S5 (see Table 8.1).

Table **R3** local references are computed in a similar fashion: at sites S2 and S4 there are a maximum of eight references.

Table 8.1   Local references for each table at each of five possible sites.

Table	Site	Transactions T1 (frequency)	T2 (frequency)	T3 (frequency)	Total Local References
R1	S1	3 read, 1 write (1)	0	0	4
	S2	0	2 read(2)	0	4
	S3	0	0	0	0
	S4	3 read, 1 write (1)	2 read(2)	0	8 (max.)
	S5	3 read, 1 write (1)	0	0	4
R2	S1	2 read (1)	0	0	2
	S2	0	0	0	0
	S3	0	0	3 read, 1 write(3)	12
	S4	2 read (1)	0	0	2
	S5	2 read (1)	0	3 read, 1 write(3)	14 (max.)
R3	S1	0	0	0	0
	S2	0	3 read, 1 write (2)	0	8 (max.)
	S3	0	0	2 read (3)	6
	S4	0	3 read, 1 write (2)	0	8 (max.)
	S5	0	0	2 read (3)	6

Allocation Decision

Figure 8.2 presents the allocation decision. Allocate table **R1** at site S4 and allocate table **R2** at site S5. At these sites the number of local references to these tables is clearly maximized. However, table **R3** is maximized at both sites S2 and S4, so additional information is needed to choose the allocation. For instance, if maximum availability of data is a major consideration, then choose site S2 for table **R3** because site S4 already has table **R1** allocated to it; putting **R3** there as well would decrease the potential availability of data should site S4 crash. The final allocation under these assumptions: S1 is empty, S2 has table **R3**, S3 is empty, S4 has table **R1**, and S5 has table **R2**.

The advantage of the "best fit" method is its computational simplicity. The main disadvantage is in accuracy: Computing the number of local

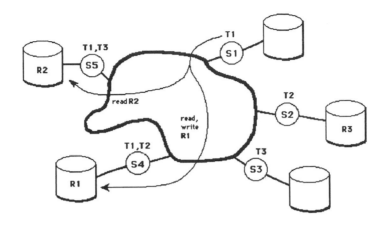

Relations: **R1, R2, R3, R4, R5**
Sites: S1, S2, S3, S4, S5
Transactions: T1, T2, T3

Figure 8.2
Nonredundant "best fit" method for data allocation, showing remote query and
update for transaction T1 originating at site S1.

references does not accurately characterize disk service time or response
time. Furthermore, it does not give any insights regarding data replication. A
better approach is to compute total block accesses or total i/o time.

8.4.2   The Redundant "All Beneficial Sites" Method

This method can be used for either the redundant or nonredundant case. It
selects all sites for a fragment allocation where the benefit is greater than the
cost for one additional copy of that fragment. You are assumed to start with
no copy or one copy of each table or fragment of a table.

The benefit at a specific site is measured by the difference in cost to do
a remote query (that is, having no additional local copy for a given fragment)
and a local query (that is, having an additional local copy of the given
fragment so the same query can be done more quickly). Total benefit for the
same additional copy of a fragment at that site is the difference between
remote and local query time per reference, multiplied by the total number of

queries (reads). Note that the difference between local and remote query times is the sum of the time required to send the remote request for service and receive the result across the network.

The cost at a specific site is the cost of all the additional remote update references for the given fragment at that site. Total cost for an additional copy of a given fragment at a specific site is the remote update time per reference multiplied by the total number of update (write) references by all user transactions at that site.

Cost/Benefit Computations

The cost/benefit computations described in this section are summarized in Table 8.2.

Table R1

Table **R1** at site S1 has the following cost: two remote updates (writes) by transaction T1 (frequency of one), one each from sites S4 and S5, multiplied by 600 milliseconds per write, totaling 1200 milliseconds. The benefit is from three queries (reads) by transaction T1 at site S1, multiplied by the difference between a remote and local query (500–100=400 milliseconds), totaling 1200 milliseconds.

Table **R1** at site S2 has the cost of three remote updates by transaction T1 (frequency of one)—one each from sites S1, S4, and S5—multiplied by 600 milliseconds per write, totaling 1800 milliseconds. The benefit is from two queries (reads) by transaction T2 at site S2 (frequency of two), multiplied by the difference between a remote and local query (400 milliseconds), totaling 1600 milliseconds.

Table **R1** at site S3 has the cost of three remote updates by transaction T1 (frequency of one)—one each from sites S1, S4, and S5—multiplied by 600 milliseconds per write, totaling 1800 milliseconds. There is no benefit, because no transaction accesses table **R1** locally at site S3.

Table **R1** at site S4 has the cost of two remote updates by transaction T1 from sites S1 and S5 (frequency of one), multiplied by 600 milliseconds per write, totaling 1200 milliseconds. The benefit is three queries by transaction T1 (frequency of one) and two queries by transaction T2 (frequency of two), multiplied by 400 milliseconds, totaling 2800 milliseconds.

Table **R1** at site S5 has the cost of two remote updates by transaction T1 from sites S1 and S4 (frequency of one), multiplied by 600 milliseconds per write, totaling 1200 milliseconds. The benefit is three queries by transaction T1 (frequency of one), multiplied by 400 milliseconds, totaling 1200 milliseconds.

In summary, for table **R1** benefit exceeds cost only at site S4; thus, only one copy of **R1** is allocated to this network.

Tables R2 and R3

With similar computations we obtain the results for tables **R2** and **R3** as shown in Table 8.2.

In summary, for table **R2**, benefit exceeds cost at sites S3 and S5. For table **R3**, benefit exceeds cost at all sites except S1.

Allocation Decision

Figure 8.3 presents the allocation decision. Allocate table **R1** to site S4. Allocate table **R2** to sites S3 and S5. Allocate table **R3** to sites S2, S3, S4, and S5.

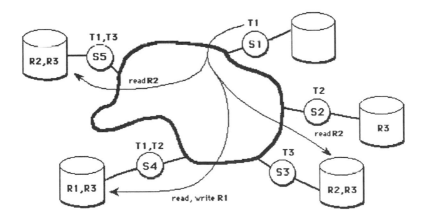

Relations: **R1, R2, R3, R4, R5**
Sites: S1, S2, S3, S4, S5
Transactions: T1, T2, T3

Figure 8.3
Redundant "all beneficial sites" method for data allocation, showing remote query and update for transaction T1 originating at site S1.

Table 8.2 Cost and benefit for each relation at five possible sites.

Table	Site	Remote Update Transactions	Remote Updates *Freq. *Time (Milliseconds)	Cost (Milliseconds)
R1	S1	T1 from S4 and S5	2*1*600	1200
	S2	T1 from S1, S4, S5	3*1*600	1800
	S3	T1 from S1, S4, S5	3*1*600	1800
	S4	T1 from S1 and S5	2*1*600	1200
	S5	T1 from S1 and S4	2*1*600	1200
R2	S1	T3 from S3 and S5	2*3*700	4200
	S2	T3 from S3 and S5	2*3*700	4200
	S3	T3 from S5	1*3*700	2100
	S4	T3 from S3 and S5	2*3*700	4200
	S5	T3 from S3	1*3*700	2100
R3	S1	T2 from S2 and S4	2*2*1100	4400
	S2	T2 from S4	1*2*1100	2200
	S3	T2 from S2 and S4	2*2*1100	4400
	S4	T2 from S2	1*2*1100	2200
	S5	T2 from S2 and S4	2*2*1100	4400

In the cases where benefit and cost are equal, consider whether either cost or benefit (or both) is likely to change in the near future or if greater availability is important. Adjust the allocation accordingly. If cost exceeds benefit at all sites for a given fragment, then pick the site for a single allocation where the difference between cost and benefit is minimized.

Note that there exist many more elaborate fragmentation and data allocation strategies than are covered here; however, this text has highlighted the major issues to provide a simple method when quick analysis is needed.

Table 8.2, continued

Table	Site	Query (Read) Sources	No. of Reads*Frequency* (Remote–Local Time)	Benefit (Milliseconds)
R1	S1	T1 at S1	3*1*(500–100)	1200
	S2	T2 at S2	2*2*(500–100)	1600
	S3	none	0	0
	S4	T1 and T2 at S4	(3*1+2*2)*(500–100)	2800
	S5	T1 at S5	3*1*(500–100)	1200
R2	S1	T1 at S1	2*1*(650–150)	1000
	S2	none	0	0
	S3	T3 at S3	3*3*(650–150)	4500
	S4	T1 at S4	2*1*(650–150)	1000
	S5	T1 and T3 at S5	(2*1+3*3)*(650–150)	5500
R3	S1	none	0	0
	S2	T2 at S2	3*2*(1000–200)	4800
	S3	T3 at S3	2*3*(1000–200)	4800
	S4	T2 at S4	3*2*(1000–200)	4800
	S5	T3 at S5	2*3*(1000–200)	4800

8.5   Summary

We have seen that distributed database design requires much more analysis than centralized databases, but that there exists a set of basic principles we can use for everyday design decisions. We have also seen that both nonredundant and redundant data allocation methods can be simply expressed and implemented to minimize the time to execute a collection of transactions on a distributed database. The methods take into account the execution times of remote and local database transactions for query and update and the frequencies of these transactions.

The advantages of the "all beneficial sites" method, compared to the "best fit" method, are its computational simplicity, its greater attention to the relative weights of service time for reads and writes, and its applicability to either the nonredundant or redundant data alternatives. It has no disadvantages relative to "best fit," but it does have some general limitations regarding the difficulty of obtaining the average query and update times over all applications and the fact that it ignores the details of network topology and protocols. In a new case study in Chapter 9, we will look at a practical extension of "all beneficial sites" that overcomes these limitations.

Literature Summary

[Case72]	Casey, R.G. "Allocation of Copies of a File in an Information Network," *Spring Joint Computer Conf.*, 1972, AFIPS Press, Vol. 40, 1972.
CePe84]	Ceri, S., and Pelagatti, G. *Distributed Databases: Principles and Systems*, McGraw-Hill, New York, 1984.
[CPW87]	Ceri, S., Pernici, B., and Wiederhold, G. "Distributed Database Design Methodologies," *Proc. of the IEEE*, May 1987, pp. 533–546.
[Chu69]	Chu, W.W. "Optimal File Allocation in a Multiple Computer System," *IEEE Trans. on Computers*, C-18,10(Oct. 1969), pp. 885–889.
[Chu84]	Chu, W.W. *Distributed Data Bases, Handbook of Software Engineering*, C.R. Vick and C.V. Ramamoorthy (editors), Van Nostrand Reinhold, 1984.
[CoGe80]	Coffman, E.G. et al. "Optimization of the Number of Copies in Distributed Databases," *Proc. of the 7th IFIP Symposium on Computer Performance Modelling, Measurement and Evaluation*, Springer-Verlag, New York, May 1980, pp. 257–263.
[FiHo80]	Fisher, M.L., and Hochbaum, D. "Database Location in Computer Networks," *J ACM* 27, 4(Oct. 1980).

[FHS80]   Fisher, P., Hollist, P., and Slonim, J. "A Design Methodology for Distributed Databases," *Proc. IEEE Conf. Distributed Computing*, Sept. 1980, IEEE, pp. 199–202.

[Heba77]   Hebalkar, P.G. "Logical Design Considerations for Distributed Database Systems," *IEEE COMPSAC*, Nov. 1977, pp. 562–580.

[MaRi76]   Mahmood, S., and Riordan, J. "Optimal Allocation of Resources in Distributed Information Networks," *ACM Trans. Database Systems* 1,1(March 1976), pp. 66–78.

[MoLe77]   Morgan, H.L., and Levin, K.D. "Optimal Program and Data Allocation in Computer Networks," *Comm. ACM* 32,5(May 1977), pp. 345–353.

[TCOU89]   Teorey, T.J., Chaar, J., Olukotun, K., and Umar, A. "Distributed Database Design: Some Basic Concepts and Strategies," *Database Programming and Design* 2,4(April 1989), 34–42.

9

An Example of Distributed Database Design

This chapter presents a distributed database design problem that involves the development of a global schema and a fragmentation and allocation of data. The designer is given a conceptual ER model for the database, a description of the transactions, and a generic network environment. A stepwise solution to this problem is then given in detail, based on mean value assumptions about work load and service.

Most textbooks and courses on distributed database systems lack concrete examples of how the database design process can be extended to include data fragmentation and data allocation strategies. The problem presented here has been carefully designed to provide enough complexity to challenge the advanced database student or practitioner, but to be small enough to avoid the drudgery of repetitive hand computation. On this latter point, as the solution is developed, it should become obvious where software tools would be helpful to evaluate large-scale designs.

9.1   A Distributed Database Design Problem

Given the database description that follows [Spro76] and the ER diagram representation of that description in Fig. 9.1, we develop a global schema of 3NF (and BCNF) relations. Then we design a data fragmentation and an initial nonredundant data allocation based on the needs of individual users at remote sites, given the network topology in Fig. 9.2. Finally, we design an optimal data allocation schema using the "all beneficial sites" method for allocating redundant data [CePe84, CPW87, TCOU89], weighing the design decisions against an exhaustive enumeration of transaction costs and feasible allocations.

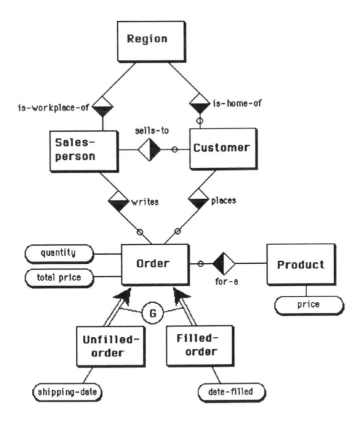

Figure 9.1
Entity-relationship diagram.

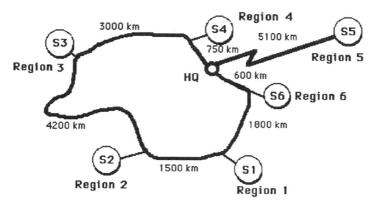

Figure 9.2
Network topology for the "order" database.

9.1.1   Database Description

A customer places an order through a particular salesperson for a given quantity of a specific product that is to be shipped by a certain shipping date. Once the order is filled, the data is saved for future reference, possibly at a site that is different from where data about the active (unfilled) orders is saved. Customers are considered to be located in certain marketing regions, and a salesperson serves customers within a particular region. The headquarters (HQ) of the company is located at a site that is separate from any regional office.

The database serves to provide information for management decision making—marketing and sales planning, for example—as well as to track orders, customers, and salespersons so that customer service is maximized. It also helps management make decisions regarding shipping.

Cardinalities (initially)

Regions=6

Salespersons=1200

Customers=240,000

Orders (filled)=2,000,000

Orders (unfilled) average level of 2000 per week per region

Products=10,000

Entities and their attributes (average field width)

Region	reg_no(2), reg_name(15), mgr_name(20), addr(30), phone(10)
Salesperson	sales_id(6), sales_name(20), addr(30), phone(10)
Customer	cust_id(8), cust_name(20), addr(30), phone(10), company(20)
Product	prod_no(10), prod_type(15), prod_name(20), price(10)
Order	order_no(12), ord_date(6), prod_no(10), quantity(5), shipping_date(6), date_filled(6), total_price(10)

Note: The designer is allowed to extend these entities and attributes in any way—by adding foreign keys, for example.

9.1.2   Database Transactions

Database transactions are relatively simple queries and updates. After each transaction a frequency is specified, and the source is given as either the HQ or one of the regions. If the regional frequency is given, the total frequency is that number multiplied by six, the total number of regions. Assume that the search key value is known when the query is made.

Database Queries

Q1. Which salespersons service a particular region? [20/day/HQ]

Q2. What are the unfilled orders for a particular salesperson? [50/day/region]

Q3. Who are the customers in a particular region? [20/day/HQ]

Q4. To which customers has a particular salesperson sold in a particular region? [50/day/region]

Q5. What are the details of the unfilled orders for a particular customer? [100/day/region]

Q6. How many new orders have there been this past month for all products in each region? [1/month/HQ]

Q7. What unfilled orders are for more than $10,000 and who sold those orders? [1/day/HQ]

Q8. For a given order, filled or unfilled, what is the name and address of the customer and the salesperson? [150/day/region]

Q9. For a given customer, who is the salesperson? [200/day/region]

Q10. Which unfilled orders are currently past any of their shipping dates, and for what products are they? [1/day/HQ]

Database Updates

U1. Add a new customer. [one batch of 50/day/region]

U2. Move a salesperson to a different region. [2/week/HQ]

U3. Place a new order. [400/day/region]

U4. Mark an order as filled (shipped). [2400/day/HQ]

U5. Update the product catalog with new products. [one batch of 100/quarter/HQ]

Note 1: Assume that a deletion results in setting the data to null, but no reorganization.

Note 2: week=5 days, month=21 days, quarter=63 days, year=252 days (shipping dates).

9.1.3 Network and Local Site Specifications

A variety of simplifying assumptions are given so that gross estimates of transaction response times can be made. Network contention is assumed to be nil because database design decisions are normally independent of total network load.

1. The generic packet switched network, including an overseas site, S5, runs at 56 kilobits per second (see Fig. 9.2). Pick the shortest distance between two sites and assume a simple protocol with no overhead: Send a one-packet query or update and receive a result of one packet or more with no processing overhead, only disk and transmission delays. Packet size=block size=2000 bytes.

2. The propagation delay is the speed of light, approximately 300 kilometers per millisecond. Note: This translates to 3.3 microseconds per kilometer, which is idealistic. Alternatively, a common assumption of 5 microseconds per kilometer (or 200 kilometers per millisecond) is used to take cable degradation into account. This model also assumes that station latency overhead is negligible.

3. Trba (random block access)=40 milliseconds, tsba (sequential block access)=10 milliseconds for a 2000-byte block. Local disk capacity: Assume it is sufficient to hold all the allocated data.

4. Local query and update: Compute access times based on disk i/o for read and rewrite.

5. Remote query and update: Compute access times based on disk i/o for read and rewrite, plus network propagation and transmission delays for the query/update, including the actual data being transferred to answer the query/update. Pick an intelligent (near-optimal) query processing strategy for each query and update; absolute optimality is not necessary.

6. Assume that all relations are initially sorted by the primary key.

7. Assume that the local database systems contain sufficient indexing so that all searches for individual records (tuples), based on the key value, take one random block access; if a rewrite is necessary for an update, it takes one sequential block access. When joins of relations are required, do appropriate selections and projections first to reduce the cost of a join. If necessary, one or both relations may need to be sorted on the attribute used in the join; however, you can specify any attribute for sorting a table before it is initially stored. Assume that all data is uniformly distributed over the six regions.

9.2 Global Schema and Fragmentation Design

In this part of the design problem we will

- perform an analysis of the transactions
- make global schema design decisions
- perform normalization
- implement fragmentation and nonredundant allocation

9.2.1 Analysis of the Transactions

Two methods are commonly used to determine which transactions to consider in the design process: either all transactions or a dominant subset. A dominant subset is frequently used when an exhaustive enumeration would be prohibitive; it is selected on such criteria as high frequency of execution, high volume of data accessed, response time constraints, and explicit priority. We will look at the exhaustive enumeration approach first to create a standard for comparison with approximation method, such as dominant subsets of transactions.

Since at this point we are not considering time constraints or priorities of transactions, our selection of a dominant subset will be based primarily on frequency of execution and volume of data searched. Our initial analysis will be to estimate the number of records accessed during each transaction, given some simplifying assumptions about database retrievals and updates (see Table 9.1). Later, as we know more details about physical storage and network distribution parameters, the analysis can be refined.

The dominant transactions in this group are queries Q2 through Q5 and update U1. All other transactions appear to have a significantly lower data volume than this subset. We will test this method and its refinements against exhaustive enumeration in Section 9.3.3.

9.2.2 Global Schema Design Decisions

The transformation from the entity-relationship model to the relational model is very straightforward in most cases, since the relationships in Fig. 9.1 are, for the most part, binary and one-to-many. In such cases we create a table (relation) from each entity in the relationship and add a foreign key in relations that represent the "many" side. The foreign key is the primary key of the parent entity, that is, the entity on the "one" side of the relationship.

The only additional relationship to consider is the generalization of order from unfilled_order and filled_order. In this case we make the simplifying decision that both unfilled_order and filled_order will have the same scheme, with the attribute date_filled set to null in unfilled_order. We will also assume that filled orders will be physically near each other and

Table 9.1 Analysis of all transactions.

Tr.	Tr./day	Data volume: Approx. number of records accessed (per region)	Total records/day
Q1	20	1200 salesperson records (get all salespersons per region)	24Kb
Q2	50*6	2000 unfilled_order records (get all unfilled_orders per region)	600Kb
Q3	20	40,000 customer records (get all customers per region)	800Kb
Q4	50*6	40,000 customer records (scan all customers, check salesperson)	12Mb
Q5	100*6	2000 unfilled_order records (scan all unfilled_orders, check customer)	1.2Mb
Q6	1/21	10,000 product count records— assume a 20-byte count record for each product is maintained by U3 for each new order (scan all count records, check product number and region number)	.5Kb
Q7	1	[2000 unfilled_order records]*6 (scan unfilled_orders, check total price and salesperson)	12Kb
Q8	150*6	1 order record, filled or unfilled+1 salesperson record+1 customer record (access order based on key, check customer and salesperson names and addresses)	2.7Kb
Q9	200*6	1 customer record+1 salesperson (access customer based on key, check salesperson)	2.4Kb
Q10	1*6	[2000 unfilled_order records] (scan unfilled_orders, check shipping date)	12Kb
U1	1*6	40,000+40,050 customer records (scan all customers, rewrite to maintain sort by primary key)	480.3Kb
U2	.4	100 salesperson records+1 rewrite+401 salesperson records (scan half of salespersons in a region, delete with one rewrite; scan all salespersons to do the insert, then rewrite whole table)	.3Kb

Table 9.1, continued

Tr.	Tr./day	Data volume: Approx. number of records accessed (per region)	Total records/day
U3	400*6	1 unfilled_order record+1 rewrite+1 count record+rewrite (access last unfilled_order and rewrite with new order, then update the product count per month)+access product for price	12Kb
U4	2400	1 unfilled_order record+1 rewrite+1 filled_order record+1 rewrite (index to an unfilled_order, delete and rewrite; index to a filled_order and rewrite)	9.6Kb
U5	1/63	10,000+10,100 product records (scan all products and rewrite with 100 more products) +write 100 product_count records	.3Kb

unfilled_orders physically near each other on each local computer's disk subsystem. Alternatively we could have consolidated both types of order into a single table, order, to be separated physically by whether or not date_filled has a null value. Analysis of the trade-offs between these two alternative designs would occur at the physical level, using the parameters discussed in Section 9.1.

Following is a feasible set of relation schemes in standard SQL. All relations are assumed to be sorted by primary key as noted in the assumptions.

Initial table definitions (SQL)

create table **region** (reg_no char(2) not null unique,
        reg_name   varchar(256),
        mgr_name   varchar(256),
        mgr_addr   varchar(256),
        mgr_phone   char(10),
        primary key (reg_no))

create table **salesperson** (sales_id char(6) not null unique,
        sales_name   varchar(256),
        sales_addr   varchar(256),

```
            sales_phone      char(10),
            reg_no           char(2) not null,
            primary key (sales_id),
            foreign key (reg_no) references region
                on delete set default
                on update cascade)
```

```
create table customer (cust_id      char(8) not null unique,
            cust_name        varchar(256),
            cust_addr        varchar(256),
            cust_phone       char(10),
            company          varchar(256),
            reg_no           char(2) not null,
            sales_id         char(6) not null,
            primary key (cust_id),
            foreign key (reg_no) references region
                on delete set default
                on update cascade,
            foreign key (sales_id) references salesperson
                on delete set default
                on update set default)
```

```
create table product (prod_no      char(10) not null unique,
            prod_type        varchar(256),
            prod_name        varchar(256),
            price decimal (10,2) not null,
            primary key (prod_no))
```

```
create table product_count (prod_no char(10) not null unique
            prod_count       char(10)
            primary key(prod_no),
            foreign key (prod_no) references salesperson
                on delete cascade
                on update cascade)
```

create table **unfilled_order** (order_no char(12) not null unique,

ord_date	date,
quantity	char(5) not null,
total_price	decimal (10,2) not null,
shipping_date	date not null,
date_filled	date default ' ',
prod_no	char(10) not null,
cust_id	char(8) not null,
sales_id	char(6) not null,

        primary key (order_no),
        foreign key (prod_no) references **product**
           on delete set default
           on update cascade,
        foreign key (cust_id) references **customer**
           on delete cascade
           on update cascade,
        foreign key (sales_id) references **salesperson**
           on delete set default
           on update cascade)

create table **filled_order** (order_no char(12) not null unique,

ord_date	date,
quantity	char(5) not null,
total_price	decimal (10,2) not null,
shipping_date	date, not null,
date_filled	date not null,
prod_no	char(10) not null,
cust_id	char(8) not null,
sales_id	char(6) not null,

        primary key (order_no),
        foreign key (prod_no) references **product**
           on delete set default
           on update cascade,
        foreign key (cust_id) references **customer**
           on delete cascade
           on update cascade,

foreign key (sales_id) references **salesperson**
on delete set default
on update cascade)

9.2.3   Normalization of the Global Schema

Normal forms were derived from the FDs in the table that follows.

Table	FDs
region	reg_no->reg_name, mgr_name, mgr_addr, mgr_phone
salesperson	sales_id->sales_name, sales_addr, sales_phone, reg_no
customer	cust_id->cust_name, cust_addr, cust_phone, company, sales_id, reg_no
	sales_id->reg_no
product	prod_no->prod_type, prod_name, price
product_count	prod_no->prod_count
unfilled_order	order_no->ord_date, quantity, total_price, shipping_date,
(or filled_order)	date_filled, prod_no, cust_id, sales_id
	cust_id->sales_id

The **region, salesperson, product,** and **product_count** tables are in BCNF. The **customer, unfilled_order**, and **filled_order** tables are considered to be in 2NF because of the existence of a transitive FD. There is no delete anomaly because of the replication of the dependent attributes elsewhere.

9.2.4   Fragmentation and Nonredundant Allocation

Only horizontal data fragmentation is considered here. Vertical fragmentation involves modifications to the relational schema, and its methods are well documented in [CePe84]. In general, horizontal fragmentation decisions can be made by studying the relationships between transactions and the relational schema. In a variation of the "best fit" method, we analyze each table in terms of the data volume (records/day) for all transactions that use that table, and note where the transactions originate. From Table 9.1 we can make the following nonredundant data allocations, noting in parenthesis the transactions that use each table.

The **region** (no transactions) table is very small and is used only by the HQ; therefore, it is left whole and unfragmented at the HQ site.

The **product (Q6, U3, U5)** and **product_count (Q6, U3, U5)** tables are used mostly at the regions by the dominating transaction U3. However, there is no obvious need to partition them because each application needs to access the whole tables. Thus they are left unfragmented at each of the regions (see alternative to A below which is an exception to nonredundancy when fragmentation is not needed and the regions are symmetric).

The **salesperson (Q1, U2)** table should remain unfragmented at HQ since it is used only for a full table scan in Q1 by the HQ. Although the salesperson's id is imbedded in other relations in the various regions for use in queries Q2, Q4, Q8, and Q9, any retrieval of further salesperson information can be made in a single random access, since the primary key is known in each case. The HQ allocation would have the additional benefit of making update U2 much easier, since only the region number (reg_no) would have to be changed to affect a location change for a salesperson.

The **filled_order (Q8, U4)** table should remain unfragmented at HQ because the data volume for U4 at HQ dominates the data volume for Q8 at the regions.

The **customer (Q3, Q4, Q9, U1)** table is used more at the regional level (Q4, Q9, U1) than at the HQ level (Q3). Therefore we initially fragment the customers by regions.

The **unfilled_order (Q2, Q5, Q7, Q8, Q10, U3, U4)** table has many transactions at the HQ and at the regional level. If we total the data volume for HQ(Q7, Q10, U4) and regions (Q2, Q5, Q8, U3), we find that the regional activity is much higher. Therefore we initially fragment the unfilled_orders by regions.

Fragmentation done in this manner is clearly heuristic. In this problem, we wish to study the most obvious alternative data allocation strategies for **product** and **product_count, salesperson, customer, unfilled_order,** and **filled_order**.

Alternative allocation strategies (cases):

1.   keep unfragmented and store only at headquarters (HQ)
2.   fragment and store by region
2A. keep unfragmented and replicate at each region

3. Combine cases 1 and 2: store unfragmented at HQ; replicate fragments at the regions

3A. Combine cases 1 and 2A: store unfragmented at HQ and replicate at all regions

9.3 Redundant Data Allocation Methods

In this section we will consider cost/benefit analysis, exhaustive enumeration, dominating transactions, and the "all beneficial sites" method and variations of it.

9.3.1 Cost/Benefit Analysis: Basic Performance Statistics

To produce a redundant data allocation, one needs only to consider allocating additional copies of a table at sites where there are queries that use that table. Thus, one need not consider, for example, placing a copy of region 1's **salesperson** table at site 2, since site 2 would never query or update this

Table 9.2 Tables' physical characteristics, given 2000 bytes per block.

Table	Cardinality	Size (Bytes)	Blocking Factor	Total Blocks	Blocks/ Region
region	6	77	25	1	1
salesperson	1,200	68	29	42	7
customer	240,000	96	20	12,000	2,000
unfilled_order	2,000	69	28	72	12
filled_order	2,000,000	69	28	71,429	11,905
product	10,000	55	36	278	278 (unfrag.)
product_count	10,000	20	100	100	100 (unfrag.)

information. This results in the following regional fragments being considered for redundant allocation: **salesperson, customer, unfilled_order,** and **filled_order.**

First we convert the logical schema specification into 2000-byte block allocations, which are shown in Table 9.2.

As an example of how the computations are conducted, let us analyze the i/o time to execute Q1, "Which salespersons service a particular region?"

CASE 1: Salesperson data stored unfragmented at HQ

This query requires a scan of 1200 salesperson records (42 blocks) at the HQ and a selection of only those from the targeted region. Ignoring the processing overhead and system contention, we calculate simple elapsed time in terms of i/o service time for the 42 blocks:

Simple elapsed time=42 blocks*tsba=42*10 ms=420 ms

Note that SQL query optimizers will do these computations automatically. It is recommended that you use the SQL optimizer, if possible, to explain the query plan before analyzing it. The system plan could be quite different from a plan based on your assumptions.

CASE 2: Salesperson data fragmented and stored by region only

Since the query is initiated by HQ, the targeted region must be accessed and its fragment fully scanned and transmitted to HQ. This involves transmission of a single packet from HQ to that region, followed by transmission of seven packets of salesperson data from the region to HQ. Our simplified model of wide area networks assumes that each regional request and reply is done sequentially, and that within each regional reply, the propagation delay occurs exactly once and multiple-packet replies occur serially. Propagation and transmission delays for this simple network are summarized in Table 9.3; the average propagation delay is 9.2 milliseconds.

simple elapsed time=propagation delay from HQ to the targeted region
+request packet transmission delay from HQ to the targeted region
+local disk i/o time for the query at the targeted region
+propagation delay back to HQ
+reply packet transmission delay back to HQ

Table 9.3 Network topological features and delays.

Region	Distance to HQ (Kilometers)	Propagation delay to HQ (Milliseconds)	Transmission delay to HQ (Milliseconds)
1	2400	8.0	285.7
2	3900	13.0	285.7
3	3750	12.5	285.7
4	750	2.5	285.7
5	5100	17.0	285.7
6	600	2.0	285.7
		(Average=9.2 ms)	

Block size (packet size)=2000 bytes
Transmission speed=56 kilobits per second

=9.2 ms+285.7 ms+7 blocks*10 ms/block
+9.2 ms+7 packets*285.7 ms

=2374 ms

**CASE 3: Salesperson stored at HQ and
replicated in fragments in each region**

This query takes the minimum of cases 1 and 2 because case 3 provides for two paths to the same data.

Obviously, if Q1 were the only transaction, storing the unfragmented salesperson data at HQ (case 1) would minimize simple elapsed time, disregarding any reliability constraints. On the other hand, if the link were improved to T1 speed (1.544 megabits per second), then fragmenting the data at the regions (case 2) would produce the best performance. However, there are many more query and update transactions to consider; Table 9.4 summarizes the cost of each transaction for each of the three data allocation cases. Since U4, "Mark an order as filled (shipped)," is among the more complex transactions, the details of its simple elapsed time computation are shown.

CASE 1: Unfilled_orders and filled_orders stored unfragmented at HQ

We still assume that **unfilled_order** and **filled_order** are physically separated at the HQ. This update involves strictly local accesses, using an index to find the appropriate unfilled order, marking the deletion, and rewriting the block. Then another index is consulted to find the appropriate point in **filled_order** to insert the new record. This involves one access to get the appropriate block and another to rewrite that block with the new record.

> simple elapsed time = access unfilled_order block+rewrite block
> +access filled_order block+rewrite block
> =1 trba+1 tsba+1 trba+tsba
> =40 ms+10 ms+40 ms+10 ms
> =100 ms

**CASE 2: Unfilled_orders and filled_orders fragmented
and stored by region only**

In this case the local update time is the same as in case 1 because the updates involve only random accesses to data, followed by sequential rewrites. We assume that the reply from an update is a single packet.

> simple elapsed time=request propagation delay+request transmis
> sion delay
> +local update time+reply propagation delay
> +reply transmission delay
> =9.2 ms+285.7 ms+100 ms+9.2 ms+285.7 ms
> =689.8 ms

**CASE 3: unfilled_orders and filled_orders stored at HQ
and replicated in fragments in each region**

This case requires that both copies of the data be updated.

> simple elapsed time=simple elapsed time for the HQ update
> +simple elapsed time for the regional update
> =100 ms+689.8 ms
> =789.8 ms

Thus U4 would be best served by the data allocation scheme for case 1. Table 9.4 summarizes all costs for each of the transactions.

Table 9.4 Simple elapsed time, in milliseconds, for three data allocation schemes (cases) for a single execution of each transaction.

Trans.	Freq./day	Case 1 Unfrag. @ HQ	Case 2 Frag. @ reg.	Case 3 Replicated @ HQ&reg.
Q1	20 @ HQ	42 blk*10 =420 ms	9.2+285.7+7*10 +9.2+7*285.7 =2374 ms	minimum (1&2)=420 ms
Q2	50*6 reg.	local: 72 blk*10 =720 remote: 9.2+285.7 +9.2+12*285.7 =590 total: 1310	12 blk*10 =120	minimum (1&2)=120
Q3	20@ HQ	12,000 blk*10 =120,000	local: 2000 blk*10 =20,000 remote: 9.2+285.7 +2000*285.7+9.2 =571,704 total=591,704	minimum (1&2)=120,000
Q4	50*6 regs.	local: 12,000*10 =120,000 remote: 9.2+285.7 +10*285.7 =3152 total=123,152	2000 blk*10 =20,000	minimum (1&2)=20,000
Q5	100*6 reg.	same as Q2	same as Q2	same as Q2
Q6	1/21 @ HQ (20B count per product)	100 blk*10 =1000	local: 6*100 blk*10 =6000 remote: 6*(9.2+285.7 +9.2+100*285.7) =173,245, total: 179,245 (Case 2A)	minimum (1&2)=1000 (Case 3A)

Table 9.4, continued

Trans.	Freq./day	Case 1 Unfrag. @ HQ	Case 2 Frag. @ reg.	Case 3 Replicated @ HQ&reg.
Q7	1 @ HQ	72 blk*10 =720	local: 6*72*10 =720 remote: 6*(9.2+285.7 +9.2+285.7)=3539 total: 4259	minimum (1&2)=720
Q8	150*6 reg.	local: 3 trba=120 remote: 9.2+285.7 +9.2+285.7=590 total: 710	3 trba=120	minimum (1&2)=120
Q9	200*6 reg.	local: 2 trba=80 remote: 590 total: 670	2 trba=80	minimum (1&2)=80
Q10	1 @ HQ	same as Q7	same as Q7	same as Q7
U1	1 @ regs.	local: (12,000 +12,014)*10 =240,140 remote: 590 total: 240,730	6*(2000+2003) blks*10=240,180	sum(1&2)=480,910
U2	.4 @ HQ	24 blk*10+10 +84 blk*10 = 1090	local: 4 blk*10+10 +14 blk*10=190 remote: 590 total: 780	sum (1&2)=1870
U3	400*6 regs.	local: 3 trba +2 tsba= 140 remote: 590 total: 730	3 trba +2 tsba =140 (Case 2A)	sum (1&2)=870 (Case 3A)

Table 9.4, continued

Trans.	Freq./day	Case 1 Unfrag. @ HQ	Case 2 Frag. @ reg.	Case 3 Replicated @ HQ&reg.
U4	2400 @ HQ	2*(trba+tsba) =100	local: 100 remote: 2*(9.2+285.7)=590 total: 690	sum (1&2)=790
U5	1/63 @ HQ	(278+281)*10 +1*40=5630	local: 6*(278+281) *10+6*1*40 =33,780 remote: 6*590 =3540 total: 37,320 (Case 2A)	sum (1&2)=42,950 (Case 3A)

Table 9.5 Cumulative simple elapsed time, in seconds, for three data allocation schemes for total transaction executions per day.

Trans.	Freq./day	Case 1 Unfrag. @ HQ	Case 2 Frag. @ regs	Case 3 Replicated
Q1	20 @ HQ	8.40	47.50	8.40
Q2	50*6 reg.	393.00	36.00	36.00
Q3	20 @ HQ	2400.00	11834.10	2400.00
Q4	50*6 regs.	36945.60	6000.00	6000.00
Q5	100*6 reg.	786.00	72.00	72.00
Q6	1/21 @ HQ	0.05	8.50	0.05
Q7	1 @ HQ	0.70	7.90	0.70
Q8	150*6 reg.	639.00	108.00	108.00
Q9	200*6 reg.	804.00	96.00	96.00
Q10	1 @ HQ	0.70	7.90	0.70
U1	1 @ regs.	240.70	240.20	480.90
U2	.4 @ HQ	0.40	0.30	0.70
U3	400*6 reg.	1752.00	336.00	2088.00
U4	2400 @ HQ	240.00	1656.00	1896.00
U5	1/63 @ HQ	0.10	0.60	0.70

9.3.2   Exhaustive Enumeration Method

The exhaustive enumeration method computes the entire cost of executing all transactions that use a particular table for each allocation strategy and then chooses the strategy that minimizes total cost. In this case cost is measured in simple elapsed time for queries and updates, assuming no contention either on the network or at the local sites. Cost computations are summarized for each relation in Table 9.6. Dominant transactions are shown with an asterisk.

Thus our allocation decision is:

1.   Allocate **unfilled_order** to each region, fragmented by region.
2.   Replicate **salesperson, customer,** and **filled_order** unfragmented at the HQ and fragmented at the regions.
3.   Allocate **product** and **product_count** unfragmented to each of the regions. Replication at the HQ is not recommended due to higher cost.
4.   Allocate **region** to the HQ (unfragmented), based on previous knowledge.

Note in Table 9.6 that several of the values are actually value ranges, for example, those associated with Q8 and U4. In most cases (in this example) the allocation decision for a given table can be made independently of the allocation decisions for the other tables because the transactions for those tables are either single table transactions or they are multiple table transactions with the initial nonredundant allocation of the tables at the same place(s). When this occurs we simply assume that our initial allocation will hold under further analysis. Conversely, Q8 and U4 are multiple table transactions where the nonredundant allocations are at different places. For instance, in Q8, **filled_order** and **salesperson** are initially at the HQ, but **customer** and **unfilled_order** are fragmented at the regions. For such transactions the allocation decisions for their associated tables are highly dependent on the locations of all the tables in each transaction. When this occurs we cannot make the assumption that the initial allocation will always hold. The lower bound value represents the best case where all the associated tables for that transaction are clustered for local accesses only, while the upper bound value represents the worst case allocation causing the maximum of remote accesses across the network.

In Table 9.6 the range of cost values for a given table and decision case can either be the minimum cost, greater than the minimum cost, or an

Table 9.6   Exhaustive enumeration of simple elapsed times for all transactions for each table.

Table &Trans.	Case 1: Unfrag. @ HQ only	Case 2: Frag. @ regs. only	Case 3: Replicated
salesperson			
Q1	8.40	47.50	8.40
Q8	108.00–639.00	108.00–639.00	108.00
U2	0.40	0.30	0.70
	117.00–648.00 sec	156.00–687.00 sec	**117.00 sec**
customer			
Q3*	2400.00	11834.10	2400.00
Q4*	36945.60	6000.00	6000.00
Q8	108.00–639.00	108.00–639.00	108.00
Q9	804.00	96.00	96.00
U1*	240.70	240.20	480.90
	40498.00	18278.00	**9085.00 sec**
	–41029.00 sec	–18809.00 sec	
unfilled_order			
Q2*	393.00	36.00	36.00
Q5*	786.00	72.00	72.00
Q7	0.70	7.90	0.70
Q8	108.00–639.00	108.00–639.00	108.00
Q10	0.70	7.90	0.70
U3	1752.00	336.00	2088.00
U4	240.00–1656.00	240.00–1656.00	1896.00
	3811.00	**1008.00**	4201.00 sec
	–5027.00 sec	**–2224.00 sec**	
filled_order			
Q8	108.00–639.00	108.00–639.00	108.00
U4	240.00–1656.00	240.00–1656.00	1896.00
	348.00–2295.00 sec	348.00	**2004 sec**
		–2295.00 sec	
product and **product_count**		Case 2A	Case 3A
Q6	0.05	8.5	0.05
U3	1752.00	336.00	2088.00
U5	0.10	0.60	0.70.00
	1752.00 sec	**345 sec**	2089.00 sec

overlapping cost with one or more other cases. For **salesperson**, the cost for Case 3 (replicated) is equal to the lower bound of Case 1 (HQ) and completely below the range of costs for Case 2 (fragmented at regions); thus we pick Case 3 because of the tie on minimum cost and greater availability. For **filled_order**, the cost of Case 3 falls between the range of costs for both Case 1 and Case 2. However, the upper bound cost in Cases 1 and 2 occurs when **unfilled_order** is fragmented at the regions, regardless of where **filled_order** is located, which is the actual nonredundant allocation in this example. Therefore, since the cost of Case 3 is less than the upper bound of Cases 1 and 2, we pick Case 3 as the most likely minimum cost situation.

9.3.3   Dominating Transactions

We test our hypothesis that the dominating transactions will lead to the same decisions as exhaustive enumeration by recomputing the total costs for the dominating subset (Q2* through Q5*, U1* in Table 9.6). The **salesperson** table has no dominating transactions, so no decision need be made regarding redundant allocation; thus, it remains at HQ. This is consistent with the exhaustive enumeration method. The **customer** table has dominating transactions Q3, Q4, and U1, which lead to the same decision as exhaustive enumeration. On the other hand, **unfilled_order**, with dominating transactions Q2 and Q5, results in a tie between cases 2 and 3. If the decision were randomly chosen at this point, a wrong decision could be made. Even worse, **filled_order**, with no dominating transactions, would stay fragmented at the regions when it should be kept unfragmented at the HQ.

We conclude from this test that serious problems exist in the specified method of computing dominant transactions based only on table record counts. A better approach is to account for packet traffic across the network, since the difference between a remote and local access can be quite large. If we use the nonredundant cases in Table 9.5 (cases 1 and 2) as a more detailed comparison of transaction costs, we can make better allocation decisions.

We can establish the threshold between dominating and nondominating transactions as the point in which the lower bound cost—that is, simple elapsed time—of one transaction is more than an order of magnitude greater than the upper bound of another transaction. Then the dominating subset consists of transactions Q2 through Q5, Q8, Q9, U1, U3, and U4. Recomputing times from Table 9.5 using only the newly defined dominating subset, we find that we will make the same redundant allocation decisions as we did with the exhaustive enumeration method. In general, however, it is difficult to specify an effective threshold selection criterion before looking at the performance data for a specific configuration.

9.3.4 "All Beneficial Sites" Method

The "all beneficial sites" method can be used for either redundant or nonredundant data allocation design decisions. It is particularly useful when the number of alternative strategies (cases) for the exhaustive enumeration method is prohibitively large. The "all beneficial sites" method selects all sites for a fragment allocation where the benefit is greater than the cost of one additional copy of that fragment. You may start with either no copies or one nonredundant copy. In this network, individual remote query and update times can be calculated instead of the average as used in [TCOU89]. The *benefit* at a specific site is measured by the difference in cost to do a remote query (that is, having no additional copy for a given fragment) and to do a local query (that is, having one additional copy of the fragment so the same query can be done locally). The *cost* at a specific site is the cost of all the additional remote update references for the fragment at that site.

Total cost for an additional copy of a fragment at a specific site is the remote update time per reference multiplied by the total number of update (write) requests by all user transactions at that site. Total benefit for the same additional copy of a fragment at that site is the difference between remote and local query time per request, multiplied by the total number of queries (reads).

In this example, we determined that the initial allocation was

1. **region, salesperson,** and **filled_order** at the HQ
2. **customer** and **unfilled_order** fragmented by region
3. **product** and **product_count** unfragmented at all regions

We now determine whether to replicate data or not, by computing costs and benefits for each table (see Table 9.7).

From Table 9.7 we see that costs exceed benefits for **product, product_count,** and **unfilled_order**; thus no replication of data is needed.

Table 9.7 Computation of costs and benefits for all beneficial sites.

Table(initially at) & transaction(from)	Cost of replicating	Benefit of replicating	Decision
salesperson(HQ)			
Q1(HQ)		0 (no query at regions)	replicate
Q8 (regions)		**590 ms*900/day**	at regions
U2(HQ)	780 ms*.4/day		
filled_order(HQ)			
Q8(regions)		590 ms*150/day*6 reg. = **531,000 ms**	replicate at regions
U4(HQ)	50 ms*2400/day = 120,000 ms		
customer(regions)			
Q3(HQ)		**571,704 ms*20/day**	replicate
Q4(regions)		0 (no queries at HQ)	at HQ
Q8(regions)		0 (no queries at HQ)	
Q9(regions)		0 (no queries at HQ)	
U1(regions)	240,730 ms*1/day		
unfilled_order(regions)			
Q2(regions)		0 (no queries at HQ)	do not
Q5(regions)		0 (no queries at HQ)	replicate
Q7(HQ)		3539 ms*1/day	at HQ
Q8(regions)		0 (no queries at HQ)	
Q10(HQ)		3539 ms*1/day	
U3(regions)	**730 ms*400/day*6 reg**		
U4(HQ)	**690 ms*2400/day**		
product and product_count (unfragmented at all regions)			
Q6(HQ)		(173,245)*1/21 =8250 ms	do not
U3(regions)	**730*2400/day=1752 sec**		replicate
U5 (HQ)	5590 ms*1/63=89 ms		at HQ

However, for **salesperson, customer,** and **filled_order** the benefits exceed costs and replication of the table at the HQ is justified. This result is consistent with the exhaustive enumeration method, and in fact selects from the same computations in Table 9.4.

As a minor extension of the original problem, consider the following availability constraint: A crash at one site should not cause the loss of data to any of the other sites that may need it now or in future transactions. This is partly met by redundancy in the network ring architecture, but data redundancy is also required. Because the **customer** table is the only table replicated in the unconstrained problem, we must now create additional copies of all other relations by fragmenting them at the regions and maintaining an unfragmented copy at the HQ. This satisfies the availability constraint and maximizes the local query performance at each site.

9.3.5   Variations of "All Beneficial Sites"

Numerous variations of the "all beneficial sites" method have been suggested. In the previous section we assumed an initial nonredundant allocation and looked at one-step variations from this initial allocation. Using a cumulative approach, we can make an allocation decision regarding a particular table, then assume that the next decision must be made based on the new state of the configuration, which no longer resembles the initial allocation. Both the one-step and cumulative approaches are "local optimization" methods and cannot guarantee global optimal solutions.

A more practical approach involves computing actual wait times in the network and local sites rather than just i/o service times. This results in more realistic elapsed times instead of simple elapsed times for use in comparing different allocation decisions. However, it requires much more knowledge about system contention, which may not be available. Extensions of "all beneficial sites" to account for data availability in a partially reliable network are discussed in [CePe84].

9.4   Summary

A distributed data allocation problem can be solved by a step-by-step solution approach that includes conceptual ER modeling; transformation to normalized relations; fragmentation for a nonredundant data allocation; and, finally, determination of a redundant data allocation scheme. A variety of practical data allocation strategies can be evaluated using a simple block access analysis of local databases and a packet propagation and transmission analysis of a simple network configuration for distributed databases. The "all beneficial sites" method has the most potential to be an effective substitute for exhaustive enumeration when scaling up for large complex databases.

Literature Summary

[CePe84]	Ceri, S., and Pelagatti, G. *Distributed Databases: Principles and Systems,* McGraw-Hill, New York, 1984.
[CPW87]	Ceri, S., Pernici, B., and Wiederhold, G. "Distributed Database Design Methodologies," *Proc. IEEE,* May 1987, pp. 533–546.
[Spro76]	Sprowls, R.C. *Management Data Bases*, Wiley/Hamilton, Santa Barbara, CA, 1976.
[Teor89]	Teorey, T.J. "Distributed Database Design: A Practical Approach and Example," *SIGMOD Record* 18,4(Dec. 1989), pp. 23–39.
[TCOU89]	Teorey, T.J., Chaar, J., Olukotun, K., and Umar, A. "Distributed Database Design: Some Basic Concepts and Strategies," *Database Programming and Design* 2,4(April 1989), pp. 34–42.

Exercises

Problem 9-1

First use the "best fit" method based on frequency of applications to determine a feasible nonredundant allocation for the three unfragmented tables (R1, R2, R3) among the three equidistant sites (S1, S2, S3). Then use the "all beneficial sites" approach to determine where to replicate the tables, using the following workload and configuration parameters. Assume that each site has adequate sequential and random (hashing) access methods for disk files.

Workload (applications)

Query 1: requires a 3-way join (single full scan, no sort required) of tables R1, R2, and R3.

Query 2: requires a random access to one record in R2.

Update 1: requires a random access to one record in R1, and a rewrite of that record.

Update 2: sequential scan of table R2 and a rewrite of every record.

Type of application	Origin of application	Application frequency
Query 1 (on R1,R2,R3)	Site S1	10
Query 2 (on R2 only)	Sites S1, S2, S3	10 from each site
Update 1 (on R1 only)	Site S2	100
Update 2 (on R2 only)	Site S3	50

Tables

R1 fits exactly into 100 blocks. Blocking factor=20.
R2 fits exactly into 100 blocks. Blocking factor=10.
R3 fits exactly into 100 blocks. Blocking factor=50.

Critical disk and network times

trba=40 ms at all sites (disk i/o time for a random block access)
tsba=10 ms at all sites (disk i/o time for a sequential block access)
network propagation delay=10 ms; transmission delay for one packet (or block)=100 ms

Problem 9-2

Repeat Problem 9-1 using the "best fit" method based on total block accesses for each application (block accesses per application execution times frequency) instead of just frequency of the application. Why does this give a different result from Problem 9-1?

Problem 9-3

The following problems refer to a modification of the problem first presented in [TeFr82], a fictitious environment based roughly on the *"Star Trek"* concept. It is now to be distributed over interplanetary space with nodes on Earth, Mars, Jupiter's moon Io, and Neptune's moon Triton.

Data Requirements Description (Processing Independent)

The Space Federation governs 100 galactic sectors, which it patrols with 25 starships assigned to approximately four sectors apiece. There are 100 cargo ships assigned the task of bringing fuel, equipment, and supplies to these starships. Because each starship is unique, cargo ships must be specially built to service each one and cannot service any other starship. More than one cargo ship is assigned to a starship to ensure continued maintenance. To aid in dispatching cargo ships and assigning crew members for relief, the Federation keeps a record of all coordinates and crew rosters for each ship.

Each cargo ship belonging to the Space Federation is divided into five sections. These sections are assigned specific maintenance, navigation, and cargo manipulation duties. Each section performs an average of three different duties. Fifty crew members are assigned to a ship and each crew member works in two sections, on the average. The Federation maintains a set of personal information about each crew member.

The organization of the starship *Enterprise* is fairly simple. The starship is divided into several divisions, each of which has a division leader. Associated with each division are a number of tasks; these tasks are performed by crew members. Although a crew member will, in general, perform more than one task, no crew member performs tasks from more than one division. Some tasks require several crew members. Associated with each person on the ship (division leader and crew member) is a set of personal information. A rating of how well a task is performed is associated with the crew member and the tasks.

The sick bay of the starship *Enterprise* keeps the following information about its 10 physicians and the 1000 crew members they treat. Each physician treats an average of 400 crew members. For each crew member, the physician maintains a history of the diseases contracted and a record of the drug allergies. A crew member averages five of each of these sick log entries. The physician also notes the planets the crew member has visited (an average of

10). Associated with each planet is a list of known diseases indigenous to the planet and a description of their symptoms and treatment.

Space is not easy on starships. To keep them in top shape, the Federation maintains 10,000 space stations. Each is located at what has been determined to be an optimal set of coordinates for servicing the fleet, and each has been given the name of a famous captain or courageous cadet who died in battle. The starship manuals define 1000 standard starship repairs. Because of their complexity and special equipment requirements, each space station is constructed to handle only 50 of these repairs. Thus, any given repair can take place at only 500 of the stations. Approximately 100 mechanics work at each station. They are trained on 10 different repairs and are given a rating level associated with each specialty. The 25 Federation starships show up at these various stations for routine maintenance and whenever major difficulties that cannot be fixed by the starship engineering staff occur. The Federation keeps records of these repairs. About 1000 such repair stops have been made at each station.

Processing Requirements: Queries

1. Whenever a galactic sector appears to be having some difficulty, such as an interplanetary war, the starship associated with that sector is found and called in to resolve the problem (frequency=20%). Source: Triton, Earth.

2. The governing counsel often wants to know what galactic sectors are governed by a given starship, in particular, the starship *Enterprise* (frequency=80%). Source: Earth.

3. When a starship needs servicing it is necessary to find the closest cargo ship capable of performing the service (frequency=90%). Source: Mars, Triton.

4. Whenever a cargo ship is assigned a service operation, the Federation distributes notices to those crew members on both ships who will find relatives on the other ship. This is done by obtaining a report of all crew members with the same last names on both ships (frequency=10%). Source: Earth.

5. The commander of the ship often wants to know the personal data about the individual assigned to a given section, such as id number, hometown, languages spoken, and hobbies(frequency=90%). Source: local starship (not done on the network).

6. Every now and then, the ship is short a crew member. Other crew members are examined for replacement possibilities. What is typically looked at is the set of duties the crew member already performs (frequency=10%). Source: Earth.

7. Find the personal information and names of crew members, capable of doing task T in division D, with a rating of R or better (frequency=50%). Source: Earth.

8. Find the names of those crew members who are capable of doing all the tasks in a subset of division D's tasks (frequency=10%). Source: Earth.

9. Find the names of all the crew members commanded by a specific leader (frequency=40%). Source: Earth, Io, Triton.

10. Find the names of all the crew members that a given physician has treated (frequency=20%). Source: Earth, Io.

11. Find the names of all the planets a given crew member has visited and list their diseases, symptoms, and treatments (frequency=50%). Source: Earth, Io.

12. Find the specified treatment for a given disease, and list all crew members who are known to be allergic to this treatment (frequency=30%). Source: Earth, Io.

13. A starship is due for maintenance on a specific control system. The captain wants to find the repair station closest to its coordinates that is capable of performing the repair (frequency=30%). Source: Mars, Triton.

14. The Federation periodically checks usage patterns to see if its repair stations are appropriately distributed. It does this by listing all the starships that have had a given repair at a given station (frequency=40%). Source: Mars, Triton.

15. The *Enterprise* needs a very tricky repair. The Federation office wants to find the best mechanic for this job and the station where the mechanic works (frequency=30%). Source: Earth, Mars, Triton.

Processing Requirements: Updates

1. Occasionally a starship needs to be replaced. To ensure continuity, the entire crew of the old ship is transferred to the new one, and all divisions and tasks remain the same (frequency=1%). Source: Earth, Mars, Triton.

2. Cargo ships also need to be replaced. A crew is transferred as a group to a new ship (frequency=15%). Source: Mars, Triton.

3. A starship that loses 10 or more crew members because of battles, disease, rotation to Federation headquarters, or retirement receive an equal number of new crew members to replace them. The average number of replacements per visit (via cargo ship) is 25 (frequency=5%). Source: Earth.

4. To keep crew members fresh, they are taught how to perform new tasks within their division. After every planet visitation, 20% of the crew changes one of their tasks (frequency=25%). Source: Earth.

5. A new space station is built every few weeks (frequency=10%). Source: Earth, Mars, Triton.

Networking Requirements

1. The database resides within the Earth's planetary system, with nodes on Earth, Mars, Io, and Triton. Planetary distances (approximate averages) are listed in the following table.

	Distance (Millions of Kilometers)			
	Earth	**Mars**	**Io**	**Triton**
Earth	0	216.8	777.9	4478.8
Mars	—	0	788.8	4489.7
Io	—	—	0	4479.0

2. Assume that the speed of light is the constraining speed: 300,000 kilometers/second. Outside Earth's solar system hyperspace starship speeds can be obtained, but they are not allowed within the solar system.

3. Assume that the interplanetary distances are so great that total response time is dominated by network propagation delay; network transmission delays and local CPU and i/o processing delays are considered negligible.

4. Frequencies are used as follows: a query or update with a frequency of 10% and two sources has 10% for each source, or 20% overall.

The Problem

The goal of the distribution design is to allocate tables redundantly to a subset of the four processing centers to minimize total access time for the most dominant queries and updates. Let us define dominance by frequency of a query multiplied by the number of sources of the query greater than 60%. Dominance by frequency of update times is the number of sources of the update greater than 20%. This includes six of the queries and three of the updates. Note that access time is one-half the response time for any given query or update, given this simplified network model. If we extend this problem to include all queries and updates, does this result in a different allocation from the dominant application approach?

10

Entity Clustering

This chapter presents the concept of entity clustering, which abstracts the ER schema to such a degree that the entire schema can appear on a single sheet of paper or a single computer screen.

This has happy conscquences for the end-user and database designer in terms of developing a mutual understanding of the database contents and formally documenting the conceptual model.

10.1   Introduction

An entity cluster is the result of a grouping operation on a collection of entities and relationships. Clustering can be applied repeatedly, resulting in layered levels of abstraction with manager and end-user views at the top level, database designer views at middle levels, and both designer and programmer views at the bottom level.

Entity clustering is potentially useful for designing large databases. When the scale of a database or information structure is large and includes a large number of interconnections among its different components, it may be very difficult to understand the semantics of such a structure and to man age it, especially for the end-users or managers. In an ER diagram with 1000 entities, the overall structure will probably not be very clear, even to a well-trained database analyst. Clustering is therefore important because it provides a method to organize a conceptual database schema into layers of abstraction, and it supports the different views of a variety of end-users.

10.2   Clustering Concepts

The entity clustering technique integrates object clustering concepts with the traditional design of ER models to produce bottom-up abstraction of natural groupings of entities. Think of *grouping* as an operation to combine entities and their relationships to form a higher-level construct. The result of a grouping operation on purely elementary entities is called an *entity cluster*. A grouping operation on entity clusters or on combinations of elementary entities and entity clusters results in a higher-level entity cluster. The highest-level entity cluster, representing the entire database conceptual schema, is called the *root entity cluster*.

Figure 10.1a illustrates the concept of entity clustering in a simple case where (elementary) entities Issue, Jour_Note, and Jour_Addr are naturally bound to (dominated by) the entity Journal; and entities Publisher, Standing_Order, and Paper are not dominated. (Note that to avoid unnecessary detail, we do not include the attributes of entities in the diagrams. The Mathematical Reviews example lists attributes in a logical data dictionary, which has accompanying text to help define them.) In Fig. 10.1b the dark-bordered box around entity Journal and the entities it dominates defines the entity cluster Journal. The dark-bordered box will be called the *EC box* to represent the idea of entity cluster. In general, the name of the entity cluster need not be the same as the name of any internal entity; however, when there is a single dominant entity, the names are often the same. The EC box number in the lower right is a clustering level number used to keep track of the sequence in which clustering is done.

The higher-level abstraction, the entity cluster, must maintain the same relationships between entities inside and outside the entity cluster as occur between the same entities in the lower-level diagram. Thus the entity names

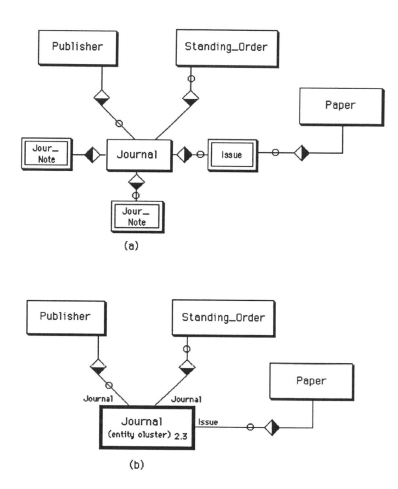

Figure 10.1
Format of an entity cluster.

inside the entity cluster must appear just outside the EC box along the path of their direct relationship to the appropriately related entities outside the box, maintaining consistent interfaces (relationships) as shown in Fig. 10.1b. For simplicity, we modify this rule slightly: If the relationship is between an external entity and the dominant internal entity (for which the entity cluster is named), the entity cluster name need not be repeated outside the EC box.

Thus, in Fig. 10.1b, we could drop the name Journal both places it occurs outside the Journal box, but we must retain the name Issue, which is not the name of the entity cluster.

The clustering concept can be expressed in terms of SQL views by treating the entity cluster as a single view, defined by the join operations over the individual entities (relations) in the unclustered form. As an example, we define an SQL view for the entity cluster in Fig. 10.1b as follows:

```
create view journal_cluster (jour_id, pub_id, st_ord_id, paper_id, iss_id,
                jour_note, jour_addr)
      as select  j.jour_id, j.pub_id, j.st_ord_id, j.paper_id, i.iss_id,
                 jn.jour_note, ja.jour_addr
      from       journal j, issue i, jour_note jn, jour_addr ja
      where      j.jour_id=jn.jour_id
      and        j.jour_id=ja.jour_id
      and        j.jour_id=i.jour_id
```

The entity cluster journal_cluster is formed by joining journal with the weak entities (relations) over the common attribute jour_id, which is the primary key of journal and foreign keys in issue, jour_note, and jour_addr. This same basic concept is used for all the entity clusters because they always keep their relationships with the external entities intact, and the internal relationships imply duplicate key values to facilitate the joins.

Relationships in entity diagrams used here are not restricted to current ER model implementations and commercial tools, but they may include n-ary as well as binary-degree relationships; optional/mandatory existence dependencies; abstractions; and, possibly, the role concept and integrity constraints of the NIAM model. Several examples from the NIAM model are adapted to the ER model here for use in the clustering scheme. In Fig. 10.2a, it is shown that multiple relationships may be constrained by an exclusion (disjoint or exclusive OR) function, which allows at most one entity occurrence among B, C, or D. The default treatment of multiple relationships is the inclusive OR, which allows any, all, or none of the entities B, C, or D to exist. Fig. 10.2b shows a two-relationship subset constraint as defined in Chapter 2.

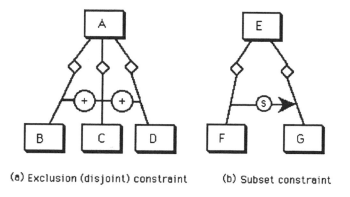

(a) Exclusion (disjoint) constraint   (b) Subset constraint

Figure 10.2
NIAM constraints adapted to the ER model.

10.3   Grouping Operations

The grouping operations are the fundamental components of the entity clustering technique. They define what collections of entities and relationships comprise higher-level objects, the entity clusters. The operations are heuristic in nature and include:

- dominance grouping
- abstraction grouping
- constraint grouping
- relationship grouping

These grouping operations can be applied recursively or used in a variety of combinations to produce higher-level entity clusters, that is, clusters at any level of abstraction. An entity or entity cluster may be an object that is subject to combinations with other objects to form the next higher level. That is, entity clusters have the properties of entities and can have relationships with any other objects at any equal or lower level. The original relationships among entities are preserved after all grouping operations, as illustrated in Fig. 10.1.

We will now study each type of grouping in turn, and then learn about their order of precedence.

10.3.1 Dominance Grouping

Dominant objects or entities normally become obvious from the ER diagram or the relationship definitions. Each dominant object is grouped with all its related nondominant objects to form a cluster. Weak entities can be attached to an entity to make a cluster (see Fig. 10.3 for the generic forms of grouping). An example of dominance grouping of the entity Book is given in Fig. 10.4. Here we see that the entity cluster is assigned the name of the dominant entity, with the cluster level designated in the lower right-hand corner.

A cluster level number is given as x.y, where x is the next level above the highest level of entities and entity clusters being grouped. Elementary

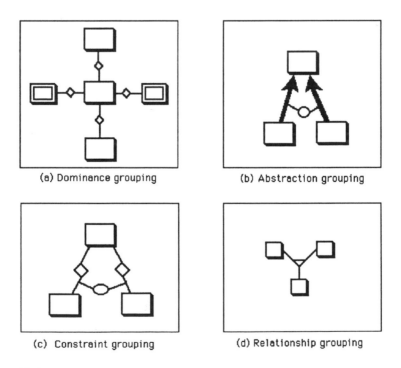

(a) Dominance grouping   (b) Abstraction grouping

(c) Constraint grouping   (d) Relationship grouping

Figure 10.3
Grouping operations (generic forms).

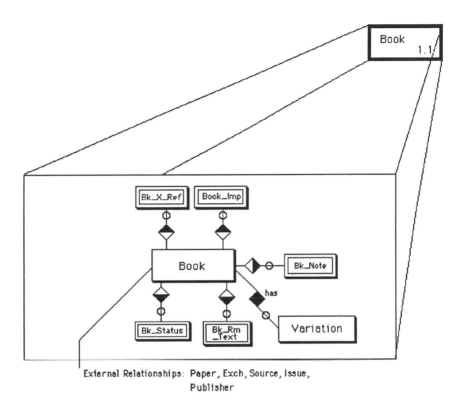

Figure 10.4
Example of dominance grouping: Book.

entities are considered to be at level 0. The y value represents a unique identification number given to each cluster at level x.

10.3.2   Abstraction Grouping

Multilevel data objects using such abstractions as generalization, subset generalization, and aggregation can be grouped into an entity cluster. The difference in notation for these three cases is shown in Fig. 10.5. The supertype or aggregate entity name is used as the entity cluster name. An example abstraction grouping is shown in Fig. 10.6, where Individual is defined as a generalization of the possibly overlapping subtypes (subsets), Author and Reviewer.

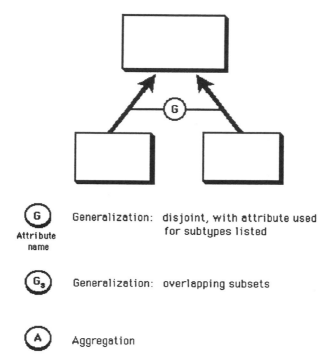

Generalization: disjoint, with attribute used
                 for subtypes listed

Generalization: overlapping subsets

Aggregation

Figure 10.5
Notation for abstraction grouping.

10.3.3   Constraint Grouping

Constraint-related objects that extend the ER model to incorporate the integrity constraints of NIAM can be grouped into an entity cluster. In Fig. 10.7 we see that Standing_Order is associated with either Journal, Publisher, or Series, constrained with an exclusive OR. The entity cluster name is assigned the name of the dominant (parent) entity, Standing_Order.

10.3.4   Relationship Grouping

The n-ary relationships of degree 3 or more can potentially be grouped into an entity cluster. The cluster represents the relationship as a whole, such as

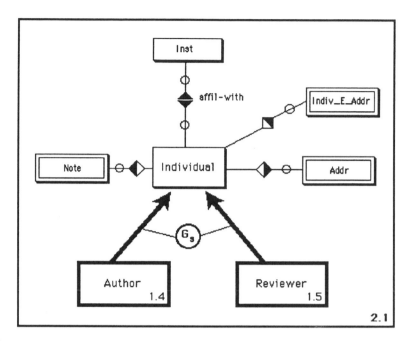

Figure 10.6
Example of abstraction grouping: Individual.

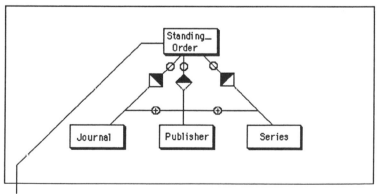

Figure 10.7
Example of constraint grouping: Standing_Order.

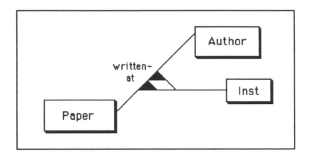

Figure 10.8
Example of (n-ary) relationship grouping.

the relationship relation that would be defined when transforming the n-ary relationship into a set of equivalent normalized relations. A specific example is illustrated in Fig. 10.8, in which the relationship written-at and its associated entities are grouped into the single entity cluster, Paper_Inst_Auth. Note that for all relationship groupings, the entity cluster name is merely the name of the relationship. Also note that, in these examples of grouping types, external relationships are not shown.

10.3.5 Cohesion

Grouping operations have an order of precedence that is defined in terms of *cohesion*, a term borrowed from software module design. Cohesion is a measure of the degree of internal cohesiveness of a module [SMC74]. For our purposes, the term describes the internal strength of the relationship among entities within an entity cluster. The spectrum of cohesion of entity clusters is defined as follows.

Greatest cohesion

Dominance grouping — A strong entity surrounded by related weak entities has high cohesion because of the "existence" dependency on a single entity. In some cases the dominated entities are nonweak entities, but the functional dominance is clearly defined.

Abstraction grouping	Cohesion is not as strong as existence dependency or dominance, but it is high because of a strong parent-child relationship between a supertype and its subtypes.
Constraint grouping	Moderately strong parent-child relationship exists between an entity and related entities, using constraint relationships.
Relationship grouping (n-ary)	Ternary and higher n-ary relationships have a low relationship cohesion because of the lack of dominance of any single entity in many of these relationships.
No relationship	Cohesion results only from entities belonging to the same functional area.

The concept of cohesion within entity clusters provides the criterion for choosing the order of grouping for a large database with potentially conflicting entity constructs. For instance, in Fig. 10.6 the entity Reviewer has a supertype entity, Individual, and in Fig. 10.9 (entity cluster 1.5) Reviewer has a subordinate weak entity, Reviewer_Status. According to the precedence rules, the relationship with the weak entity is grouped first, then the abstraction relationship is grouped. (However, in this case, the abstraction is actually not grouped because of the constraint that a functional area boundary cannot be crossed. See step 2 in Section 10.4.)

10.4   Clustering Technique

The grouping operations and their order of precedence determine the individual activities needed for clustering. We now learn how to build a root entity cluster from the elementary entities and relationships defined in the ER modeling process. This technique assumes that a top-down analysis has been performed as part of the database requirement analysis and that it has been documented so that the major functional areas and subareas are identified. Functional areas are often defined by an enterprise's important organiza-

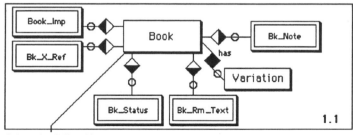

External relationships: Paper, Exch, Source, Issue, Publisher, Series

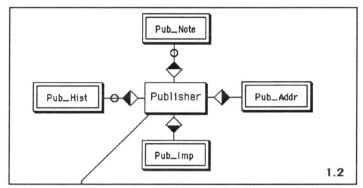

External relationships: Journal, Book, Standing Order, Series

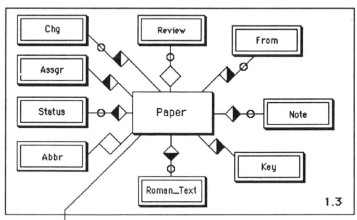

External relationships: Reviewer, Author, Book, Issue, Classifications, Language, Institution

Figure 10.9
Entity clusters at the first level.

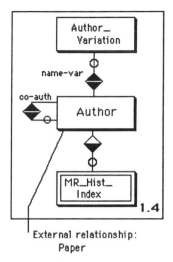

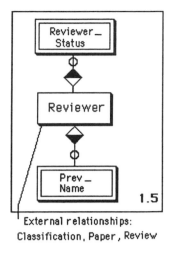

Figure 10.9, continued

tional units; business activities; or, possibly, by dominant applications for processing information. As an example, recall Fig. 3.3, which showed the four major functional areas for the Mathematical Reviews publishing application. Note that the functional areas are allowed to overlap. Using an ER diagram resulting from the database requirement analysis, such as shown in Fig. 3.3, clustering involves a series of bottom-up steps using the basic grouping operations. The list that follows explains these steps.

1. *Define points of grouping within functional areas.* Locate the dominant entities in a functional area through the natural relationships, local n-ary relationships, integrity constraints, abstractions, or just the central focus of many simple relationships. If such points of grouping do not exist within an area, consider a functional grouping of a whole area.

2. *Form entity clusters.* Use the basic grouping operations on elementary entities and their relationships to form higher-level objects, or entity clusters. Because entities may belong to several potential clusters, we need to have a set of priorities for forming entity clusters. The following set of rules, listed in priority order, defines the set that is most likely to preserve the clarity of the conceptual model.

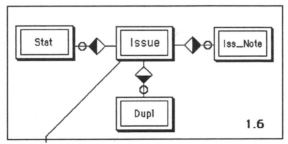

External relationships: Journal, Paper

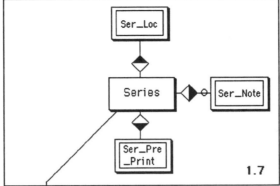

External relationships: Publisher, Book, Standing Order, Journal

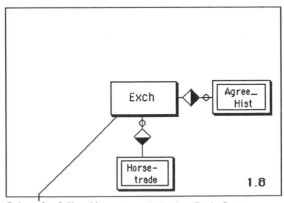

External relationships: Journal, Series, Book, Source

Figure 10.9, continued

a. Entities to be grouped into an entity cluster should exist within the same functional area; that is, the entire entity cluster must occur within the boundary of a functional area. For example, in Fig. 3.3, the relationship between Paper and Book should not be clustered. In another example, the relationship between Paper and Editor could be clustered within the Assigning functional area, but not within the Papers or Author identification areas.

b. If a conflict in choice between two or more potential entity clusters cannot be resolved (for example, between two constraint groupings at the same level of precedence), then leave these entity clusters ungrouped within their functional area. If that functional area remains cluttered with unresolved choices, then define functional subareas in which to group unresolved entities, entity clusters, and their relationships.

3. *Form higher-level entity clusters.* Apply the grouping operations recursively to any combination of elementary entities and entity clusters to form new levels of entity clusters (higher-level objects). Resolve conflicts using the same set of priority rules given in step 2. Continue the grouping operations until all the entity representations fit on a single page without undue complexity. The root entity cluster is then defined.

4. *Validate the cluster diagram.* Check for consistency of the interfaces (relationships) between objects at each level of the diagram. Verify the meaning of each level with the end-users.

This technique could feasibly be implemented with software whose diagrams are created and accessed with the simple open, close, group, and ungroup operations found in available object-oriented drawing packages.

Example: Entity Clustering

During initial interviews for the Mathematical Reviews database, a number of factors strongly suggested that some entities and relationships be grouped into clusters (step 1). First was a managerial request for a one-page overview diagram. It was clear that an overview diagram that included all weak entities was neither readily understandable nor provided emphasis where appropriate. Second, end-users felt that entities that had either a number of weak entities or a number of relationships needed their own overview diagrams to summarize numerous assertions. Third, when a number of major entities interacted in a functional area, a representation was needed that emphasized salient functional relationships, not those between a major entity and its weak entities.

By the end of the initial interviews, numerous entity clusters were identified (step 2). Instances of dominance grouping were the easiest clusters to identify, because many major entities had a number of multivalued attributes that did not interact often with other entities. As a result, this type of cluster was always contained within a major functional area. Examples are shown in Fig. 10.9 for Book, Publisher, Paper, Author, Reviewer, Issue, Series, and Exch.

A second phase of interviews involved verification of both the initial assertions and functional area entity clusters (step 3). Functional areas were considered critical, because many users understood data requirements through mastery of their area's processing requirements. Having all related entities in one diagram made it easier to discover omissions and other errors. Each of the four major functional areas was reviewed with end-users. An example for the ordering area is shown in Figs. 3.3 and 10.10.

During this process a number of instances arose in which potential clusters were not used because they could not meet all data requirements. For example, author identification procedures require that languages be maintained for authors in a paper-specific fashion. This leads to the ternary relationship depicted in Fig. 10.8, which could be the basis for a cluster via relationship grouping. Although this meets the needs of the author identification function, the Author and Paper entities are also separated in other functional areas (Author is not part of the Paper functional area). In addition, Author is a member of the Individual generalization hierarchy. If the ternary relationship grouping were performed, Author would then not meet the other data requirements in a semantically natural fashion. In part, such instances arose here because of the unusual amount of overlap between functional areas in this specific application. However, dominant entities often participate in more than one functional area, and the designer has to make decisions concerning competing clusters based on maximum clarity.

Continued user interviews, which tended to be relatively brief and limited in scope, resulted in successive refinement of the basic design. Some elementary entities were added, and entity clusters were modified. Higher-level diagrams were modified for better clarity (step 4). See Fig. 10.11 for an example of an entity cluster at level 2, Source, which is composed of subtypes that are either elementary entities or level 1 entity clusters. In Fig.

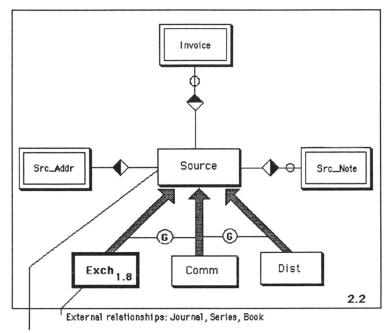

2.2

External relationships: Journal, Series, Book

External relationships: Publisher, Standing_Order, Letter_Hist

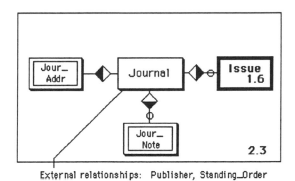

2.3

External relationships: Publisher, Standing_Order

Note: See Figure 10.6 for entity cluster 2.1 Individual.

Figure 10.10
Entity clusters at the second level.

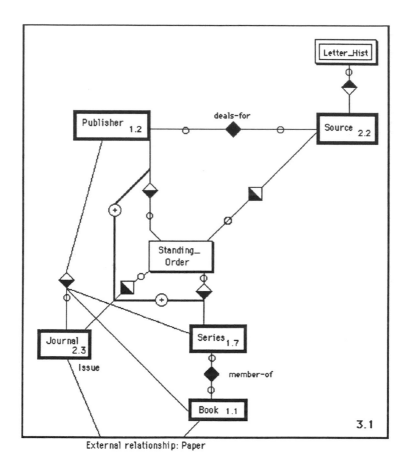

External relationship: Paper

Figure 10.11
Standing_Order entity cluster at the third level.

10.11 the entity cluster, Standing_Order, is composed of a variety of lower-level entity clusters and elementary entities. Figure 10.12 shows the root entity cluster resulting from the analysis. As a summary, Fig. 10.13 shows a conceptual representation of all the clustering levels for this application.

Real-life end-users have expressed enthusiasm for the ER diagrams, noting the ease with which they could be read and the amount of information conveyed. Cluster diagrams are considered useful because the designers and end-users can quickly agree on the "picture" of the system. A sufficient number of users had no problem with the diagrams, and the graphics encouraged widespread participation.

Entity clusters successfully supported multiple end-user views. In general, users do not reference all relationships for the entities from other functional areas, thus the entity cluster provided the level of abstraction to which they are accustomed. The use of functional areas as an organizing principle fits naturally into the users' approach to their data.

The case study illustrates a trade-off in clarity between a collection of entities and entity clusters at one level and a single, higher-level entity cluster that encompasses those components. It is conceivable that the higher-level entity cluster has so many relationships that the lines, relation-

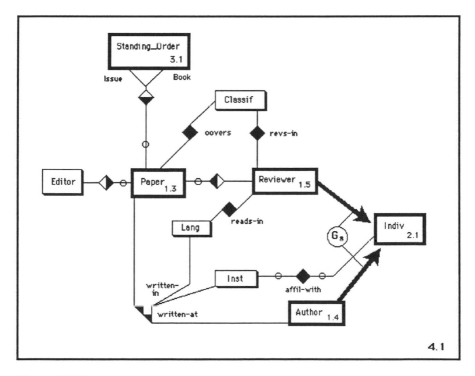

Figure 10.12
Root entity cluster.

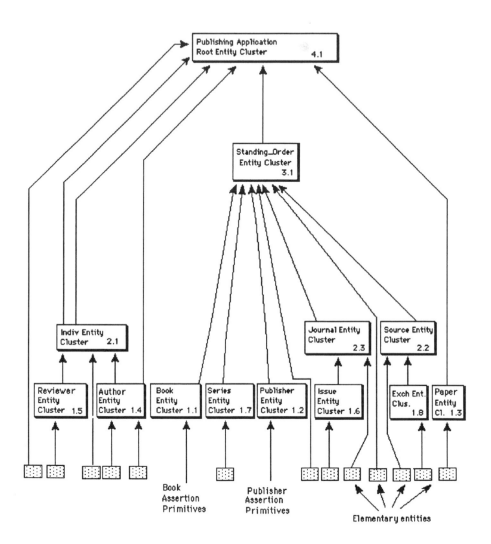

Figure 10.13
Summary of entity cluster levels for the publishing application.

ship boxes, and relationship names extending from it tend to clutter the diagram and seriously degrade clarity. This could be remedied by an automated tool having a "show relationships" function that would display the labeled lines or give a list of relationships that are not included in the initial diagram to avoid undue clutter.

10.5 Summary

Entity clustering promotes the simplicity that is vital for fast end-user comprehension as well as the complexity at a more detailed level to satisfy the database designer's need for extended semantic expression in the conceptual model. An entity cluster is a grouping of entities and their corresponding relationships into a higher-level abstract object. This grouping operation can be modeled by an SQL view that specifies the join of relations formed from the entities grouped into the entity cluster.

Grouping operations can be classified by dominance of an entity over other entities such as an entity surrounded by weak entities that are dependent on it for their existence, abstraction grouping such as generalization, constraint grouping, and n-ary relationship grouping. Applying these grouping operations to a usable abstraction requires the definition of a precise method that specifies points of grouping within functional areas of the database model, formation of entity clusters from elementary entities and relationships, and further abstractions into higher-level entity clusters until the ER model can be represented on a single page. Validation of each clustering decision requires checking for consistency of entity interfaces, that is, making sure the relationships are kept intact between entities inside an entity cluster and those external to that cluster.

Literature Summary

An entity cluster is also known in the literature as a complex object [Su83,DGL86, StRo86, PoKe86], molecular aggregation [BaBu84], or subject area [FeMi86]. The entity or object cluster concept can already be found in some database systems [BaBu84,MSOP86,Wied86]. Clustering models have been recently defined that provide a useful foundation for the proposed clustering technique [Ossh84, FeMi86, DGL86, TWBK89].

[BaBu84]   Batory, D.S., and Buchmann, A.P. "Molecular Objects, Abstract Data Types, and Data Models: A Framework," *Proc. 10th Int'l. Conf. on Very Large Data Bases,* Singapore, Aug. 1984, pp. 172–184.

[DGL86]   Dittrich, K.R., Gotthard, W., and Lockemann, P.C. "Complex Entities for Engineering Applications," *Proc. 5th ER Conf.*, North-Holland, 1986.

[FeMi86]   Feldman, P., and Miller, D. "Entity Model Clustering: Structuring a Data Model by Abstraction,"*Computer Journal* 29,4(Aug. 1986), pp. 348–360.

[MSOP86]   Maier, D., Stein, J., Otis, A., and Purdy, A. "Development of an Object-Oriented DBMS," *OOPSLA 1986 Proc.*, Sept. 1986, pp. 472–482.

[Ossh84]   Ossher, H.L. "A New Program Structuring Mechanism Based on Layered Graphs," *Proc. 11th Annual ACM SIGACT-SIGPLAN POPL*, Salt Lake City, Utah, Jan. 15–18, 1984, pp. 11–22.

[PoKe86]   Potter, W.D., and Kerschberg, L. "A Unified Approach to Modeling Knowledge and Data,"*IFIP WG 2.6 Working Conf. on Knowledge and Data*, University of South Carolina, Elsevier, North-Holland, New York, Sept. 1986, 32 pp.

[StRo86]   Stonebraker, M., and Rowe, L.A. "The Design of Postgres,"*Proc. ACM-SIGMOD Intl. Conf. on Management of Data*, May 1986, pp. 340–355.

[Su83]   Su, S.Y.W. "SAM*: A Semantic Association Model for Corporate and Scientific Statistical Databases," *Inform. Sciences* 29, 2–3(May–June 1983), pp. 151–199.

[TWBK89]   Teorey, T.J., Wei, G., Bolton, D.L., and Koenig, J.A. "ER Model Clustering as an Aid for User Communication and Documentation in Database Design,"*Comm. ACM* 32, 8(Aug. 1989), pp. 975–987.

[Wied86]   Wiederhold, G. "Views, Objects, and Databases,"*IEEE Computer* (Dec. 1986), pp. 37–44.

Exercises

Problem 10-1

In the ER clustering methodology, the basic objects are defined as

a. entity
b. relationship
c. attribute
d. entity cluster

Consider each of these objects as an entity type, and draw their actual relationships in terms of an ER diagram. Assume that each instance of an object of any of these four types has a unique identity (for example, the attribute employee_name occurs only once in the database).

Problem 10-2

Assume that the ER diagrams in Figures 7.1 and 9.1 are two views to be integrated into a single ER model. Proceed with this view integration and then define entity clusters from the integrated model. Define the root entity cluster.

References

[Abri74]   Abrial, J. "Data Semantics," *Data Base Management, Proc. IFIP TC2 Conf.*, Cargese, Corsica, North-Holland, 1974.

[Ariav86]   Ariav, G. "A Temporally Oriented Data Model," *ACM Trans. Database Systems* 11,4(Dec. 1986), pp. 499–527.

[APLV81]   Atzeni, P., Batini, C. Lenzerini, M., and Villanelli, F. "INCOD: A System for Conceptual Design of Data and Transactions in the Entity-Relationship Model," *Entity-Relationship Approach to Information Modeling and Analysis,* ER Institute, Saugus, CA, 1981.

[Bach69]   Bachman, C.W. "Data Structure Diagrams," *Database* 1,2(1969), pp. 4–10.

[Bach72]   Bachman, C.W. "The Evolution of Storage Structures," *Comm. ACM* 15,7(July 1972), pp. 628–634.

[Bach77]   Bachman, C.W. "The Role Concept in Data Models," *Proc. 3rd Int'l. Conf. on Very Large Data Bases*, Tokyo, Oct. 6–8, 1977, IEEE, New York, pp. 464–476.

[BaLe84]   Batini, C., and Lenzerini, M. "A Methodology for Data Schema Integration in the Entity Relationship Model," *IEEE Trans. on Software Engr.* SE-10,6(Nov. 1984), pp. 650–664.

[BLN86]   Batini, C., Lenzerini, M., and Navathe, S.B. "A Comparative Analysis of Methodologies for Database Schema Integration," *ACM Computing Surveys* 18,4(Dec. 1986), pp. 323–364.

[BaBu84]   Batory, D.S., and Buchmann, A.P. "Molecular Objects, Abstract Data Types, and Data Models: A Framework," *Proc. 10th Int'l. Conf. on Very Large Data Bases,* Singapore, Aug., 1984, pp. 172–184.

[BaMc72]   Bayer, R., and McCreight, E. "Organization and Maintenance of Large Ordered Indexes," *ACTA. Inf.* 1,3(1972), pp. 173–189.

[BBG78]   Beeri, C., Bernstein, P., and Goodman, N. "A Sophisticate's Introduction to Database Normalization Theory," *Proc. 4th Int' l. Conf. on Very Large Data Bases*, Berlin, Sept. 13–15, 1978, IEEE, New York, pp. 113–124.

[Bern76]   Bernstein, P. "Synthesizing 3NF Relations from Functional Dependencies," *ACM Trans. Database Systems* 1,4(1976), pp. 272–298.

[BeGo81]   Bernstein, P.A., and Goodman, N. "Concurrency Control in Distributed Database Systems," *ACM Computing Surveys* 13,2(June 1981), pp. 185–222.

[BlEs77]   Blasgen, M.W., and Eswaran, K.P. "Storage and Access in Relational Data Bases," *IBM Syst. J.* 16,4(1977), pp. 363–377.

[BPP76]   Bracchi, G., Paolini, P., and Pelagatti, G. "Binary Logical Associations in Data Modelling," *Modelling in Data Base Management Systems, Proc. IFIP TC2 Conf.*, Freudenstadt, North-Holland, 1976.

[BHHS85]   Braind, H., Habrias, H., Hue, J., and Simon, Y. "Expert System for Translating an E-R Diagram into Databases," *Proc. 4th Int' l. Conf. on Entity-Relationship Approach*, Chicago, IEEE Computer Society Press, Silver Spring, MD, 1985, pp. 199–206.

[BMS84]   Brodie, M.L., Mylopoulos, J., and Schmidt, J. (editors). *On Conceptual Modeling: Perspectives from Artificial Intelligence, Databases, and Programming Languages*, Springer-Verlag, New York, 1984.

[Bube77]   Bubenko, J. "The Temporal Dimension in Information Modelling," *Architecture and Models in Data Base Management Systems*, G. Nijssen (editor), North-Holland, 1977.

[Card85]   Cardenas, A.F. *Data Base Management Systems* (2nd Ed.), Allyn and Bacon, Boston, 1985.

[Case72]   Casey, R.G. "Allocation of Copies of a File in an Information Network," *Spring Joint Computer Conf.*, 1972, AFIPS Press, Vol. 40, 1972.

[CePe84]   Ceri, S., and Pelagatti, G. *Distributed Databases: Principles and Systems*, McGraw-Hill, New York, 1984.

[CNW83]   Ceri, S., Navathe, S.B., and Wiederhold, G. "Distribution Design of Logical Database Schemes," *IEEE Trans. on Soft. Engr.* SE-9,4(1983), pp. 487–504.

[CPW87]   Ceri, S., Pernici, B., and Wiederhold, G., "Distributed Database Design Methodologies," *Proc. IEEE*, May 1987, pp. 533–546.

[Chen76]   Chen, P.P. "The Entity-Relationship Model—Toward a Unified View of Data," *ACM Trans. Database Systems* 1,1(March 1976), pp. 9–36.

[Chen87]   Chen and Associates, Inc. *ER Designer* (User Manual), 1987.

[Chu69]   Chu, W.W. "Optimal File Allocation in a Multiple Computer System," *IEEE Trans. on Computers* C-18,10(Oct. 1969), pp. 885–889.

[Chu84]   Chu, W.W. *Distributed Data Bases, Handbook of Software Engineering*, C.R. Vick and C.V. Ramamoorthy (editors), Van Nostrand Reinhold, 1984.

[ClWa83]   Clifford, J., and Warren, D. "Formal Semantics for Time in Databases," *ACM Trans. Database Systems* 8,2(1983), pp. 214–254.

[CFT84]   Cobb, R.E., Fry, J.P., and Teorey, T.J. "The Database Designer's Workbench," *Information Sciences* 32,1(Feb. 1984), pp. 33–45.

[Codd70]   Codd, E. "A Relational Model for Large Shared Data Banks," *Comm. ACM* 13,6(June 1970), pp. 377–387.

[Codd74]   Codd, E. "Recent Investigations into Relational Data Base Systems," *Proc. IFIP Congress*, North-Holland, 1974.

[CoGe80]   Coffman, E.G. et al., "Optimization of the Number of Copies in Distributed Databases," *Proc. of the 7th IFIP Symposium on Computer Performance Modelling, Measurement and Evaluation*, Springer-Verlag, New York, May 1980, pp. 257–263.

[Date84]   Date, C.J. *A Guide to DB2*, Addison-Wesley, Reading, MA, 1984.

[Date86]   Date, C.J. *An Introduction to Database Systems*, Vol. 1 (4th Ed.), Addison-Wesley, Reading, MA, 1986.

[Date87]   Date, C.J. "The Twelve Rules for a Distributed Data Base," *Computerworld*, June 8, 1987.

[Date89]   Date, C.J. *A Guide to the SQL Standard* (2nd Ed.), Addison-Wesley, Reading, MA, 1989.

[DeMa78]   De Marco, T. *Structured Analysis and System Specification*, Yourdon Press, New York, 1978.

[DGL86]   Dittrich, K.R., Gotthard, W., and Lockemann, P.C. "Complex Entities for Engineering Applications," *Proc. 5th ER Conf.*, North-Holland, 1986.

[DKM86]   Dittrich, K.R., Kotz, A.M., and Mulle, J.A. "An Event/Trigger Mechanism to Enforce Complex Consistency Constraints in Design Databases," *SIGMOD Record* 15,3(Sept. 1986), pp. 22–36.

[DuHa89]   Dutka, A.F., and Hanson, H.H. *Fundamentals of Data Normalization*, Addison-Wesley, Reading, MA, 1989.

[ElWi79]   Elmasri, R., and Wiederhold, G. "Data Model Integration Using the Structural Model," *Proc. ACM SIGMOD Conf.*, Boston, ACM, New York, 1979, pp. 319–326.

[EHW85]   Elmasri, R., Hevner, A., and Weeldreyer, J. "The Category Concept: An Extension to the Entity-Relationship Model," *Data and Knowledge Engineering* 1,1(1985), pp. 75–116.

[ElNa89]   Elmasri, R., and Navathe, S.B. *Fundamentals of Database Systems*, Addison-Wesley/Benjamin/Cummings, Redwood City, CA, 1989.

[Ever86]   Everest, G.C. *Database Management: Objectives, System Functions, and Administration*, McGraw-Hill, New York, 1986.

[Fagi77]   Fagin, R. "Multivalued Dependencies and a New Normal Form for Relational Databases," *ACM Trans. Database Systems* 2,3(1977), pp. 262–278.

[FeMi86]   Feldman, P., and Miller, D. "Entity Model Clustering: Structuring a Data Model by Abstraction," *Computer Journal* 29,4(Aug. 1986), pp. 348–360.

[Ferg85]   Ferg, S. "Modeling the Time Dimension in an Entity-Relationship Diagram," *Proc. 4th Int'l. Conf. on the Entity-Relationship Approach*, Chicago, IEEE Computer Society Press, Silver Spring, MD, 1985, pp. 280–286.

[FiHo]   Fisher, M.L., and Hochbaum, D., "Database Location in Computer Networks," *J ACM* 27,4(Oct. 1980), pp. 718–735.

[FHS80]   Fisher, P., Hollist, P., and Slonim, J. "A Design Methodology for Distributed Databases," *Proc. IEEE Conf. Distributed Computing*, Sept. 1980, IEEE, pp. 199–202.

[FHJF85]   Fong, E., Henderson, M., Jefferson, D., and Sullivan, J. *Guide on Logical Database Design*, NBS Spec. Pub. 500–122, U.S. Dept. of Commerce.

[Gadr87]   Gadre, S.H. "Building an Enterprise and Information Model," *Database Programming and Design* 1,1(Dec. 1987), pp. 48–58.

[GaSa79]   Gane, C.P., and Sarson, T. *Structured System Analysis: Tools and Techniques,* Prentice-Hall, Englewood Cliffs, NJ, 1979.

[Gray81]   Gray, J. "The Transaction Concept: Virtues and Limitations," *Proc. 7th Int'l. Conf. on Very Large Data Bases*, Sept. 1981, IEEE, New York, pp. 144–154.

[GrAn87]   Gray, J.N., and Anderson, M. "Distributed Computer Systems: Four Cases", *Proc. IEEE* 75,5(May 1987), pp.719–729.

[Gros86]   Grosshans, D. *File Systems Design and Implementation*, Prentice-Hall, Englewood Cliffs, NJ, 1986.

[HaMc82]   Hammer, M., and McLeod, D. "Database Description with SDM: A Semantic Database Model," *ACM Trans. Database Systems* 6,3(Sept. 1982), pp. 351–386.

[Harb88]   Harbron, T.R. *File Systems Structures and Algorithms*, Prentice-Hall, Englewood Cliffs, NJ, 1988.

[Hawr84]   Hawryszkiewycz, I. *Database Analysis and Design*, SRA, Chicago, 1984.

[Heba77]   Hebalkar, P.G. "Logical Design Considerations for Distributed Database Systems," *IEEE COMPSAC*, Nov. 1977, pp. 562–580.

[HeYa87]   Hevner, A.R., and Yao, S.B., "Querying Distributed Databases on Local Area Networks," *Proc. IEEE* 75,5(May 1987), pp. 563–572.

[Howe83]   Howe, D. *Data Analysis and Data Base Design*, Arnold, London, 1983.

[HuKi87]   Hull, R., and King, R. "Semantic Database Modeling: Survey, Applications, and Research Issues," *ACM Computing Surveys* 19,3(Sept. 1987), pp. 201–260.

[Inmo87]   Inmon, W.H. "Optimizing Performance with Denormalization," *Database Programming and Design* 1,1(Dec. 1987), Premier Issue, pp. 34–39.

[IrKh81]   Irani, K.R., and Khabbaz, N.G. "A Combined Communication Network Design and File Allocation for Distributed Databases," *2nd Intl Conf. on Distributed Systems*, Paris, IEEE Computer Society Press, April 1981.

[ISO82]   ISO/TC97/SC5/WG3-N695 Report. "Concepts and Terminology for the Conceptual Schema and the Information Base," J. van Griethuysen (editor), ANSI, New York, 1982, 180 pp.

[ISAN89]   ISO-ANSI Database Language SQL2 and SQL3, ANSI X3H2-89-110, ISO DBL CAN-3(working draft), J. Melton (editor), February 1989.

[JaNg84]   Jajodia, S., and Ng, P. "Translation of Entity-Relationship Diagrams into Relational Structures," *J. Systems and Software* 4, pp. 123–133.

[JaKo84]   Jarke, M., and Koch, J. "Query Optimization in Database Systems," *ACM Computing Surveys* 16,2(June 1984), pp. 111–152.

[Kent81]   Kent, W. "Consequences of Assuming a Universal Relation," *ACM Trans. Database Systems* 6,4(1981), pp. 539–556.

[Kent83]   Kent, W. "A Simple Guide to Five Normal Forms in Relational Database Theory," *Comm. ACM* 26,2(Feb. 1983), pp. 120–125.

[Kent84]   Kent, W. "Fact-Based Data Analysis and Design," *J. Systems and Software* 4(1984), pp. 99–121.

[KoSi88]   Korth, H.F., and Silberschatz, A. *Database System Concepts*, McGraw-Hill, New York, 1986.

[LCC84]   Lee, R.M., Coelho, H., and Cotta, J.C. "Temporal Inferencing on Administrative Databases," *Information Systems* 10,2(1985), pp. 197–206.

[LeSa83]   Lenzerini, M., and Santucci, G. "Cardinality Constraints in the Entity-Relationship Model," *The Entity-Relationship Approach to Software Engineering*, G.C. Davis et al.(editors), Elsevier, North-Holland, New York, 1983, pp. 529–549.

[Lien81]   Lien, Y. "Hierarchical Schemata for Relational Databases," *ACM Trans. Database Systems* 6,1(1981), pp. 48–69.

[Lien82]   Lien, Y. "On the Equivalence of Data Models," *J. ACM* 29,2(1982), pp. 333–362.

[Ling85]   Ling, T. "A Normal Form for Entity-Relationship Diagrams," *Proc. 4th International Conf. on the ER Approach*, Chicago, IEEE Computer Society Press, Silver Spring, MD, 1985, pp. 24–35.

[Loom83]   Loomis, M.E.S. *Data Management and File Processing*, Prentice-Hall, Englewood Cliffs, NJ, 1983.

[Maci89]   Maciaszek, L. *Database Design and Implementation*, Prentice-Hall International, 1989.

[MaRi76] Mahmood, S., and Riordan, J. "Optimal Allocation of Resources in Distributed Information Networks", *ACM Trans. Database Systems* 1,1(March 1976), pp. 66–78.

[Maie83] Maier, D. *Theory of Relational Databases*, Computer Science Press, Rockville, MD, 1983.

[MSOP86] Maier, D., Stein, J., Otis, A., and Purdy, A. "Development of an Object-Oriented DBMS," *OOPSLA 1986 Proc.*, Sept. 1986, pp. 472–482.

[MaTe88] Mantei, M.M., and Teorey, T.J. "Cost/Benefit Analysis for Incorporating Human Factors into the Software Lifecycle," *Comm. ACM* 31,4(April 1988), pp. 428–439.

[Mark87] Mark, L. "Defining Views in the Binary Relationship Model," *Inform. Systems* 12,3(1987), pp. 281–294.

[Mart82] Martin, J. *Strategic Data-Planning Methodologies*, Prentice-Hall, Englewood Cliffs, NJ, 1982.

[Mart83] Martin, J. *Managing the Data-Base Environment*, Prentice-Hall, Englewood Cliffs, NJ, 1983.

[McGe74] McGee, W. "A Contribution to the Study of Data Equivalence," *Data Base Management*, J.W. Klimbie and K.L. Koffeman (editors), North-Holland, 1974, pp. 123–148.

[McKi79] McLeod, D., and King, R. "Applying a Semantic Database Model," *Proc. 1st Int'l. Conf. on the Entity-Relationship Approach to Systems Analysis and Design*, Los Angeles, North-Holland, 1979, pp. 193–210.

[MoLe77] Morgan, H.L., and Levin, K.D. "Optimal Program and Data Allocation in Computer Networks," *Comm. ACM* 32,5(May 1977), pp. 345–353.

[MTM89] Moyne, J.R., Teorey, T.J., and McAfee, L.C. "Time Sequencing and Ordering Extensions to the Entity Relationship Model and Their Application to the Automated Manufacturing Process," submitted to *IEEE Trans. on Data and Knowledge Engr.*

[NaCh83] Navathe, S. and Cheng, A. "A Methodology for Database Schema Mapping from Extended Entity Relationship Models into the Hierarchical Model," *The Entity-Relationship Approach to Software Engineering*, G.C. Davis et al.(editors), Elsevier, North-Holland, 1983.

[NaGa82]   Navathe, S., and Gadgil, S. "A Methodology for View Integration in Logical Database Design," *Proc. 8th Int' l. Conf. on Very Large Data Bases*, Mexico City, 1982, pp. 142–152.

[NEL86]   Navathe, S., Elmasri, R., and Larson, J. "Integrating User Views in Database Design," *IEEE Computer* 19,1(1986), pp. 50–62.

[NSE84]   Navathe, S., Sashidhar, T., and Elmasri, R. "Relationship Merging in Schema Integration," *Proc. 10th Int' l. Conf. on Very Large Data Bases*, Singapore, 1984, pp. 78–90.

[NvS79]   Nijssen, G., van Assche, F., and Snijders, J. "End User Tools for Information Systems Requirement Definition," *Formal Models and Practical Tools for Information System Design*, H. Schneider (editor), North-Holland, 1979.

[Oren85]   Oren, O. "Integrity Constraints in the Conceptual Schema Language SYSDOC," *Proc. 4th Int' l. Conf. on the Entity-Relationship Approach*, Chicago, IEEE Computer Society Press, Silver Spring, MD, 1985, pp. 288–294.

[Ossh84]   Ossher, H.L. "A New Program Structuring Mechanism Based on Layered Graphs," *Proc. 11th Annual ACM SIGACT-SIGPLAN POPL*, Salt Lake City, Utah, Jan. 15–18, 1984, pp. 11–22.

[Parn72]   Parnas, D.L. "On the Criteria to be Used in Decomposing Systems into Modules," *Comm. ACM* 15, 12(1972), pp. 1053–1058.

[PaSp86]   Parent, C., and Spaccapietra, S. "Enhancing the Operational Semantics of the Entity-Relationship Model," in *Database Semantics* (DS-1), T.B. Steel, Jr., and R. Meersman (editors), Elsevier, North Holland, 1986, pp. 159–173.

[PeMa88]   Peckham, J., and Maryanski, F. "Semantic Data Models," *ACM Computing Surveys* 20,3(Sept. 1988), pp. 153–190.

[PoKe86]   Potter, W.D., and Kerschberg, L. "A Unified Approach to Modeling Knowledge and Data," *IFIP WG 2.6 Working Conf. on Knowledge and Data*, University of South Carolina, Elsevier, North-Holland, New York, Sept. 1986, 32 pp.

[Rein85]   Reiner, D., Brodie, M., Brown, G., Friedell, M., Kramlich, D., Lehman, J., and Rosenthal, A. "The Database Design and Evaluation Workbench (DDEW) Project at CCA," *Database Engineering* 7,4(1985), pp. 10–15.

[Rein86]   Reiner, D., Brown, G., Friedell, M., Lehman, J., McKee, R., Rheingans, P., and Rosenthal, A. "A Database Designer's Workbench," *Proc. 5th ER Conference*, Dijon, North-Holland, 1986, pp. 347–360.

[Rodg89]   Rodgers, U. "Denormalization: Why, What, and How?" *Database Programming and Design* 2,12(Dec. 1989), pp. 46–53.

[RoSt87]   Rowe, L., and Stonebraker, M. "The Postgres Data Model," *Proc. 13th Intl. Conf. on Very Large Data Bases*, Brighton, England, Sept. 1–4, 1987.

[Sacco87]   Sacco, G.M. "The Fact Model: A Semantic Data Model for Complex Databases," *ESPRIT '86: Results and Achievements*, Elsevier, North-Holland, 1987, pp. 587–594.

[Saka83]   Sakai, H. "Entity-Relationship Approach to Logical Database Design," *Entity-Relationship Approach to Software Engineering*, C.G. Davis, S. Jajodia, P. A.Ng, and R.T. Yeh (editors), Elsevier, North-Holland, New York, 1983, pp. 155–187.

[SSW80]   Scheuermann, P., Scheffner, G., and Weber, H. "Abstraction Capabilities and Invariant Properties Modelling within the Entity-Relationship Approach," *Entity-Relationship Approach to Systems Analysis and Design*, P. Chen (editor), Elsevier, North-Holland, 1980, pp. 121–140.

[ScSo80]   Schkolnick, M., and Sorenson, P. "Denormalization: A Performance Oriented Database Design Technique," *Proc. AICA 1980 Congress*, Bologna, Italy, AICA, Brussels, 1980, pp. 363–377.

[Seli79]   Selinger, P. G., Astrahan, M.M., Chamberlin, D.D., Lorie, R.A., Price, T.C. "Access Path Selection on a Relational Database Management System," *Proc. 1979 ACM SIGMOD Internat'l. Conf. on Management of Data*, ACM, New York, pp. 23–34.

[Smit85]   Smith, H. "Database Design: Composing Fully Normalized Tables from a Rigorous Dependency Diagram," *Comm. ACM* 28,8(1985), pp. 826–838.

[SmSm77]   Smith, J., and Smith, D. "Database Abstractions: Aggregation and Generalization," *ACM Trans. Database Systems* 2,2(June 1977), pp. 105–133.

[Spro76]   Sprowls, R.C. *Management Data Bases*, Wiley/Hamilton, Santa Barbara, CA, 1976.

[StMa88]   Stein, J., and Maier, D. "Concepts in Object-Oriented Data Management," *Database Programming and Design* 1,4(April 1988), pp. 58–67.

[SMC74]   Stevens, W., Myers, G., and Constantine, L. "Structured Design," *IBM Syst. J.* 13,2(1974), pp. 115–139.

[StRo86]   Stonebraker, M., and Rowe, L.A. "The Design of Postgres," *Proc. ACM-SIGMOD Intl. Conf. on Management of Data*, May 1986, pp. 340–355.

[Su83]   Su, S.Y.W. "SAM*: A Semantic Association Model for Corporate and Scientific Statistical Databases," *Inform. Sciences* 29, 2–3(May–June 1983), pp. 151–199.

[Swee85]   Sweet, F. "Process-Driven Data Design," *Datamation* 31, 16(1985), pp. 84–85, first of a series of 14 articles.

[TeHe77]   Teichroew, D., and Hershey, E.A. "PSL/PSA: A Computer Aided Technique for Structured Documentation and Analysis of Information Processing Systems," *IEEE Trans. Software Engr.* SE-3,1(1977), pp. 41–48.

[TeFr82]   Teorey, T., and Fry, J. *Design of Database Structures*, Prentice-Hall, Englewood Cliffs, NJ, 1982.

[Teor89]   Teorey, T.J. "Distributed Database Design: A Practical Approach and Example," *SIGMOD Record* 18,4(Dec. 1989), pp. 23–39.

[TCOU89]   Teorey, T.J., Chaar, J., Olukotun, K., and Umar, A. "Distributed Database Design: Some Basic Concepts and Strategies," *Database Programming and Design* 2,4(April 1989), pp. 34–42.

[TWBK89]   Teorey, T.J., Wei, G., Bolton, D.L., and Koenig, J.A. "ER Model Clustering as an Aid for User Communication and Documentation in Database Design," *Comm. ACM* 32,8(Aug. 1989), pp. 975–987.

[TeYa90]   Teorey, T.J., and Yang, D. "Usage Refinement for ER-to-Relation Design Transformations," to appear in *Information Sciences* (1989).

[TYF86]   Teorey, T.J., Yang, D., and Fry, J.P. "A Logical Design Methodology for Relational Databases Using the Extended Entity-Relationship Model," *ACM Computing Surveys* 18,2(June 1986), pp. 197–222.

[TsLo82]   Tsichritzis, D., and Lochovsky, F. *Data Models*, Prentice-Hall, Englewood Cliffs, N.J., 1982.

[Ullm88]   Ullman, J. *Principles of Database and Knowledge-Base Systems*, Vols. 1 and 2, Computer Science Press, Rockville, MD, 1988.

[VeVa82]   Verheijen, G., and Van Bekkum, J. "NIAM: An Information Analysis Method," *Information Systems Design Methodologies*, Olle, Sol, and Verryn-Stuart (editors), North-Holland, 1982, pp. 537–590.

[Wied83]   Wiederhold, G. *Database Design* (2nd Ed.), McGraw-Hill, New York, 1983.

[Wied86]   Wiederhold, G. "Views, Objects, and Databases," *IEEE Computer* (Dec. 1986), pp. 37–44.

[Wied87]   Wiederhold, G. *File Organization for Database Design*, McGraw-Hill, New York, 1987.

[Wilm84]   Wilmot, R. "Foreign Keys Decrease Adaptability of Database Designs," *Comm. ACM* 27,12(Dec. 1984), pp. 1237–1243.

[Yao85]   Yao, S.B. (editor). *Principles of Database Design*, Prentice-Hall, Englewood Cliffs, NJ, 1985.

[YoCo79]   Yourdon, E., and Constantine, L.L. *Structured Design*, Prentice-Hall, Englewood Cliffs, NJ, 1971.

[YuCh84]   Yu, C., and Chang, C. "Distributed Query Processing," *ACM Computing Surveys* 16,4(Dec. 1984), pp. 399–433.

[ZaMe81]   Zaniolo, C., and Melkanoff, M. "On the Design of Relational Database Schemas," *ACM Trans. Database Systems* 6,1(1981), pp. 1–47.

Index